Writers of Wales

Hester Lynch Thrale Piozzi

Editors:
Jane Aaron
M. Wynn Thomas
Andrew Webb

Founding Series Editors:
R. Brinley Jones
Meic Stephens†

Other titles in the Writers of Wales series:
Christopher Meredith (2018), Diana Wallace
B. L. Coombes (2017), Bill Jones and Chris Williams
Owen Rhoscomyl (2016), John S. Ellis
Dylan Thomas (2014), Walford Davies
Gwenlyn Parry (2013), Roger Owen
Welsh Periodicals in English (2013), Malcolm Ballin
Ruth Bidgood (2012), Matthew Jarvis
Dorothy Edwards (2011), Claire Flay
Kate Roberts (2011), Katie Gramich
Geoffrey of Monmouth (2010), Karen Jankulak
Herbert Williams (2010), Phil Carradice
Rhys Davies (2009), Huw Osborne
R. S. Thomas (2006), Tony Brown
Ben Bowen (2003), T. Robin Chapman
James Kitchener Davies (2002), M. Wynn Thomas

Writers of Wales

Hester Lynch Thrale Piozzi

Michael John Franklin

University of Wales Press
2020

© Michael John Franklin, 2020

All rights reserved. No part of this book may be reproduced in any material form (including photocopying or storing it in any medium by electronic means and whether or not transiently or incidentally to some other use of this publication) without the written permission of the copyright owner except in accordance with the provisions of the Copyright, Designs and Patents Act 1988. Applications for the copyright owner's written permission to reproduce any part of this publication should be addressed to the University of Wales Press, University Registry, King Edward VII Avenue, Cardiff CF10 3NS.

www.uwp.co.uk

British Library Cataloguing-in-Publication Data
A catalogue record for this book is available from the British Library.

ISBN 978-1-78683-540-6
e-ISBN 978-1-78683-541-3

The right of Michael John Franklin to be identified as author of this work has been asserted by him in accordance with sections 77, 78 and 79 of the Copyright, Designs and Patents Act 1988.

The publisher acknowledges the financial support of the Welsh Books Council.

Typeset in Wales by Eira Fenn Gaunt, Cardiff
Printed by CPI Antony Rowe, Chippenham, Wiltshire

*For Elinor Estelle,
a.k.a. the bilingual 'Duchess of Dorset'*

Contents

Acknowledgements ix
List of illustrations xi

1 Hester Lynch Salusbury: 'a thousand pretty Tricks, [. . .] a Thousand pretty Stories and [. . .] a Thousand pretty Verses'   1

2 The Two Hesters 'have *murder'd* Peace & Happiness at Home'   21

3 The Arrivals of Queeney and the Great Cham   29

4 Hester Brewster, or, 'Women have a manifest Advantage over Men in the doing Business'   53

5 'Like a Rocket She rises, and leaves us to Stare'   71

6 'To revise my past Life, & resolve upon a new one'   93

7 'To hie *home* and dye like a Hare upon the old *Farm*, near the Place I was *kindled* at'   119

8 'Each bold Cambrio Briton's a Stranger to Fear'   144

Notes 167
Bibliography 181
Index 187

Acknowledgements

If Hester Lynch Thrale Piozzi richly merits an honoured place in the pantheon of great Welsh writers, she certainly deserves this belated and slim volume in the UWP series Writers of Wales. To consider her as a Welsh writer in English has been my aim and has proved an unalloyed enjoyment; I can only hope that the generous general reader will derive some pleasure from my attempt. At the very least, the prodigious range of her innovative writings and genre experimentation should emerge as impressively apparent. Immensely proud of her aristocratic Welsh blood, she bravely refused to accept the restrictions on female authors in her time. Hester Piozzi's poems, letters, political pamphlets, journals, hoaxes, memoirs, marginalia and major published volumes all reveal the insatiable curiosity of the scholar. It is most encouraging that her works are receiving renewed critical attention as she is reassessed by cultural historians and, especially, by contemporary feminism.

   I am pleased to record a particular debt to the profound and pioneering work of William McCarthy in his *Hester Thrale Piozzi: Portrait of a Literary Woman* (1985), a most readable model of precision. In preparing this book I have used the printed materials of the British Library, the National Library of Wales, Aberystwyth, the New York Public Library, the Beinecke Library at New Haven, the Houghton Library at Harvard, the John Rylands Library, Swansea University, and the Firestone Library, Princeton. I am happy to acknowledge my gratitude to the helpful efficiency of the library staff at all these institutions. I should especially like to register my thanks to John McCrory of the John Rylands Library, Emma Butterfield of the National Portrait Gallery, Céline Gorham, Registrar

Acknowledgements

of the Beaverbrook Art Gallery and Rosemary Williams of the Inter-Library Loan department here at Swansea. For thoughtful and encouraging conversations and camaraderie, I am very grateful to all my colleagues in Elizabeth Montagu Correspondence Online: *http://www.elizabethmontagunetwork.co.uk/emco/*. For many years Elizabeth was Hester's friendly rival for personal celebrity, and Frances Burney opined: 'As to Mrs. Montagu, she reasons well, and harangues well, but wit she has none. Mrs Thrale has almost too much; for when she is in spirits, it bursts forth in a torrent almost overwhelming.' Finally, my sincere thanks, for her cheerful efficiency and helpful kindness, to Sarah Lewis at the University of Wales Press. As ever, my deepest debt is to Caroline.

Illustrations

1. Bodfel Hall, Llannor, Pwllheli, Caernarfonshire. Coflein. NMR Site Files Catalogue Number: C554943.

2. Bachegraig House, Tremeirchion, Flintshire, 1776, by Richard Bernard Godfrey, engraver (b. 1728). National Library of Wales, Aberystwyth.

3. Portrait of Hester Thrale and her daughter Hester, c.1777, by Joshua Reynolds (1723–92). By kind permission of the Beaverbrook Art Gallery, Fredericton, New Brunswick, Canada.

4. 'The Southwark Macaroni', cartoon of Henry Thrale. Published according to the Act of 24 August 1772, by M. Darly, 39 Strand, London. Etching 1915, 0313.163 © The Trustees of the British Museum.

5. Samuel Johnson (1709–84), engraved by William Holl, after Joshua Reynolds, and published in *The Gallery of Portraits with Memoirs*, vol. 7 (London: Knight, 1837).

6. Thrale Place, otherwise known as Streatham Place or Streatham Park, drawn and engraved by William Ellis, published 1 August 1792, by Harrison & Co., 18 Paternoster Row, London, *Copperplate Magazine, or Monthly Cabinet of Picturesque Prints, Consisting of Views in Great Britain and Ireland*, 5 vols (Harrison and Co., London, 1792–1802), vol. 1, print 14. 1862,0712.924. © The Trustees of the British Museum.

7   Hester Lynch Piozzi (née Salusbury, later Mrs Thrale) by unknown Italian artist; oil on canvas 1785–6. NPG 4942. © National Portrait Gallery, London.

8   'Frontispiece for the second edition of Dr Johnson's Letters' by James Sayers; etching, published by Thomas Cornell 7 April 1788. NPG D9898. © National Portrait Gallery, London.

9   Portrait; half length, seated to left; elbow resting on ledge; wearing hat and cloak tied around neck, vignette. Engraved by Henry Meyer from an original Drawing by John Jackson in 1811. Stipple. A, 2.50. © The Trustees of the British Museum.

10 Brynbella, the Seat of G. Piozzi Esqr., engraved by J. Bluck (fl. 1791–1819); J. Baker, artist, Tremeirchion, Flintshire. National Library of Wales, Aberystwyth.

1

Hester Lynch Salusbury: 'a thousand pretty Tricks, [...] a Thousand pretty Stories and [...] a Thousand pretty Verses'

A failed adventure park three miles west of Pwllheli – 'Bodvel Hall means a fun day out for the family, with an Animal Farmyard, [...]' – was the birthplace of our writer of Wales. In the sixteenth century, Bodvel had been the home of a real adventurer, John Wynn, who used Ynys Enlli as a piratical base while employed as County Commissioner for the Suppression of Piracy. But by 1739 it had become haven to a young couple whose marriage reinforced the familial ties between the Salusburys of Bachegraig and Lleweni and the Cottons of Combermere. Tall, dark and handsome, with a quick wit and a quicker temper, John Salusbury was himself something of an adventurer. Although in many ways a gigolo and sponger par excellence, his thoughtful generosity was acknowledged by his kinsman Thomas Pennant, whose love of natural history was first stimulated by Salusbury's gift of Francis Willoughby's *Ornithology* (1678).[1] John's cousin and wife, Hester Maria, was 'for all personal and mental Excellence the most accomplished' and virtuous of women, with the most beautifully piercing eyes.[2] She was the toast of the Denbigh Assembly Rooms, but, hopelessly fascinated by him, had married for love. However, the relationship of this spirited couple was strained and tempestuous. Hester's daughter would later describe it as physically abusive:

for a Woman to contend with a Man She is shut up with at a Distance from Society, where the natural Roughness of the Sex is not restrained; & Gallantry can obtain no Reputation; is so dangerous, that I wonder almost how She escaped with her Life [. . .] after several Miscarriages from Frights, Contests, Falls &c my Mother did produce a live Child. (*Thraliana*, 1: 281)

'After two or three dead things', our Welsh writer, Hester Lynch Salusbury, was born alive on 16 January 1741. Her arrival changed everything; as she herself realized: 'Now they had a Centre of Unity in their Offspring.' While Bodfel Hall, the converted gatehouse of a grand Renaissance-style mansion never brought to completion, continually reminded her parents of their hopes for better things, the *enfant gâté* of the gatehouse began her career of charming others. As our writer reflected over thirty years later:

My Mother nursed up her Infant Daughter my simple Self, to play a thousand pretty Tricks, & tell a Thousand pretty Stories and repeat a Thousand pretty Verses to divert Papa at his Return. Rakish Men seldom make tender Fathers, but a Man must Fondle something, and Nature pleads her own Cause powerfully when a little Art is likewise used to help it forward. (*Thraliana*, 1: 281)

The growing Hester early perfected her powers of pleasing and performing. With much of the Salusbury property mortgaged, money was a perennial problem, and genteel poverty encouraged her parents to use Hester's precocious charms to gain an inheritance. Their daughter not only became the focus of their love, but the centre of their intellectual and financial aspirations: '*I* was their Joynt Play Thyng, & although Education was a Word then unknown, as applied to Females, they had taught me to read, & speak, & think, & translate from the French, till I was half a Prodigy'.[3]

Selling up their household goods at Bodfel, the family briefly lived with Hester's childless maternal uncle, Sir Robert Salusbury Cotton, at Lleweni Hall, a truly palatial Elizabethan mansion in the beautiful Denbighshire vale of Clwyd. Suits of armour and heraldic hatchments 'struck my infant eyes with wonder and delight', intensifying Hester's fascination with her own genealogy. She imbibed the romance of Salusbury descent from Adam of Salzburg, son of the Duke of Bavaria, rewarded with Lleweni for his service to William the Conqueror, and of Sir John Salusbury y Bodiau, whose two thumbs on each hand helped him slay a white lioness ('llewen') in the Tower of London, a feat celebrated by the lion rampant argent device on his shield. *Sat est prostrasse leoni* (It is enough to have conquered a lion) was the family motto and perhaps an appropriate one for a future literary lioness. Hester's parents were both descended from Catrin of Berain, 'Mam Cymru' ('Mother of Wales'), whose first husband was yet another John Salusbury, and whose four marriages intermingled the bluest blood of north Wales.

Sir Robert proved a doting uncle, nicknaming Hester 'Fiddle' on account her restless mental and physical energy. Hester records a *tête-à-tête* conversation between five- and fifty-two-year-old lions beneath the armorials of the *Old Hall*:

> 'Come now, dear,' said he, 'that we are quite alone, tell me what you expected to see here at Llewenney.' 'I expected,' replied I, 'to see an old baronet.' 'Well, in *that* your expectation is not much disappointed; but why did you think of such stuff?' 'Why just because papa and mamma was always saying to me and to one another at Bodvel, what the old baronet would think of this and that: they did it to frighten me I see now; but I thought to myself that kings and princes were but men, and God made *them* you know, Sir, and *they* made old baronets.' (*Autobiography*, 2: 11).

Sir Robert was delighted with his niece, but could not brook his brother-in-law's proud sensitivities. When it was suggested that the latter might apply for a colonial post, leaving his wife and daughter in the security of Lleweni: '"No, no, Sir Robert," was the haughty answer, "if I go for a soldier, *your* sister shall carry the knapsack, and the little wench may have what I can work for."' John Salusbury had burnt his boats and though Sir Robert offered them the use of his grand house in Albemarle Street and there were promises of a £10,000 bequest for Hetty in the baronet's will, the family had to leave for London. There, Hester Lynch captivated the Duke and Duchess of Leeds, honing her performance skills while fed dramatic lines and delicious sweetmeats on David Garrick's lap, and being taught Satan's speech to the sun from *Paradise Lost* by James Quin, England's leading actor. She recalled viewing the solar eclipse of 14 July 1748 'thro' smok'd Glasses', but the following month saw the eclipse of her parents' rose-tinted expectations: Sir Robert Salusbury Cotton died intestate, everything went to his younger brother, the eccentric fourth baronet, Sir Lynch Salusbury Cotton, MP for Denbighshire, and Hester had lost her first chance of acquiring heiress status.

In the following year the proud and restless John Salusbury set out to repair the family fortunes as part of Lord Halifax's expedition to Nova Scotia, having received the impressive-sounding post of 'Register and Receiver of His Majesty's Rents' through the influence of his friend Dr Edward Crane, prebendary of Westminster. He lamented at the quayside: 'My Dear Love, To live an Individual—not thought of by any body—Is of all Others, the Most Forelorne State: and, Except Thy Dear Self, Wife, I am the Very Man'.[4] Constantly apprehensive concerning threats to the settlement from the Indians and the French, his journal reveals the self-pity Hester remembered thirty years later:

> My Father was a Man of quick Parts, much Gentleman like Literature, and a Vein of humour very diverting and seemingly inexhaustible: his Conversation was showy however, not solid; few Men were ever more certain to please at Sight; but though his Talk did not consist in telling Stories, it fatigued his Hearers, who as he was not rich—made no Ceremony of letting him see it. His Sensibility—quickened by Vanity & Idleness was keen beyond the Affectation of any other Mortal, and threw him into Hypocondriack Disorders in spite of a Manly Vigorous Person, & of a Constitution eminently strong: his Affections and Aversions were proportionably violent—he adored his Wife, he doated on his Brother, and his anxious Tenderness for me would often pass the Bounds of common or of *un*common Attention. (*Thraliana*, 1: 127)

Mother and child lived on an £125 annuity, at Mrs Butler's, a Catholic mantua-maker in Great Queen Street, or with Mrs Haynes, a Methodist milliner in St James's Square. Hester later recalled that her mother's steely resolve 'to live upon Air if possible', or at least on vegetables and water, was impairing her health, but significantly she never touched wine on any occasion. Summer brought invitations from Sir Lynch Salusbury Cotton at Lleweni, or joyous holidays with 'my own Dear Grandmamma', Philadelphia Lynch Cotton, at East Hyde in Berkshire. Hester recalled:

> I was kicking my heels on a corn binn, and learning to drive of the old coachman; who, like every body else, small and great, delighted in taking me for a pupil. Grandmamma kept four great ramping warhorses, *chevaux entiers*, for her carriage, with immense long manes and tails, which we buckled and combed; and when, after long practice, I showed her and my mother how two of them (poor Colonel and Peacock) would lick my hand for a lump of sugar or fine white bread, much were they amazed; much more when my skill in guiding them round the courtyard on the break could no longer be doubted or denied, though strictly prohibited for the future. (*Autobiography*, 2: 15–16)

Mother and daughter were frequent visitors to their neighbours at Offley Park just over the border in Hertfordshire: Sir Henry Penrice, a widower and Judge of the High Court of Admiralty, and his highly educated daughter Anna Maria both delighted in the company of the two Hettys. The fearless equestrienne acquired another sobriquet: 'little Spright on Account I guess of my Activity and Paleness' (*Thraliana*, 1: 291). Hester's uncle, Dr Thomas Salusbury, who had been given power of attorney to transact all her father's affairs in his absence, visited East Hyde. One day, 'bursting out into Tears of Joy [he] took my Mother suddenly in his Arms & kissed her—told her that he was to be married to Miss Penrice the Heiress of Offley' (*Thraliana*, 1: 292). Sir Henry retired, Thomas succeeded him as Admiralty Judge with its accompanying knighthood, and married Anna Maria on 20 November 1751.

With the return of her father on leave from Nova Scotia, 'all was Gayety, Transport, & Frenzy of Enjoyment', but his Flintshire agent, Edward Bridges reported that Salusbury credit had 'sunk down to the Lowest Ebb'. With no immediate cash forthcoming from Offley and Lord Halifax urging him to return to Nova Scotia with new instructions for the governance of the colony, John reluctantly complied. He set sail again on the Jason with the new governor, Peregrine Hopson, on 7 June 1752 in an angry mood. By the time they reached Madeira he had quarrelled with Hopson, and he stupidly wrote home with the needless information that 'he had fought a Duel at Madera with Capn [James] Young of the Sphinx, for showing Hopson (whom he hated)—more Civilities than him'. Having briefly mentioned his regret at their separation, John continued to vent his spleen, this time upon his brother: 'how his Estate was frittering away thro' Sir Thomas's Management who was minding nothing but his Wife [Anna Maria]'. On receiving this letter Hester Maria simply communicated John's uneasiness to Sir Thomas, who in early March 1753 successfully petitioned the Board of Trade to allow his return to settle his private affairs.

His capable wife and 'miserable dog' of a brother had coolly sorted everything out, but – like the petulant overgrown child he was – 'He came home gloriously out of humour; said there was no need to have taken from him his Estate & his place too' (*Thraliana*, 1: 294). Much had happened in his absence: Sir Henry Penrice's death on the 10 August 1752 had placed Sir Thomas in command of a fortune which the newspapers reported as 'upwards of One Hundred and Fifty Thousand Pounds'. John found his wife and daughter comfortably lodged in Jermyn Street and preparing for a move to a house in Dean Street where they kept a manservant and two maids. The reunion he had longed for was achieved, and his little family 'might have been very happy, if my Father's violent Temper had not put peace & Quietness out of the Question'. Daily young Hester was learning from her mother feminine skills which she would draw upon throughout her life, the chief of which was how to soothe thin-skinned male egos.

Earlier lessons learnt at Lleweni and practised to perfection on Sir Robert Cotton ensured success as Hester now exerted her charm upon Sir Thomas and Lady Anna Maria Salusbury. Mother and daughter were frequently installed at the commodious seventeenth-century brick manor house of Offley Park, and Anna Maria, 'a Woman of extensive Acquirements' grew to love Hester 'as her own Daughter and destined Heiress'.[5] Anna Maria thought it a 'pity I should not learn Latin, Italian, and even Spanish, in all of which she was conversant' (*Autobiography*, 2: 17). The pupil was eager and not averse to obtaining patronage:

> And now I was set to learn Italian to flatter Lady Salusbury who was an Adept in that Language; & I used to write her Letters in it, and make long Translations, Dedicating them to her, forsooth, for which, tho' people said She was covetous, I never missed my Reward. Indeed She was extremely kind & Indulgent to me, gave me fine Silks, Pearls and a thousand Things. (*Thraliana*, 1: 295)

In the learning of Spanish, the manipulation of Hester's education to coincide with Anna Maria's interests emerges with greater clarity. Her aunt was a woman of great piety and had been greatly moved by the Lisbon earthquake of All Saints' Day 1755. Hester's 'mother, who was particularly fond of Spanish literature, made me translate a sermon in that language, written and preached in the Jewish synagogue at London by Isaac Netto,—whose name is all I can bring back to mind,—and dedicate it to my dear aunt, Anna Maria Salusbury' (*Autobiography*, 2: 17–18). Nieto's sermon, preached at the Bevis Marks synagogue on 6 February 1756, the Day of Fasting and Humiliation appointed by the government to mark this ominous visitation of providence, might seem strong stuff for a girl of fifteen. Opening with a Ta'anit text stressing the need for repentance and good works and a quotation from Deuteronomy 10:16: 'Circumcise therefore the Fore-skin of your Hearts, and be no more Stiff-necked', Nieto did not rule out 'natural Causes for Earthquakes', but argued that God is 'the effective Causes of all Causes', and the trembling of the earth should be read as a terrible warning.[6] The sermon made a huge impact upon the young translator, far beyond the 'set of pearl and garnet ornaments' with which she was rewarded for her efforts.[7] Throughout her life Hester was fascinated by earthquakes, their physical causes and their place within the apocalyptic nightmares of millenarianism; her moving interview with a woman survivor of the 1783 Messina earthquake, published in her *Observations*, turned fashionable travel writing into documentary journalism, earning her a place in the history of women in science.[8]

The young scholar's love of *Don Quixote* led to the pleasure of reading it in the original, and her translation of sections of the novel, even before 'My Father had made me translate the Life of Cervantes prefixed to the Novel'.[9] Lacking the wit to seek the assistance of printed translations, she 'plodded and blundered on & translated the Verses into Rhymes of my own', but arguably her teenage version of the 'Epitafio' on Cervantes is more harmonious than the crude rendering of John Ozell's published translation.[10]

One evening, when the celebrated artist William Hogarth, an intimate friend of her father, joined Hester and her cousins in playing the board Game of the Goose he was caught by her excited expression and this resulted in Hogarth's request that she should model for *The Lady's Last Stake*:

> [L]ook here said he I am doing this for you—you are not 14 Years old yet I think, but you will be 24; and this Portrait will then be like you. 'Tis the Lady's last Stake—See how She hesitates between her Money and her Honour, Take you care; I see an Ardour for Play in your Eyes and in Your heart—don't indulge it, I shall give you this Picture as a Warning, because I love you now, you are so good A Girl. (*Autobiography*, 2: 309)

In fact, gambling was never to prove to Hester's taste, and she subsequently remarked modestly that 'he had scarcely attempted a likeness, having made his rash lady a beauty'. So what did our ardent heroine look like? Her impoverished parents could scarcely afford a portrait, so we must have recourse to later canvases, or a thirty-seven-year-old's glance in the cheval-glass:

> The Height four feet eleven only, and the Waist though not a taper one quite in proportion. The Neck rather longish, and remarkably white—so much as to create Suspicions of its being painted—This however is particular only because the Woman is a brown one, with Chestnut Hair

& Eyebrows of the same Colour strongly mark'd over a pair of large—but light Grey Eyes. The Complexion however is perfectly clear—the Red very bright, & the White eminently good & clean. So much for Colour; Expression there is none I think; and the Grace—which resembles that of Foreigners—is more acquired than natural; for Strength & not Delicacy was the original Characteristick of the Figure. (*Thraliana*, 1: 321)

Another frequent visitor at Offley who had seen the light of mischievous intellect in Hester's eyes was Dr Arthur Collier, a friend of Sir Thomas, a civil lawyer, who championed female education. Having taught Greek and Latin to the novelist Sarah Fielding, he seemed to Anna Maria an ideal preceptor for her niece. In 1758 he was 51 and she was 17 and the attraction was mutual; she later described him as 'my truest, my most disinterested Friend'. He was just what she needed after years of praise, an exacting teacher, combative to the point of contentiousness, to sharpen her intellect. Yet, according to Hester, most people found his disputatious disposition disagreeable:

[H]e loved to talk better than to hear, & to dispute better than to please; his Conversation too was always upon such Subjects as the rest of Mankind seem by one Consent to avoid. Duration and Eternity, Matter & Motion, Whig & Tory, Faith and Works were his favourite Topicks; and upon these or other Metaphysical Disquisitions would he be perpetually forcing his Company—while by his Superiority in Logic, & constant Exercise in all the Arts of Ratiocination, he delighted to drive them into Absurdities they were desirous to keep clear of, & then laugh at the ridiculous Figures that they made: All this however being done with an Air of great Civility made him more a painful than an offensive Companion, & People generally left the Room with a high Opinion of that Gentleman's Parts and a confirmed Resolution to avoid his Society. (*Thraliana*, 1: 16)

Collier's conversation was good practice for the future friend of Dr Johnson. A letter from early in her tuition – their later correspondence was often in Latin – complaining about her grammatical errors, provides a flavour of their relationship:

> My Dear Child, You are enough to make a Parson Swear [. . .] there must be something strangely wrong in your Head that so plain and simple a doctrine will not make its way into your understanding. In the very first sentence of your yesterdays Letter there are but seven words and six faults. (Clifford, p. 26)

The pupil–teacher relationship had something of the erotic: as Swift had written: 'Each girl, when pleased with what is taught, / Will have the teacher in her thought.' Hester esteemed Collier as 'a Man of perfect Worth, profound Erudition, and polish'd Manners: a Man who engrossed my whole Heart, & deserved it' (*Thraliana*, 1: 297).

To win the approval of her proud family and her exacting mentor Hester produced a range of occasional verse reflecting her omnivorous reading and her youthful compassion. 'I was now completely a spoyl'd Child, and wrote Odes for the Peace & Verses upon every, & upon no Occasion. Imitations of English poets too, which I fancied tolerable: but which in looking over my Copies of late, appeared to me Insupportable'.[11] One of the earliest, 'Forrester; or the old Hunter's Petition for Life addressed to Sir Thomas Salusbury', written in 1758 'to save dear Forester from being shot because grown superannuated', takes the theme of man's right to end the life of animals. Forrester admires the beautiful young horse Tudor who has supplanted him as Sir Thomas's favourite mount, but begs to be allowed his natural span:

> Safe to thy Care my Master I confide,
> And cede to thee my Glory & my Pride.
> Till the poor panting Prey appears in View
> Each eager Sportsman ardent to persue; [. . .]
> Then shall our Owner's heart with Pleasure bound
> To hear thy Praise from ev'ry Tongue resound:
> And now—when all have gain'd their glorious Ends,
> That Death upon whose Life their Sport depends,
> Haply his Hand caressive may repay
> The pleasing Labours of thy well-spent Day;

> His hand—to which my utmost wish aspires,
> The only Boon his Forrester desires,
> That friendly hand in Confirmation given
> That I may live the Term allow'd by Heaven.
> (*Thraliana*, 1: 37–40; 40)

Hester returned to the critique of René Descartes's concept that animals were mindless automata in 'a little odd metaphysical toy to divert Doctor Collier after the death of his dog', entitled 'Pompey, or a Doggerel Epistle from Pompey in the Shades—to his Master in Doctor's Commons':

> That Brutes were mere Machines he swore
> Sans passive Will, or active Pow'r;
> And all their Actions bad or good
> Effects of circulating Blood:
> Automatons by secret Springs
> Made to perform surprizing Things.
> (*Thraliana*, 1: 17–20; 18)

Collier's efforts in making Hester 'perform surprizing Things' were augmented by the tutorial assistance of another of her father's less rakish friends: the Revd Dr. William Parker, rector of Saint James's, Westminster, and a chaplain in ordinary to George II and George III. This Fellow of the Royal Society increased her competency in Latin and finessed her French, sharing her interests in European earthquakes and talking dogs.[12] Having read her 'Pompey', Parker's 5-line impromptu response, concluding with the couplet 'Dogs should hence forward bark in Rhyme, / And Doggrel Verse be true Sublime', revealed a poet inferior to his pupil. Accordingly the verses he addressed 'To Miss Salusbury—Express from Parnassus' culminate in the nine Muses vying with the three Graces for Hester's inclusion in their number as acknowledged 'Genius of the British Isle', a tussle only to be resolved by Apollo's decision that she should join the ranks of both: 'Henceforth acknowledge every Pen, / The Graces four—the Muses Ten' (*Thraliana*, 1: 21–3; 23).

Collier was increasingly impressed with Hester's poems and sent them to his circle of friends, which included James 'Hermes' Harris, the philosopher and musical patron, whose brilliant *Hermes, or, A Philosophical Inquiry Concerning Universal Grammar* (1751) had provided his sobriquet. He complimented Hester with the gift of a copy of its 1760 edition in four volumes, interleaved with blank pages for her comments and queries. Furthermore, Harris, encouraged her literary endeavours, which were frequently sent to the London newspapers. Her early poems, like her translations from the Romance languages, demonstrate an intriguing blend of imitation and individuality. In her 'Irregular Ode on the English Poets', composed on New Year's Day 1759, celebration of the diversity of 'Britannia's Genius' is artfully accomplished through emulation, and the stanza upon Spenser reveals the extent to which Hester has been seduced by the power of words:

> So the soft Maid doth still in Secret sigh
> For him who first did cause her Love-sick Smart;
> Which never shall remove until She die,
> His image is imprinted in her Heart,
> Ne can a Second Love oblige it to depart.
> (*Thraliana*, 1: 63–6; 64)

The death of Anna Maria on 7 March 1759 at the age of 41 after a severe miscarriage left Hester's uncle distraught. The storms of the following January which felled her aunt's favourite tree presented the dutiful niece with an opportunity to memorialize her aunt in 'Verses on the Fall of the Great Ash Tree in Offley Park', which concluded with a sixteen-line paean to her merits. The grieving husband recited it to all his visitors, but Hester acknowledged mixed motives in her account of its reception: 'This trifling Performance brought Tears into my Uncle's Eyes, and Money into my Pocket for having celebrated so artfully, I will own the Virtues of a Woman he remembered with Gratitude and Esteem' (*Thraliana*, 1: 77). The mention of 'Performance' and 'artfully' celebrated, together with her father's contribution of a line to the poem, underscore the fact that familial encouragement and expectations had weighed so heavily upon the child that performativity and theatricality were now at the heart of her own self-fashioning. This is disturbing as is her apparent awareness of private conversation between her aunt and uncle, presumably – and remarkably – relayed to her by the former: '[She] told her husband she should die more happily, persuaded that he would not marry, as he was so attached to the good girl she now considered as her own' (*Autobiography*, 2: 17).

It seems clear that Offley Park had for years been suffused with powerful cross-currents of emotion all focused upon future possession of the estate. Hester's recollections of Anna Maria recorded that she 'loved my Uncle passionately & me tenderly as his favourite plaything: my Mother She rather fear'd as her Superior in Knowledge & Elegance; and my Father she hated heartily as who can wonder?' Continual gratitude can prove a tiresome duty, but it still comes as something of a shock to read Hester's later annotation: 'The kind & constant Partiality She shew'd me claim'd all my Gratitude, but as I always lov'd & hated after my Mother—I never did *much love her*' (*Thraliana*, 1: 295).

After the demise of her generous aunt, 'Father could hardly be moderate in his Joy'; the family were installed at Offley, and her uncle 'said that he had ten thousand Pounds ready for me whenever a proper Match might be offer'd'. As the immediate heir 'both to the Welch Estate and the Hertfordshire one [. . .] I was looked up to—as the principal Person of the Family—my Influence was courted by every one.' Following her aunt's death, Hester's 'supposed' estate of Offley was now

> haunted by young men who made court to the niece, and expressed admiration of the horses. Every suitor was made to understand my extraordinary value. Those who could read, were shown my verses; those who could not, were judges of my prowess in the field. It was my sport to mimic some, and drive others back, in order to make Dr. Collier laugh, who did not perhaps wish to see me give a heart away which he held completely in his hands. (*Autobiography*, 2: 18)

In the concluding stanza of her 'Irregular Ode on the English Poets', dated New Year's Day 1758, Hester had celebrated a young poet, placing him in the best of company:

> While easy Marriott tunes the vocal Lyre,
> While Gray—that great Original we own,
> And gentle Mason sits sublime on Nature's peaceful Throne.

Hester's suitor was Dr James Marriot, a young advocate and friend of her uncle's at Doctors' Commons, 'who made Love to me and Verses on me, English ones and French ones [. . .] the prettiest verses in French of any Englishman I know'.[13] Marriott was a correspondent of Voltaire who also recognized him as a talented poet: 'A man who writes such charming verses as you do must have a great deal of courage to occupy himself with people's quarrels'.[14] His Italian was also pretty good, and the fifth stanza of his 'Verses from Ariosto addressed to Miss Salusbury' praises its dedicatee as a modern rival to 'Gay Sappho' and Corinna:

> But now I see the pleasing Visions rise,
> One female triumphs, and extends her Praise;
> Her Labours now the wond'ring World surprize
> Ordain'd to flourish thro' a Length of Days.
> (*Thraliana*, 1: 33–4; 34)

This indefatigable seeker after patronage found that, as a suitor for the hand of 'heiress' Hester, flattery would get him nowhere. Her irascible duellist father stood like the rampant Salusbury lion at the gate, barring entry to any prospective fortune-hunter. The colour drained from the gay and volatile face of Dr Marriott when a threatening letter informed him that if he continued 'to insult my poor child [. . .] I will be avenged on you, much to the detriment of your person'.[15] As the black paternal moods produced by such 'Ill humour generally fell heavy on my poor dear Mother [. . .] I used to keep clear of Solicitations to Marriage with more assiduity than other Girls use to procure them' (*Thraliana*: 1: 296).

In many respects Hester was more concerned with achieving literary fame. Indeed, her 'free Translation' of Louis Racine's first 'Épitre sur l'homme' which she entitled 'Essay on Man', displays growing intellectual and literary confidence. The modern critic, William McCarthy, whose work has effectively rebutted the idea that Hester's literary career was entirely dependent on the commanding influence of Samuel Johnson, points out in his edition of her 'Essay on Man' that it represents 'the only English translation of Racine's 'Épitre', and only the second English translation of any Racine poem'.[16] Exhilarated by what she termed 'the racy season of life', she deliberately revisited the French poet's earlier attack upon Pope as a Pelagianist and Spinozan deist. Displaying a deliberate perversity which delighted in controversy, she used Pope's own aphorisms against him, to critique a poet who had proved such a formative influence upon her. For Hester, as for many European intellectuals, horror at disasters such as the Lisbon earthquake had made it impossible to accept early Enlightenment optimism:

> No longer Pope, in Death and Reason's Spite
> Shall vainly think whatever is, is right.
> ('Essay on Man', ll. 218–19)[17]

Parker was delighted with it: 'I never saw any French Poetry that was so nervous [muscular], or that pleased me as much as your Translation'.[18] She later recalled the impact of her reading Joseph Warton's proto-Romantic *Essay on the Genius and Writings of Pope* (1756): 'I felt its Beauties, repeated its Precepts, wearied my Parents with Quotations, and my Tongue with Praises, of this—shall I call it unlucky Volume [. . .] made a Writer & a Critic of H:L:P'.[19]

Politics, hunting, the lure of Wales, and the introduction of two Offley neighbours were to conspire to make a 'Wife & a Childbearer' of H.L.S. In late March 1761, Lord Halifax was nominated to the lord-lieutenancy of Ireland, and both the Salusbury brothers jumped at the chance of joining his entourage to Holyhead and showing their patron 'the wonders of Wales'. After the tour, Sir Thomas drove back to Offley while Hester's father stayed on for some time attending to Bachegraig affairs. When John Salusbury returned from Flintshire he discovered his brother infatuated by the attentions of Mrs Sarah King, a 'blooming Widow' with obvious designs upon the Offley estate. John was also appalled that in his absence his wife and his brother were conniving and contriving to arrange a marriage between his daughter and a rich brewer. The twenty-year-old Hester at the centre of all this collusion could hardly view things with an unjaundiced eye. She judged Mrs King as a creature of 'rapacious Avarice' and her 'most tender Affection for his Person' as pretended; how might it be otherwise when the sixty-year-old Sir Thomas was 'loaded with fat, & bloated with hard Drinking no Object as I believe of any Passion but Disgust' (*Thraliana*, 1: 303). As for the 'Beau Brewer' (her father's coinage) or the 'model of perfection and *'real sportsman'* (her uncle's), Hester and her mother had been expected to like him and, from his introduction, the latter certainly did:

> Mr. Thrale applied himself so diligently to gain my mother's attention—aye, and her heart, too,—that there was little doubt of her approving the pretensions of so very showy a suitor—if suitor he was to me, who certainly had not a common share in the compliments he paid to my mother's wit, beauty, and elegance. (*Autobiography*, 2: 19)

No suitor was good enough for Hester's father, especially not one of yeoman origins, and Hester hardly felt she had one, for 'nothing resembled love *less* than Mr. Thrale's behaviour'. Henry Thrale was a tall, handsome, unaffected, intelligent and rich thirty-three-year-old, but he took 'less Notice of Me than any other man I had ever seen come to the House almost' (*Thraliana*, 1: 303). Perhaps this was calculated to intrigue her.

'[T]he principal Person of the Family' was being sidelined while the vanities of mother and uncle were being expertly massaged by Thrale and King. Clearly Hester must compensate by honing her writerly and critical skills to shine on a more extensive stage than that of Offley Park. Fascinated by the prospect of seeing her work in print, Hester began sending in pseudonymous letters and verses to the papers, especially the newly founded *St James's Chronicle*: '[I]t was my sport to see them reading, studying, blaming or praising their own little whimsical girl's performances' (*Autobiography*, 2: 28). Inspired by what her father had told her of the Mi'kmaq indigenous natives of Nova Scotia, and what she had read of the ferocious Anglo-Cherokee War of 1759–60, she composed her 'American Eclogue'. Enclosed in a letter sent to the printer of the *Chronicle*, she describes it as 'an *Indian* fragment which I picked up in *North America* six Months ago, and got a Countryman of mine, a *North Briton*, to translate for me into *Fingalian* Prose'. The italics of this artful young correspondent pressed all the right buttons. They connected two topical and engrossing concerns: the Ossian controversy, intensified by the publication of *Fingal* two months earlier, and the nature of Britain's courageous adversaries in her New World empire. A sensitive and humane third-century Celtic warrior-poet is linked to the innate nobility of the North American 'savage', via a 'north British' 'translator' from the north of Wales. Entitled 'The Lamentations of Samoset, a Chief of the Oneydoes, over his Son, who fell in Battle', this is part of the father's elegiac eulogy:

> And is my Warrior fallen indeed? Does his Ghost pursue the Foe? And it shall pursue them, my Son, to the Shore of the pointed Wave, where the Sun sets in the West, and Quenches, till Morn, the Flames of his Hair in the cool Caves of the silent Ocean.[20]

The *Chronicle*'s editor, Nathaniel Thomas, a Cardiff man, failed to notice that the two speakers in the Eclogue belonged to the previous century: Samoset was the first Native American to greet the Pilgrims at Plymouth in the spring of 1621, and his interlocutor Squanto, last of the Patuxet, was Samoset's interpreter. Thomas had fallen for Hester's spoof, hook, line and sinker, and he placed the following message in his own italics: '*The Continuance of this Correspondent's Favours is desired*'.[21]

And so it was; in July of the same year, that the *St James's Chronicle* was again favoured – this time by a political squib. This concerned the dislodging from ministerial office of William Pitt and Thomas, Duke of Newcastle, by the Earl of Bute, a Scots peer, former tutor and now favourite of George III. An amusing and detailed allegory of the history of Albion Manor (England), it culminates in the dismissal of its faithful old steward: 'they have turned off old Tom (Newcastle), and made a dirty Scotch Boy (Bute) Steward that used to dry-rub old Madam's Jointure-House'.[22] Hester's Whiggish intervention in the acrimonious debate between supporters and opponents of the widely detested Bute ministry hit its mark. Political journalism had rarely been more hard fought with Tobias Smollett's newly founded *The Briton* rebuffed by the anti-ministerial and ironically titled *The North Briton* of John Wilkes.[23] Loathing of Bute was all that Hester shared with 'Liberty' Wilkes, but her political talent, like his, resided in the pen.

The following week the *St James Chronicle* printed an apparent announcement under the title 'ALBION MANOR' which opens:

> MR. WILKES returns his most sincere Thanks to the Right Honourable and Noble Personage, for an original Answer from John, the present Steward of Albion Manor, to the Letter of Thomas, the late Steward, which was printed in the SAINT JAMES'S CHRONICLE of Saturday last.[24]

Many readers would have thought that this referred to the member for Aylesbury, especially as nearby columns contained a substantial extract from *The North Briton*. The remainder of the copy consisted of an advertisement for the weekly magazine *Political Controversy*, edited by John Caesar Wilkes, which assembled arguments from both sides of the dispute. Very few would have known that this was the pseudonym of an opportunist journalist and piratical publisher named Brookes whose imposition Wilkes deeply resented. Be that as it may, Hester's letter was reprinted in *Political Controversy*, immediately followed by the promised letter signed by the new steward of Albion Manor, John (Bute), deploring the customs of the old servants and stoutly defending the new Master (George III).[25] The bold assurance and sheer political nous of Hester's imaginative entrée into the venomous world of anti-Bute propaganda displayed the untameable nature of this twenty-one-year Welsh woman. She was not merely amusing her parents but modifying contemporary political rhetoric, as was displayed when Smollett himself followed Hester's lead by creating his own allegory of the estate of Mr Fitz-George and his troublesome servants in *The Briton* of 20 November 1762.

Pseudonymous intervention in Westminster feuding, however, could only provide a temporary relief from the problems facing 'her own' estate and the scheming partialities of her own troublesome relatives. The brothers had quarrelled and John had taken his family to London, first to Dean Street and then to Masefield Street, where the continuing visits of Henry Thrale 'to my mother [were] rendered terrifying to *me* every day from papa's violence of temper' (*Autobiography*, 2: 21). John Salusbury raged against this Bankside 'whoring fop', who had the effrontery to display a miniature of the celebrated courtesan Polly Hart on the outside of his snuffbox. His fury was exacerbated by his wife's partiality towards Thrale: he forgot that she had married a gigolo herself. His unwilling daughter should not be sold 'for a Barrel of Porter' to a man who would give her the pox.

At the eye of this turmoil, Hester found a comforting stillness in her relation with her tutor, but ironically it was a confidential letter from Dr Collier, written in Latin, that precipitated the tragic crisis. Its purport was to let her know that Sir Thomas was about to marry Mrs King and that she should not breathe a syllable until Collier himself came to 'break the dreadful Tydings to my Father'. Possessed by his compulsive monomania and misreading Hester's distress, John Salusbury accused his daughter of receiving clandestine letters from Thrale, and a cruel evening of bitter recriminations culminated in Hester's fainting. By the time she revived, the anguished father had read the letter and was profusely apologizing to the wronged daughter: 'poor unhappy soul! and in this fond misery spent we the hours till four o'clock in the morning'. At nine he set out to seek the advice of Dr Crane and of his brother-in-law, Sir Lynch Cotton, but on that fateful day, 18 December 1762, he dropped down dead of an apoplectic stroke and the fifty-five-year-old John Salusbury 'was brought us home a corpse, before the dining hour' (*Autobiography*, 2: 22).

There were many expressions of grief and shock from his wide circle of friends, including Lord Halifax, but his sudden death struck at the heart of his family who had adored him despite all his faults. Sir Thomas, struck by remorse, cleared his brother's debts and made profuse promises of support for his niece and sister-in-law. As his grief subsided, however, so did his generosity and it was left to Dr Crane, and particularly Dr Collier, to persuade Sir Thomas to make good his promise to settle a fortune on his niece before he remarried. Collier urged Hester to write a letter of earnest supplication to her uncle but her Salusbury pride would not let her. In some respects she was very much her father's daughter and, as Collier wrote: 'his sweetest Angel in a passion' was more frightening than the fiercest 'Lions and Tygers'.[26] She decided she would be a writer and work to support herself and her mother, avoiding both the Scylla of being a craven suitor to Sir Thomas and the Charybdis of an apparently loveless suitor like Thrale. Increasingly her mother seemed convinced that more reliance might be placed upon the sheet-anchor fortune of Thrale's Anchor Brewery, despite her daughter's reluctance to sleep between Southwark sheets in a Borough bed.

2

The Two Hesters 'have *murder'd* Peace & Happiness at Home'

Torn between her mother's desire to see her well married and what her mother viewed as her tutor's disinclination to her marrying anyone, Hester's romantic visions of a love-match were gradually eroded. Jealous of his influence and angry at his gullibility in believing Sir Thomas's promises, her mother forbade Hester to correspond with her beloved tutor. Hester senior now felt free to encourage Thrale's visits, which culminated in this awkward but undeniably heartfelt first proposal of the 28 June 1768 from the usually stolid and phlegmatic brewer, reflecting a failure of nerve the preceding evening and a fresh determination to be accepted by both Hesters:

> Mr. Thrale presents His most respectfull compliments to Mrs. & Miss Salusbury & wishes to God He could have communicated His Sentiments to them last night, which is absolutely impossible for Him to do to any other Person breathing; He therefore most ardently begs to see Them at any Hour this afternoon, & He will at all Events immediately enter upon this very interesting Subject, & when once begun, there is no Danger of His wandering upon any other: in short, see them, He must, for He assures them, with the greatest Truth & Sincerity, that They have *murder'd* Peace & Happiness at Home.[1]

There is almost something touching about this clumsy letter with its attempt to enlist the *fin' amour* trope of the beauteous murderer, confused by Thrale's persistent use of the third person plural and diluted by the unromantic phrase 'Happiness at Home'. Such nervousness would seem unexpected from a man later to be lampooned as 'The Southwark Macaroni', whom Sir Thomas had met 'at the house of Mr. Levinz, a well-known *bon vivant* [...] who kept a gay house and a gay lady at Brompton, where he entertained the gay fashionists of 1760' (*Autobiography*, 2: 20).² It remains something of a mystery exactly why 'Mr. Thrale deigned to accept my undesired hand'. He claimed it was not the £10,000 dowry her uncle had promised, gallantly adding 'that if I had been 10,000$^£$ *in Debt*, he would have been happy to pay the Debt & then married me' (*Thraliana*, 1: 306). In this apparently passionless marriage of convenience one thing that united the couple was respect for Hester's mother, whose aristocratic hauteur symbolized for Thrale exactly what he was gaining from the match. Very little is known about Mary, his own mother, who had died in 1760; uncertainty concerning her maiden name, which might have been Dobbins, would seem to emphasise her obscurity. Yet Henry Thrale, whose foxhounds were famed throughout Surrey, seems never to have been embarrassed by his humble origins. On learning that the family cottage, in which his father, Ralph, had been born, was now the Salusbury dog kennel, he was vastly amused at the appropriateness.

A few days later Hester received a letter, dated 30 June 1763, from her frustrated lover, James Marriott, who had sent her a copy of his *Poems written chiefly at the University of Cambridge* (1761) and had probably heard of the engagement. It mingled the passionate: 'You have never been out of my thoughts', with the admonitory.

> Those brilliant endowments wch are natural to you or which you have acquired may make you envied and shunned by y^r own sex, and even distrusted by ours, and if not valued as they deserve by the Man who shall possess y^r Person may make you perhaps unhappy and secretly unbeloved, for all you should be adored.

Rejecting his concern for her happiness, the dutiful daughter returned 'both his Book and his Letter which she hopes will convince him that she does not chuse his correspondence'.³ Yet while the details of her dowry and jointure were negotiated and the wedding plans arranged, her life, her liberty and her pursuit of happiness engrossed her thoughts. As a self-solacing gesture she penned her first published poem, her final poem as an unmarried woman, 'Imagination's Search after Happiness: An Allegorical Fable', published in the *St James's Chronicle* of 8–10 September 1763.[4] Imagination enthusiastically seeks for her lover, Happiness, in 'Love's gay temple' until reprimanded by the 'eye severe' of blushing Delicacy:

> I never thought to see you here
> Without a Veil too—Fye my Dear!
> To seek your Lover! and is this
> A likely Seat for sober Bliss?

Ascending the steep path, slippery with human blood, to the glittering palace of Ambition:

> Her Lover's Form on high was plac'd,
> To tempt her Steps along;
> But when the Phantom She embrac'd,
> It vanish'd and was gone.

Despairing of finding her lover midst the 'Consumptive Care and dropsy'd Pride'of the Realms of Riches, Imagination suddenly hears a sweet female voice: '"Come to my Cot, and live with me / *In unreproved pleasures free*"' in the company of Peace, Content and Contemplation:

> 'Your Lover will no longer fly,
> 'Tis his to court when we deny,
> And fly when we pursue.'
> The Virgin weigh'd, and found her wise,
> Nor scorn'd to own herself to blame;
> But took fair Piety's Advice—
>   Uncall'd the Lover came.

Having taken the advice of family rather than piety, the imaginative nymph Hester summoned all her Celtic courage during the following weeks, stoically schooling herself to accept the inevitable. Within a month, unlov'd the Bridegroom came, and the 'bartered' bride was married on Tuesday, 11 October, St Anne's Soho, at the age of twenty-two.

The honeymoon was an enthralling family affair as the couple – encumbered with her mother, her uncle, and the officiating clergyman and distant relative, the Revd Thelwall Salusbury, whom she loathed – set off at a sedate pace on the six-mile rural drive to Streatham Park. The erstwhile heiress of Offley was singularly unimpressed with her first sight of the brick villa that her father-in-law, Ralph, had built in 100 acres of Tooting Common, which the Duke of Bedford allowed him to enclose in exchange for a ten years' supply of ale and porter at Woburn Abbey. 'And what a House it was then!' she recalled, almost three decades, and very many improvements, later, 'a little squeezed miserable Place with a wretched Court before it [. . .] Such Furniture too!' (*Thraliana*, 2: 782). And so her married life began. Like Imagination in Piety's Cot, Hester in Thrale's villa enjoyed '*unreproved pleasures free*' in the company of Peace, Contemplation, Content, and her rug-making mother:

> My Mother lived with me & I was content; I re'd to her in the Morning, played at Back Gammon with her at Noon, & worked Carpets with her in the Evening. Mr Thrale profess'd his Aversion to a *Neighbourhood*, in wch my Mother perfectly agreed with him, so we visited nobody; he sometimes brought a Friend from London, and that She had more Wit than to oppose, tho' she did not encourage it. His sisters each came once in a formal way, my Mother charged me not to be free or intimate with 'em, & none of them pleased me enough to make me wish to break her Injunction. Mean Time my Husband went every day to London & returned either to dinner or Tea, said he always found two agreable Women ready to receive him, & thus we lived on Terms of great Civility & Politeness, if not of strong Alliance and Connection. (*Thraliana*, 1: 306–7)

It is hard for a young, attractive and vivacious woman of twenty-two completely to abandon her visions of romance. Theirs had been a marriage of convenience, but she felt it should be possible to capture the love of her handsome husband, to be elevated in his eyes, which were 'of the deepest Blue', above the status of being regarded merely as one of the 'two agreable Women' to whom he returned. Hester tried all the elements of the repertoire she had used to captivate as a child. In retrospect she wryly commented on her simple naiveté:

> I was [. . .] silly enough to expect that my husband's heart was to be won by the same empty Tricks that had pleased my Family & my Uncle. so I wrote Verses in *his* Praise instead of *theirs*—& while we remained at Streatham between Octr. 11th—our Wedding Day, & the Time we went to Southwark for the Winter: (while he was at Harrow on a Visit—& I sat at home to *spin*) *This* was my Amusement.[5]

This amusement, which – perhaps intentionally – symbolizes the fact that Hester was more spinster than wife, is reflected in her 'Rondeau to Mr. Thrale at Harrow':

> As much in vain my Wheel I seize
> My Temper, not my Flax I teize,
> No subject now my Thoughts can please
>   But Harrow on the Hill:
>
> And while my Heart in earnest *burns*,
> Your Stay the murmuring Spindle mourns
> Impatient till my Love returns.
>   (from 'Harrow on the Hill', *Thraliana*, 1: 272)

Hester was no Arianrhod in her spinning tower, but she knew the spindle and spinning wheel were symbols of female virtue and diligence, of creativity and domesticity. The multivalent employments, both wheel and rondeau, to which she turns are more than amusements: they represent the centripetal role she desires to play in her own household. 'Your Stay' primarily denotes Thrale's sojourn at Harrow, but it also reminds the reader of what she aspires to be, and it is not only the spindle that mourns his impassive indifference. An 'Ode to a Robin Redbreast', written two months after her wedding, urges the little bird to sing the sweets of 'Nuptial Bliss', midst 'Streatham's calm Retreats':

> Where Love and Peace and Pleasure join,
> A wreath for Hymen's Brows to twine;
> Where You like me have most Delight to prove
> The Joys of rural Life—and sweet connubial Love.
> (*Thraliana*, 1: 55–6)

Hester's ode is a poem of desideration expressing a self-consolatory longing for what it describes, as if asserting that Streatham was a bower of marital bliss might bring it about. Such poems, dismissed or devalued by her stolid and obtuse partner,[6] were far from the 'empty Tricks' which Hester termed them, for they embodied, during a winter of lonely discontent, the therapeutic power of creative expression.

Hester needed coping strategies: she was totally mastered by two despotic personalities, her mother and her husband, and she dared not cross either. With Thrale she soon learned how to avoid being thwarted or refused: self-abnegation she found preferable to the prospect of facing the depressing reality of her own absolute powerlessness. It is profoundly saddening to read of her self-censorship:

> Was I to propose a Journey Mr Thrale would refuse to let me take; or desire a Tree to be cut down or planted, and he should—as he most undoubtedly would—give me a coarse Reply and abrupt Negative, it would make *me* miserable: to have one's own un Importance presented suddenly to one's Sight, and one's own Qualities insolently undervalued by those who do not even *pretend* to possess them—is sufficiently mortifying. (*Thraliana*, 1: 269)

Any fighting spirit was simply knocked out of the unloved Hester. Her favourite horse-riding had been forbidden her by her parents when she was the valued potential heiress and bankable asset; now her sportsman husband proscribed it as unfeminine. Wintering at Southwark might have offered compensations, but husband and mother conspired to prevent her from entering polite society, with the latter choosing to ignore the fact that, for Thrale, London society meant clubbing and womanizing. In the Borough as in the country the patriarchal Henry even forbade her superintendence of their cuisine: 'his Wife was not to stink of the Kitchen',[7] yet his nostrils seemed oblivious of the sour and acrid South Bank smells of brewing, tanning and vinegar-making which drifted through the windows of Thrale's severe four-storeyed stone townhouse, adjoining the brewery in Deadman's Place, off Dirty Lane. The Borough, traditionally known for its breweries, brothels and bear-baiting, was not a place to which she might invite persons of any *ton*. The house was situated near the entrance to the wet and sloppy brew yard, in which were quarters for the counting-house and collecting clerks, storehouses, vaults, the brewhouse with its enormous coppers, forty massive porter vats and associated mash tuns, coopers' sheds, stables for a hundred dray and mill horses, dung pits, coal-stores and so on.

In Southwark as at Streatham, Hester learned that domesticity was far from blissful:[8] 'She lived with her Husband a Life so completely domestic that She really never went out to dinner with a Friend or ever saw the Inside of a Theatre from the Day She married till her eldest Daughter could accompany her'.[9] She was quick to see the irony of the fact that the nine-acre plot on which Thrale's house stood included both part of a former burial ground and the site of Shakespeare's Globe:

> For a long time, then—or I thought it such—my fate was bound up with the old Globe Theatre; the alley it had occupied having been purchased & thrown down by Mr. Thrale to make an opening before the windows of our dwelling house. When it lay desolate in a black heap of rubbish, my mother, one day in a joke, called it the Ruins of Palmyra. (*Autobiography*, 2: 33)[10]

Her mother was not slow to remove herself to their former house in Dean Street in the then fashionable area of Soho. Thither Hester travelled for daily visits generally from noon till five, and such willing thraldom was yet a very real human bondage, as she acknowledged in a remarkably revealing passage of *Thraliana*:

> Mother & I had never been twelve hours apart from each other till I married, nor ever more than twelve Days apart afterwards. Mr Thrale was originally her Choice for me, not mine for myself, however we never differed on that or any other Occasion—her Pleasure was my Delight, her Will my Law, nor had my husband & I been ever alone together without her for five Minutes till after the nuptial Ceremony was past. (1: 55)

Meanwhile on 8 November 1763 her uncle, Sir Thomas, had married Mrs Sarah King, who soon 'weaned his Affections away from me', but his neglect in remitting Hester's mother's jointure created a breach between them so deep that she 'would 'cry for whole Days' if Hester so much as suggested that she wished to visit Offley. Such blatant emotional blackmail frequently went unremarked by the dutiful daughter, but occasionally it was recalled with a natural resentment. Thrale spent his mornings in the counting-house and his evenings at the opera or at Carlisle House, where Teresa Cornelys, the 'Circe of Soho Square', organised for aristocrats and their friends exclusive and notorious balls and masquerades, gaming tables, champagne and Johann Christian Bach concerts. Needless to say Hester was never invited. Shut away from the world, she lived, as Johnson was later to remark, like Thrale's kept mistress. Her mother 'was the only Creature that I saw; & if She was not in Spirits, what a Life I must lead! [. . .] if I did not keep my Mother in good humour what Chance had I for Comfort?' (*Thraliana*, 1: 308).

3

The Arrivals of Queeney and the Great Cham

The spring of 1764 raised Hester Thrale's spirits with forward-looking thoughts: she was pregnant and her husband was pleased. He decided that the lying-in must be in Southwark – 'sorely against my Will—if any Will I had'. On 17 September, despite his keen desire for a male heir, Thrale was delighted to be introduced to 'his beautiful Daughter', christened Hester Maria after her grandmother. On her daughter's thirtieth birthday Hester recalled the 'cruel Agony' of her first labour. What the new mother did not realise was that she would have to endure perpetual pregnancies for the next fourteen years, producing twelve children, only four of whom survived to maturity. When the lying-in month was over, Hester's mother returned to Soho and Hester resumed her 'Occupation of daddling after her, carrying the Child with me as I had the honour of suckling it'. Breastfeeding so weakened her slight body that she 'became a perfect shadow; & they were forced for very Shame to let me off that Duty, and get me an Ass to suck myself' (*Thraliana*, 1: 308). She did not seem to be in control of her own life or her own body. It was only with reluctance that 'they', a cabal of mother and master (in which the former, with her awareness that breast is best, would here have dominance), allowed her to abandon this 'Duty'. 'They' would both know that she would lose the contraceptive effect of breast-feeding, lasting at least six months, but it would appear that Thrale's unwillingness to practise coitus interruptus, or to use sheep-gut condoms (of which, as a womanizer, he would have been intimately aware) condemned her to continual pregnancy. Four months after Hester Maria's birth, Hester was pregnant with her second child, and so the exhausting cycle was established.

In many respects a pregnant wife suited Thrale as, while he awaited the arrival of a male child, he felt even more free to indulge himself with high-class prostitutes and rakish friends such as the 'King of Hell' Simon Luttrell, first Earl of Carhampton, and Peter King, sixth Baron King, who disgusted Samuel Johnson: 'It is a Mind in which nothing has grown up of itself & where whatever has been translated—has degenerated' (*Thraliana*, 1: 169). Such were the bachelor cronies Thrale would bring to Southwark, and more than a century later, on being told by Edward Mangin that his mother thought she had once seen Mrs Thrale, beautiful and sparkling in diamonds at the theatre in the winter of 1764, Hester philosophically replied:

> I never possessed a diamond in my life, never was in a theatre from my first wedding day, till my daughter born in 1764 went with me; and never was considered through the early periods of my life as even tolerably pretty. The person Mrs. Mangin saw was Polly Hart, Mr. Thrale's mistress, whose picture he wore on his box. (*Autobiography*, 1: 441)

There was one friend, however, whose treatment of a prostitute, a certain 'Miss Hooper', was very different. Discovering her real name to be Ann Elliot, and bewitched by her hazel eyes and chestnut-brown hair, he took her as his mistress and protégée, training her as an actress and creating the part of Maria for her in his successful comedy *The Citizen* (1761). This was the witty and scholarly Irish playwright, poet, critic, editor, barrister, and actor Arthur Murphy, and Hester relished his company. Here, at last, for Hester there was a meeting of minds, and Murphy, who had been a close friend of Johnson's for a decade, wanted to introduce the Great Cham to the Thrales. Hester's 'fate', in a very real sense, was to be 'bound up with the theatre' – Murphy's Drury Lane rather than Shakespeare's Globe – for this introduction would completely change the nature of Hester's life and establish her as a writer.

Knowing Johnson's interest in the emergence of labouring-class writers, Hester and Murphy hit on the idea of inviting James Woodhouse, the Staffordshire 'shoemaker poet', whose *Poems on Sundry Occasions* (1764) had sold very well. Johnson took the bait and Murphy brought him to dine at Deadman's Place at four on Wednesday, 9 January 1765. As she rose to welcome him, we can imagine the absolute contrast between these two, Hester at 24, elegant, petite and still something of a shadow of her normal slim self, and this huge 55 year-old ungainly dancing bear of a man. She noted his stoop and rounded back, his features distorted by scrofula, his negligent appearance, stained and shabby clothing, his nervous twitching and extraordinary gestures. Discourse at the dinner table was dramatically punctuated by 'his howls, and his indescribable but really pathetic slow semi-circuits of his head', and bouts of clumsy voraciousness.[1] Johnson was not overly impressed by the poems of Woodhouse, but he let him down gently, advising his fellow Staffordshire writer to 'Give nights and days, Sir, to the study of Addison'. Hester began to appreciate the truth of what Oliver Goldsmith had said of him: 'Johnson, to be sure, has a roughness in his manner: but no man alive has a more tender heart. He has nothing of the bear but his skin'.[2] Despite his aggressiveness and incivility, the Thrales' tolerance of many of his idiosyncrasies led to an intimacy with Johnson, who became a regular dinner guest.

The presence of Johnson served as a powerful catalyst in Brewery House: it removed the stale and stultifying veil of polite civility that had characterized their unloving relationship. The play of mind and intellect allowed both husband and wife to reveal aspects of their personalities that had been little in evidence in their relationship. They slowly began to appreciate each other: she saw how in such company Henry's cool reserve could melt to reveal a mordant wit; as he thawed, he released the spirited enthusiasm of her Welsh *hwyl*. Thrale was no great talker, but he operated as a species of deep-cover agent provocateur of contentious ideas. He found, as Frances Burney later recalled, 'a singular amusement in hearing, instigating, and provoking a war of words, alternating triumph and overthrow, between clever and ambitious colloquial combatants'.³ Hester revelled in such combative conversation, and her effervescent volubility encouraged, and provided an admirable foil for, Johnson's erudite pronouncements. Johnson more than filled the place of Hester's former mentor Collier; she was flattered that he took her sufficiently seriously as a poet and translator not only to praise and criticise her efforts, but also to suggest collaboration. He was toying with the idea of following Chaucer as a translator of Boethius' *De consolatione philosophiae*, and he playfully suggested that she should collaborate and present him with a translation of one of its poems each week when he came to dinner. Although this project may have represented displacement therapy on Johnson's part (his edition of Shakespeare was long overdue), Hester enjoyed the task, producing twice as many as he did, and this is one of the five on which they collaborated:

> *VAINLY the Tyrian purple bright,*
> *Vainly the pearl's pellucid white,*
> *The tyrant Nero strove t'adorn,*
> *Who liv'd our hatred and our scorn;*
> His choice our sacred seats disgrac'd,
> His conduct human kind debas'd:
> If such on earth can bliss bestow,
> Say, what is happiness below?
> (Book III, Metre 4; Hester's lines in italics)[4]

It was an exciting time for Hester but she found her second pregnancy totally exhausting. She remarked in her 'Family Book', a record which Johnson had suggested: 'I never had a Day's Health during the whole Gestation'.[5] Sea air was prescribed, and the Thrales invited Johnson to join them in their Brighton cottage. He was checking the proofs of his Shakespeare edition, and his letter of 13 August 1765, the first she ever received from him, reveals very early signs of an almost childlike dependence upon Hester and her opinion of him. His rhetorical question, 'Where should pleasure be sought, but under Mrs Thrale's influence?', might be taken as complimentary hyperbole, but the tone of the last paragraph with its beseeching 'Do not blame me' is more than apologetic; its final sentence, 'If you cannot think I am good, pray think I am mending', seems close to puerile regression.

By the time Johnson arrived in Brighton, he was furious to learn that the Thrales had suddenly returned to Southwark. Their departure was occasioned by the news of the death of Alexander Hume, one of the Borough MPs, and Henry's long-held political ambition to represent Southwark as his father had done in the 1740s. He announced his candidature on 23 September, and the heavily pregnant Hester helped him compose his addresses to the electors. Four days later another little girl, Frances, was born on 27 September 1765 and died after only nine days, a victim of infantile diarrhoea. Johnson forgot his anger in the face of their loss and enthusiastically added his weight to the campaign. There was little time for grieving in the midst of canvassing and campaigning, and, as her health and spirit returned, the trio ran a very effective campaign. As Hester recalled, 'I grew useful now—*almost* necessary; wrote his Advertisements, looked to the Treats; & People to whom I was till then unknown, admired how happy Mr Thrale must be—in such a *Wonder* of a Wife'.[6]

Yet if some of the electors of Southwark were envying Thrale's happiness, Hester herself was still regretting what she termed 'my odd kind of Life'. When 'the Wonder of a Wife' wondered at her husband's 'cold Carriage to me', Johnson had cruelly retorted:

> Why, how for Heaven's Sake Dearest Madam should any Man delight in a Wife that is to him neither Use nor Ornament? He cannot talk to you about his Business, which you do not understand; nor about his Pleasures which you do not partake; if you have Wit or Beauty you shew them nowhere so he has none of the Reputation; if you have Economy or Understanding you employ neither in Attention to his Property. You divide your Time between your Mamma & your Babies & wonder you do not by that means become agreeable to your Husband.' (*Thraliana*, 1: 309)

Such advice from a man whose own household, as Hester soon discovered, veered between the chaotic and the rancorous, was a bitter pill for any young wife to swallow. But our shock at the effrontery of this new friend's ignorance and insensitivity is as nothing compared with our virtual disbelief at the meekness of her response: '[I] gently hinted to my Mother that I had some Curiosity about the Trade, which I would may be one day get M\[r] Thrale to inform *me* about as well as the Jacksons who I observed had all his Confidence.' The maternal scorn at her daughter's apparent willingness to debase herself as '*My Lady Mashtub*' is deeply predictable, but the fact that Hester's jealousy is aroused by Thrale's close relationship with his chemist friend Humphrey Jackson FRS, rather than by any of his adulterous amours, is in many respects quite remarkable. The woman who was to become a prime mover of fashionable sociability here reveals a fascination with trade and commercial sociability which entangles social and sexual chemistry with the chemistry of brewing and of male friendship. This is especially interesting when we consider that Thrale had met with earlier refusals from women who could neither bear the nature of his business nor the thought of living in the Borough (*Autobiography*, 2: 24). Hester's inquiring mind was indeed curious about the source of their wealth. She knew that women have traditionally been associated with brewing, but she would have to wait several years before she could convince everyone that producing beer was woman's business.

Thrale was returned as one of the two Members of Parliament for Southwark on 23 December 1765, and late sittings now became the pretext for infidelity. His wife resigned herself to her conventional domestic role, chained to childbirth and the intensive labour of producing a male heir. Johnson, for his part, was thinking of combining encouraging Hester's literary talent with helping one of his own dysfunctional household of waifs and strays. This was the blind Pembrokeshire poet Anna Williams, of whose verse he had long planned to print a subscription volume. To add substance to what would have else proved an over-slim quarto he enlisted Hester and was particularly pleased to read a humorous poem that she had recently written, 'The Three Warnings'. The fate of her baby, who had given up her life so placidly, as well as the declining health of her mother and uncle had encouraged this poem's clear-eyed focus upon death and upon how

> That love of life increas'd with years
> So much, that in our latter stages,
> When pains grow sharp, and sickness rages
> The greatest love of life appears.[7]

An uninvited wedding guest at 'neighbour Dobson's[8] wedding' feast, Death draws the happy groom aside with the grave news that he must quit his sweet bride and accompany him. Mollified by the youth's desperate pleas, Death grants a reprieve and promises that he shall have 'Three several Warnings' before his return. Farmer Dobson 'smok'd his pipe and strok'd his horse' and lived his life so contentedly that he scarcely perceived that he was growing old when his eightieth year arrived. Death had patiently waited thirty-six years but, when he reappears, Dobson craftily reminds him of the promised warnings:

> I know, cries Death, that, at the best,
> I seldom am a welcome guest;
> But don't be captious, friend, at least:
> I little thought you'd still be able
> To stump about your farm and stable;
> Your years have run to a great length;
> I wish you joy, tho', of your strength!
>
> HOLD, says the farmer, not so fast!
> I have been lame these four years past.
>
> And no great wonder, Death replies:
> However, you still keep your eyes;
> And sure, to see one's loves and friends,
> For legs and arms would make amends.

> PERHAPS, says Dobson, so it might,
> But latterly I've lost my sight.
>
> This is a shocking tale, faith;
> Yet there's comfort still, says Death;:
> Each strives your sadness to amuse,
> I warrant you hear all the news.
>
> THERE's none, cries he; and if there were,
> I'm grown so deaf I could not hear.
>
> Nay, then, the spectre stern rejoin'd,
> These are unjustifiable yearnings;
> If you are Lame, and Deaf, and Blind,
> You've had your Three sufficient Warnings.
> So, come along, no more we'll part;
> He said, and touch'd him with his dart;
> And now, old Dobson turning pale,
> Yields to his fate—so ends my Tale.

Hester's retelling of a fable motif well known in both Persian and western traditions is more sprightly than Jean de La Fontaine's 'Death and the Dying Man', its easy octosyllabics providing a sense of folk-tale inevitability. Hester's best-known poem, it was given public recitations and widely reprinted throughout the century in popular anthologies, miscellanies, chap-books and prints.

Johnson also asked her to translate Boileau's 'Epistle to his Gardener'. In the summer of 1693 Boileau was grappling with his muse and reciting aloud with wild gesticulations in his formal garden; he was in the throes of composing a heroic Pindaric ode to celebrate the taking of Namur when he observed his astonished gardener, Antoine Riquet, peering through a hedge. The resultant verse epistle, contrasting intellectual with manual labour, not only made Antoine famous but was widely judged to be far superior to the 'Ode sur la prise de Namur' that Boileau was struggling to compose. Hester successfully juxtaposed the 'mad Master' and skilled gardener as artistic creators of beauty:

> While tonsile Eughs [Yews] obey your forming hand,
> And twining Woodbines climb at your command,
> Why cannot I the mental garden till
> With equal happiness or equal skill? [. . .]
> Or when at eve you tread the tedious round
> And drag the roller up the rising ground,
> If your incautious steps the gloom pervade,
> Where your mad Master haunts the silent glade,
> And with erratick gait, and kindling eyes,
> Now stamps the ground, now gazes at the skies.[9]

Inspired both by Hester and her contributions, Johnson, who had begun to refer to the Thrales as his 'Master' and 'Mistress', now decided to add one of his own to Anna Williams's subscription volume: 'Come Mistress, now I'll write a Tale and your Character shall be in it'.[10] *The Fountains: A Fairy Tale* was more than a delightful compliment to his new Welsh friend and collaborator; in several respects it represents a ground-breaking development of the genre. It opens with Floretta wandering in a meadow beneath what Thomas Gray had recently described in his Gogynfeirdd-inspired 'The Bard' (1757) as the 'cloud-topt head' of 'huge Plinlimmon'.[11] She rescues a limed goldfinch from a hovering hawk, but rejecting her mother's suggestion that it would sing beautifully in a gilded cage, liberates it with a kiss. Seeking the bird the following day, Floretta discovers that her kindness has released a fairy, Lady Lilinet of the Blue Rock, from a spell that transformed her into a goldfinch.[12] The grateful fairy might be expected to grant a wish, but Johnson, aware that the mytheme of wishing often leads to tragedy, makes Lilinet grant Floretta the 'power to regulate [her] future life' with the ability both to make and to retract wishes by drinking of the Spring of Joy or by taking the bitter waters of the Spring of Sorrow. The initial desires of the heroine for perfect beauty, a faithful lover, 'spirit to do her own way', wealth[13] and wit are all fulfilled but subsequently reversed, except the last, for she 'resolved to keep her wit with all its consequences'(139), one of which must ultimately be resignation 'to the course of Nature'

(141). But, if Floretta's education was to mirror that of Hester, the most depressing renunciation was that of spirit, foiled by the pertinacity of her mother – 'the old lady asserted her right to govern' – and by her own realization of the eternal double standard whereby 'the vehemence of mind, which to a man may sometimes procure awe and obedience, produce to a woman nothing but detestation' (127–8). The bluestocking polyglot and translator of Epictetus, Elizabeth Carter, found Johnson's 'Fairy Tale enchantingly beautiful. But the conclusion is faulty, and leaves too melancholy an impression on one's mind.' This was unsurprising in a woman who had recently celebrated her father's enlightened educational ideas:

> Ne'er did thy voice assume a master's pow'r,
>   Nor force assent to what thy precepts taught;
> But bid my independent spirit soar,
>   In all the freedom of unfetter'd thought.[14]

Johnson, who famously valued Mrs Carter for her ability to 'make a pudding as well as translate Epictetus from the Greek', knew very well that Thrale was a man who appreciated a good dinner more than a wife conversant with the classics. More seriously, if the jealous biographer Boswell is to be believed, Johnson was impressed by Thrale's patriarchal power: 'I know no man who is more master of his wife and family than Thrale. If he but holds up his finger, he is obeyed'.[15]

Despite all his predilections for fetters, Johnson's presence within the household would enable Hester's 'independent spirit [to] soar', placing Streatham firmly on the map of British literary history. The magnet of Johnson attracted his fellow Turk's Head club-members and other distinguished figures to her dining table and tea urn. Recalling her Salusbury motto, *Sat est prostrasse leoni* (It is enough to have conquered a lion), Hester had netted a literary lion, and together they presided over this new Streatham salon, which she described as 'a sort of Receptacle for Wits & Writers'. Thrale had attempted to shut Hester from the world: now the world came to Streatham.

For Johnson, Streatham provided the best of conversation, books, food and, above all, the security of a well-ordered household. Hester was the first to acknowledge her husband's centrality in his domestication: 'Mr. Thrale had a very powerful influence over the Doctor, and could make him suppress many rough answers: he could likewise prevail on him to change his shirt, his coat, or his plate, almost before it came indispensably necessary to the comfortable feelings of his friends'.[16] Her own power over their friend was limited to health matters and she bullied the reluctant Johnson into taking the air and exercise that relieved his chronic emphysema. He could be troublesome but there were more than intellectual compensations, for he took a grandfatherly delight in young children, especially Hester's first-born, 'Miss Hetty', later 'Queen Hester', ultimately and ineradicably 'Queeney'. The court painter Johann Zoffany was engaged to capture Queeney at the age of twenty months sitting on a cushion, stroking her favourite spaniel, Belle. Observing her motherly pride, Johnson sensitively encouraged the writer in Hester to link reproduction and production by recording her daughter's physical and intellectual growth in a 'Children's Book or rather Family Book' (1766–8), which subsequently served as an intimate diary to which she confided her pent-up feelings. At the age of two, Queeney has almost outgrown the use of a pinafore back-string:

> She is perfectly healthy, of a lax Constitution, & is strong enough to carry a Hound puppy two Months old across the Lawn at Streatham [. . .] She is neither remarkably big not tall, being just 34 Inches high, but eminently pretty. She can speak most words and speak them plain enough too, but is no great Talker: she repeats the Pater Noster, the Three Christian Virtues & the Signs of the Zodiac in Watts's Verses, she likewise knows them on the Globe perfectly well. She can tell all her Letters great & small & spell little Words as D, o, g, Dog, C, a, t, Cat &c. She knows her nine Figures & the simplest Combinations of 'em as 3, 4. 34, 6, 8. 68, but none beyond a hundred. She knows all the heathen Deities by their Attributes & counts 20 without missing one.[17]

Comparative theology at two would seem quite enough to impress Johnson, but Hester would subsequently discover that, as an infant, the Lichfield 'prodigy of early understanding' came to loathe his father's caresses as they inevitably preceded a request to display his remarkable abilities; when visitors arrived he would 'run up a tree that he might not be found and exhibited' (*Anecdotes*, p. 11). There were risks in attempting to produce any live child, never mind an infant prodigy. But at last she could write in the *Family Book*: 'Henry Salusbury Thrale was born the 15: Feby 1767, strong & lively at Southwark.' The birth was much celebrated and Hester had never been in such favour; she had produced the male heir her husband so desired. Two days later the toddler Queeney's presentation to her mother of a hot-house rose, in itself an act motivated by a childlike mixture of genuine affection on a snowy morning and an understandable desire to refocus attention upon herself as senior sibling, was rewarded with a poem. 'A Fable to Miss Thrale Feb: 17: 1767', opening with an acknowledgement that roses are always welcomed by poets, 'No Rhymist e'er the Bait resisted / Since Rhymes and Roses have existed', leads into an insulting address to the flower itself as an 'Offspring of Artifice and Care', a 'Factitious Thing, by Folly bred'. The Rose, 'blush[ing] a deeper dye', responds indignantly:

> Before you hastily condemn
> My feeble Stalk my slender Stem;
> Think on Your Daughter's early Bloom
> Nor longer scorn my faint perfume:
> When with Attention, Care and Skill,
> You mould her Infant Mind at will,
> With pains the frigid Soil prepare,
> And force th'unwilling Tree to bear;
> Beneath Your fost'ring Hand she grows,
> And blooms at length—a hothouse Rose.

Perhaps, the Rose tactfully suggests, it might prove better for the maternal educator to relinquish the 'Charcoal Fires' of the forcing-house and allow her toddler artlessly to 'chear the Safe Domestic Fire':

> There, should her Prattle once beguile
> Judicious Johnson of a Smile;
> You'd soon confess your Cares repaid,
> And wonder at the progress made.
> (*Thraliana*, 1: 273–4)

Torn between fireside storytelling and forcing-house rote learning, between education as a leading forth or a cramming with facts, Hester could never quite free herself from the notion that the mother's performance would be judged upon that of the child. In the moulding of infant minds and performing of maternal duties she was always examining her own progress alongside that of her child, and in this her own mother was both a role model and a constant reproach. An obedient and only child, willing to perform as 'half a prodigy', Hester herself had then become a young intellectual still studying into her twenties. Because her own education became her primary source of fulfilment in life she expected her daughters follow in her footsteps. She recorded her private contempt for the views of her house guest, the musicologist Charles Burney:

> Dr Burney did not like his Daughter should learn Latin even of *Johnson* who offered to teach her for Friendship, because then She would have been as wise as himself forsooth, & Latin was too Masculine for Misses— a narrow Souled Goose-Cap the Man must be at last. (*Thraliana*, 1: 502)

By contrast, she applauded Johnson's support of a liberal education for women: 'it is a paltry Trick indeed to deny Women the Cultivation of their mental Powers, and I think it is partly a proof that we are afraid of them—if we endeavour to keep them unarmed' (*Thraliana*, 1: 172). Yet Johnson would also criticize her pedagogy:

> [H]e used to condemn me for putting Newbery's books into their hands as too trifling to engage their attention. 'Babies do not want (said he) to hear about babies; they like to be told of giants and castles,

and of somewhat which can stretch and stimulate their little minds.' When in answer I would urge the numerous editions and quick sale of Tommy Prudent or Goody Two Shoes: 'Remember always (said he) that the parents buy the books, and that the children never read them.' Mrs. Barbauld however had his best praise, and deserved it, no man was more struck than Mr. Johnson with voluntary descent from possible splendour to painful duty. (*Anecdotes*, p. 16)

It is typical of Hester, however, that she not only leaves the last word in their dispute to her adversary but concludes by endorsing Johnson's praise of Anna Laetitia Barbauld's children's writing and offering her own compliment to him. She knew the value and the need for 'voluntary descent', and indeed her whole life was lived between 'possible splendour' and 'painful duty'. Despite the glamour, the wit and the repartee, Johnson was an exhausting house guest, demanding attention to his various physical ailments, and a mother love to compensate for his own austere upbringing. Behind the public face of her performance as brilliant hostess, Hester's nurturing powers were drained not only by her own children, but by the overgrown child Johnson, who required psychological fostering of his creative powers.

While Queeney was making 'amazing Improvements' and little Henry was growing sturdy, nursery affairs tended to predominate, and Hester as *Mere de famille* always found 'Time for tutoring, caressing, or what is still more useful, for having one's Children about one' (*Thraliana*, 1: 158). She resented being reproached for neglecting to record Johnsonian bons mots: 'little do these wise Men know or feel, that the Crying of a young Child, or the Perverseness of an elder, or the Danger however trifling of any one—will soon drive out of a female Parent's head a Conversation concerning Wit, Science or Sentiment.' But the Great Cham knew and felt much and, despite his monumental egocentricity, he involved himself in the rearing of her children with genuine affection. One day, when she recounted her former mentor Dr Collier's opinion that the love one bore to children was in anticipation of the wise or amiable adults they might become: 'One cannot love *lumps of flesh* and little infants are nothing more', her new mentor responded:

> 'On the contrary, one can scarcely help wishing, while one fondles a baby, that it may never live to become a man for it is *so* probable, that when he becomes a man, he should be sure to end in a scoundrel.' Girls were less displeasing to him, 'for as their temptations were fewer (he said), their virtue in this life, and happiness in the next, were less improbable; and he loved (he said) to see a knot of little misses dearly.' (*Anecdotes*, p. 273)

The snow-bound New Year of 1768 found Hester pregnant for the fourth time and her husband distributing largesse to the Borough voters and, together with his fellow Southwark MP, Sir Joseph Mawbey, 1,000 Dutch lobsters to the poor prisoners of Southwark's gaols. This joint gesture would seem to indicate that Thrale was acquiescing in the radical programme of Mawbey who increasingly was lending his support to John Wilkes. The approaching election was to be dominated by the latter's return to London and crowds shouting for 'Wilkes and Liberty'. Johnson was in Oxford secretly (a secret he confided only to H.L.T) helping his young friend Robert Chambers write his Vinerian lectures, but he was also assisting Hester in the writing of electoral 'advertisements' and the postal canvassing of key electors. Like Johnson, Hester had little sympathy for Wilkes's mixture of libertinism and liberty, but her close friend the surgeon Herbert Lawrence was another enthusiastic supporter. The heavily pregnant Hester did her utmost by entertaining prominent constituents. On the 23 March Thrale headed the poll. Both he and the second-runner Mawbey were elected as the two members for Southwark. While Thrale celebrated, his exhausted wife retired to Streatham where she gave birth to 'a small Child', named Anna Maria after her 'Dear Aunt', on All Fools' Day.

Johnson wrote from Oxford on 19 April not to ask after her health but to inform Hester that he himself had 'been very much disordered': 'I have been really very bad, and am glad that I was not at Streatham, where I should have been troublesome to you, and you could have given no help so me'.[18] He wished that this baby might have been christened Elizabeth in memory of his wife who had been 20 years older than him and had died in 1752, grumbling: 'I design to love little Miss Nanny very well; but you must let us have a Bessy some other time. I suppose the Borough bells rung for the young lady's arrival.'

The unrest continued in London where Wilkes, having been elected as one of the members for Middlesex, delivered himself into custody, was freed by the mob, smuggled himself back into prison in disguise and was subsequently sentenced by Lord Mansfield to two years' imprisonment for publishing the seditious and obscene libels of the *North Briton* and the *Essay on Woman*. All this drama was playing itself out at the King's Bench prison in Southwark, and on 10 May, the opening of Parliament was mobbed by Wilkite crowds, the Riot Act was read and the soldiers fired on the crowd killing six protesters and wounding many more. This 'Massacre of St George's Fields' sparked demonstrations and strikes amongst various trades, such as watermen, coal-heavers and coopers, some of whom were employees of the Thrale brewery. Hester's response was one of mockery rather than polemic and her poem was published in the *Public Advertiser* on 20 July. Drawing upon some *un*natural history of Pliny, her squib somewhat misfires, libelling the courageous mongoose as fouler than the immoral Medmenham 'Monk' Wilkes:

> In proud —'s[19] Despight,
> See true Britons unite,
>   To huzza Mr. Wilkes as he passes:
> Though when calm we consider
> The Vice of their Leader,
>   We're apt to conclude them but Asses.
>
> Yet 'tis thus that we're told
> The Egyptians of old
>   Ador'd the still fouler Ichneumon,
> Who alone durst engage
> The fell Crocodile's Rage
>   With Courage exceeding the human.[20]

On Johnson's return to London the turbulent atmosphere of the Wilkite crisis, and especially the politically charged conversations at Streatham, were to spur him into new creativity. *'The False Alarm* [published on 17 January 1770] his first and favourite pamphlet, was written at our house between eight o'clock on Wednesday night and twelve o'clock on Thursday night; we read it to Mr. Thrale when he came very late home from the House of Commons' (*Anecdotes*, p. 41). This powerful polemic ridiculed the demagogue Wilkes with energetic wit and Swiftian irony, but shocked many liberals with the apparent contempt for the Bill of Rights shown by a writer who had been drawing court pension of £300 a year since 1762: '[T]he rabble, whencesoever they come, will always be patriots and always Supporters of the Bill of Rights'.[21]

The early summer of 1768 also saw the first and accidental meeting of Hester and James Boswell outside 7, Johnson's Court, off Fleet Street, an address that had appealed to the solipsistic Sam. Despite yet another attack of venereal disease, Boswell was basking in the success of his recently published *Account of Corsica*, containing the memoirs of the Corsican patriot Pasquale Paoli. He had come to visit Johnson who was about to depart in Hester's carriage for Streatham. In a letter of the following year Boswell reminded her of his first words: '[Y]ou and I [are] rivals for that great man. You would take him to the country, when I was anxious to keep him in town'.[22] This was a momentous meeting for 'Bozzy and Piozzi', who were to become the two major rival biographers of the great Cham. What Boswell did not fully know at this stage was exactly how Johnson's tendencies to debilitating depression were being alleviated by his close relationships with Robert Chambers at Oxford and with Hester at Streatham.

In September the Thrales took Johnson for a little tour of the North Downs of Kent to benefit his health and celebrate his birthday. As Hester records, the reasons 'he doated on a coach so' were that 'in the first place, the company was shut in with him *there*; and could not escape, as out of a room: in the next place, he heard all that was said in a carriage.' Intelligent conversation and a changing panorama ensured that 'the very act of going forward was delightful to him' (*Anecdotes*, p. 276). Johnson's fifty-ninth birthday was enjoyably spent at Went House, the property of Francis Brooke, an attorney of West Malling and old friend of the Thrales, who true to his name, had designed elaborate water features within his landscaped gardens. The bleak hours of that very night, however, were spent by Johnson in the melancholic anguish of deep despair. We know this as Hester subsequently found the following lines in an open drawer:

> Sept. 18: 1768 At night Town Malling in Kent.
> I have now begun the sixtieth[23] year of my life. How the last year has past I am unwilling to terrify myself with thinking. This day has been past in great perturbation. I was distracted at Church in an uncommon degree, and my distress has had very little intermission. I have found myself somewhat relieved by reading, which I therefore intend to practice when I am able. This day it came into my mind to write the history of my melancholy. On this I purpose to deliberate. I know not whether it may not too much disturb me.[24]

This was perhaps Hester's first insight into the 'black Dog' that regularly took possession of her friend: a complex compound of morbid fears of indolence, oblivion and insanity, and the torturing terrors of the dark night of the soul. Like Banquo, Johnson prayed that 'Merciful powers' would 'Restrain in me the cursed thoughts, that nature / Gives way to in repose!' and, like Lear, 'O! let me not be mad, not mad, sweet heaven.' Increasingly Johnson revealed his trust in Hester, confiding in her what she termed 'a Secret far dearer to him than his Life', which she never betrayed. The context of her *Thraliana* reference to Johnson's confession is revealing in a variety of ways:

> It appears to me that no Man can live his Life quite thro', without being at *some* period of it under the Dominion of *some* Woman—Wife Mistress or Friend. Pope and Swift were softened by the Smiles of Patty Blount & Stella & our stern Philosopher Johnson trusted me about the Years 1767 or 1768—I know not which just now—with a Secret far dearer to him than his Life: such however is his nobleness and such his partiality, that I sincerely believe he has never since that Day regretted his

Confidence or ever looked with less kind Affection on her who had him in her Power.—Uniformly great is the Mind of that incomparable Mortal; & well does he contradict the Maxim of Rochefoucault that no Man is a Hero to his Valet de Chambre.—Johnson is more a Hero to me than to any one—& I have been more to him for Intimacy, than ever was any Man's Valet de Chambre. (*Thraliana*, 1: 384–5)

Despite her desire for personal literary fame, Hester also saw herself within a tradition of Muse-mistress figures who have encouraged male creativity, and she was intensely conscious of the confidence with which the 'stern Philosopher' has placed himself 'in her Power'. Her references to female dominion, female power and male intellect, and the debunking of a male maxim by a woman's claim of more intense physical intimacy, all focus attention upon this dear and dangerous 'Secret', the revelation of which might be most damaging to the reputation of the 'incomparable' Great Cham. A little later in *Thraliana*, Hester unexpectedly burst out with: 'How many Times has this great, this formidable Doctor Johnson kissed my hand, ay & my foot too upon his knees!' This was immediately followed by another exclamation: 'Strange Connections there are in this odd World!' which received Hester's later marginal comment: 'a dreadful & little suspected Reason for ours God knows—but the Fetters & Padlocks will tell Posterity the Truth', together with an editorial note concerning 'item 649 in the sale of Mrs Piozzi's library and personal effects [. . .] a padlock, with a manuscript note attached —"Johnson's padlock, committed to my care in the year 1768"' (*Thraliana*, 1: 415). A morbid fear of incipient insanity might explain these articles of restraint, but Johnson discussed this fear with Boswell, and so it might seem that this cannot have been the secret exclusively confided to Hester. Johnson's secret was not his fear of insanity but that he had prevailed upon Hester to take a key therapeutic role in the treatment of his mental illness. Having conducted much research upon the topic, the hypochondriacal Johnson had filled his mind with the potential horrors that awaited him; as he explained to Boswell, 'Madmen are all sensual in the lower stages of their distemper. They are eager for gratifications to sooth their minds and divert their attention from the misery which they suffer: but when they grow very ill, pleasure is too weak for them, and they seek for pain' (Boswell, 1: 158).

A letter of early June 1773 from Johnson to Hester within the house at Streatham, written originally in French to ensure privacy, demonstrated the extent of his dependence upon Hester's warden-like ministrations:

> And if it seems better to you for me to stay in a certain place, I beg you to spare me the necessity of constraining myself, by taking away from me the power of leaving the place where you want me to be. This will not cost you more than the trouble of turning the key in the door twice a day. You must act completely as Mistress, so that your judgement and vigilance may come to the aid of my weakness.[25]

This letter was claimed by the scholarly editor of *Thraliana*, Katharine C. Balderston, to reveal Johnson's masochistic fantasies which he desired Hester to enact with him: 'It is a pathological document, the product of a sick mind'.[26] The final line of Hester's sympathetic letter in response, 'do not quarrel with your Governess for not using the Rod enough', is cited by Balderston with the comment: 'one is bound to inquire whether Mrs Thrale's role, beyond that of jailer and turnkey, was not also that of beater' (p. 10). Such tenuous and prurient speculations, encouraged by her reading of Richard von Krafft-Ebing's *Psychopathia Sexualis* (1886), insensitively attempted to replace Johnson's terrors of Hogarth's Bedlam with a taste for BDSM.

Their relationship was indeed a complex one: a compound of dominance and subservience, infantilism and correction, playfulness and clumsy courtliness, all of which were subsumed in the motherly/loverly ambiguities and knowing ambivalences of 'My Mistress'. It was appallingly self-centred of Johnson to reprimand Hester for neglecting him while she was tending the ailing Mrs Salusbury and consulting physicians; with characteristic patience and tact she recommended him to take his long-planned trip to the Hebrides: 'Dissipation is to you a glorious Medicine, and I believe Mr. Boswell will be at last your best Physician.'

If Hester was his turnkey, she also emancipated the private Johnson, freeing his letters from Ramblerian polysyllabics and liberating a more colloquial vigour. The Swan of Johnson's birthplace, Lichfield, Anna Seward, who herself had a somewhat fraught relationship with Sam, declared to her friend, the poet Mary Knowles:

> [His] long-enduring passion for Mrs Thrale was composed equally perhaps of cupboard-love, Platonic love, and vanity tickled and gratified from morn to night by incessant homage. The two first ingredients are certainly oddly heterogeneous; but Johnson, in religion and politics, in love and in hatred, in truth and falsehood, was composed of such opposite and contradictory materials, as never before met in the human mind.[27]

Although much truth lies in Seward's clear-eyed observation, as experienced from the inside their love must often have seemed mutual and fully reciprocated; he admired her intellect, her wit, her conversation and her gaiety: 'Nobody loves me as Johnson does at last—but then nobody has as much Soul to love one with' (*Thraliana*, 1. 418). He compared his love for Hester with his deep devotion to his closest male friend, the military physician Richard Bathurst:

> [Spe]aking once of His friendly Affection for me, [he s]aid kindly, I do certainly love you better [tha]n any human Being I ever saw—better I [th]ink than even poor dear Bathurst, and esteem [y]ou more, though that would be unjust too, for I have never seen You in distress, & till I have I cannot rank you with a Man who acted in such trying situations with such Uniformity of Virtue. (*Thraliana*, 1: 601)

To say he loved her better than a friend of whom, according to Arthur Murphy, 'he hardly ever spoke without tears in his eyes' amounted to a most striking compliment, but still more remarkable is his comment that he had never seen her in distress. Even taking into consideration Johnson's obtuseness and self-obsessed neurosis, this must imply that Hester was concealing her distress. Those who do so are often more distressed than those who reveal their pain secure in the hope of receiving caring support. If Hester had no such recourse in Johnson the emotional reciprocity of their relationship must have been sadly incomplete.

Hester had the key to Johnson's padlock but no key to her own. Streatham had become a salon, but it was also a nursing home and an asylum; her fetters, forged by her sense of duty, were self-imposed and manifold. When she was not indulging a negligent and serially unfaithful husband; mothering her children, together with her aged friend and her demanding mother, who loathed and were jealous of each other; or being a governess to them all; she was expected to sparkle in distinguished company. She was pregnant yet again, and in June 1769 gave birth to her fifth child, named Lucy (after her Welsh great-grandmother) Elizabeth (after Johnson's wife). For once, the baby was 'large strong and handsome likely to live'.

Hester continued proudly recording the progress of her other children in her 'Family Book': Henry, now in breeches at two years and three months, is 'remarkably strong made, course and bony:— not handsome at all, but of perfect Proportion; & has a surly look with the honestest & sweetest Temper in the World' (Hyde, p. 33). Anna Maria, by contrast 'is remarkably small bon'd & delicately framed'. Her grandmother's favourite, she lived with her in Dean Street, Soho, on account of the more salubrious air. 'She could kiss her hand at 9 Months old, & understand all one said to her: could walk to perfection, & even with an Air at a Year old & seems to intend being Queen of us all if She lives which I do not expect She is so very lean—I think she is consumptive.'

Hester's devoted attention to Queeney's education is apparent in the following:

> Hester Maria was four Years and nine Months old when I lay in with Lucy: and then I began to teach her Grammar shewing her the Difference between a substantive and an adjective as I lay in Bed; She has made since then a Progress so considerable, that She this Day 1: Feb: 1770 parsed the first Couplet of Pope's Iliad. (Hyde, p. 34)

The very next entry records Anna Maria's death on 20 March, despite all Mrs Salusbury's loving ministrations, of a distressing

'Dropsy of the Brain' (perhaps meningitis). Hester adds: 'I am now myself near five Months gone with Child, and I fear the Shock & Anxiety of this last fortnight has done irreparable Injury to my little Companion—if so I have lost two Children this Spring—how dreadful!' In her despondency she comforted herself by composing prayers for the preservation of her surviving children, her husband and her friends, together with a litany of her own sins:

> From Pride Insolence and an overweening Carriage,
> from Vanity & a Delight in vain Amusements
> Good Lord deliver me![28]

On 22 May 1770,

> I was sitting with Mr Johnson and Mr Thrale till towards 11 o'Clock at Night, I felt sudden & violent pains come on; I hasted to bed & by 1 o'clock in the Morning was delivered with very little pain of a small weakly female Infant, whom we called Susanna Arabella; The Child presented wrong but being small it did not signify. (Hyde, pp. 36–7)

The family physician Robert Bromfield declared 'he never saw but one born so very little & kept alive to a Year old'. Susanna Arabella, at least two months premature, surprised them all; she outlived all her siblings, until 5 November 1858.

Within fourteen months of Susanna's birth, and while she was worrying about the chronic discharge from Lucy's ears, on 22 July 1771 Hester was brought to bed of her seventh child and sixth daughter, Sophia, who was born post-term and was consequently a very large baby. Johnson wrote to the six-year-old Queeney from Ashbourne, where he had taken refuge from witnessing potential distress with his friend Dr John Taylor: 'Desire her to make haste and be quite well, for, You know, that You and I are to tye her to the tree, but we will not do it while she is weak'.[29] When she read this, a wry smile must have passed across the face of 'Little Mama' (as Johnson termed her). She was in bondage to the hard labour of extending the Thrale family tree, being in thrall to the lazy lust of her thoughtless husband, and Henry Thrale would certainly not be denied his marriage debt however weak she was, using her frequent pregnancies as an indulgence to excuse his adulteries.

Polly Hart had featured in Edward Thompson's poetical satire *The Metriciad* since 1761, and its eighth edition, published in Thompson's *The Court of Cupid* (1770), included this footnote: 'After this most accomplished woman had quitted Mr. Thrale, she went into keeping to Sir E. D—g' (p. 20). When Thompson was editing the *Westminster Magazine*, in a regular section also entitled 'The Court of Cupid', he featured the 'Memoirs of Miss H—t, alias Mrs. R—d—h, Mr. Th—le, and Sir Edward D[erin]g'. Polly, the daughter of a dancing master, 'fell into the wide-spreading arms of a Borough Brewer, more famed for his amours than celebrated for his beer'.[30] Established at his 'rural seat', probably his hunting-box near Croydon, 'the Borough bucks made her the Goddess of their chace'. Ironically she is described in almost Hester-like terms, having both the 'spirit to lead the Hounds in the Field, and Wit to entertain *them* in the house'.[31]

1 Bodfel Hall, Llannor, Pwllheli, Caernarfonshire. Coflein.
NMR Site Files Catalogue Number: C554943.

2 Bachegraig House, Tremeirchion, Flintshire, 1776,
by Richard Bernard Godfrey, engraver (b. 1728).
National Library of Wales, Aberystwyth.

3 Portrait of Hester Thrale and her daughter Hester, *c*.1777, by Joshua Reynolds (1723–92). By kind permission of the Beaverbrook Art Gallery, Fredericton, New Brunswick, Canada.

4 'The Southwark Macaroni', cartoon of Henry Thrale, Published according to the Act of 24 August 1772, by M. Darly, 39 Strand, London. Etching 1915, 0313.163 © The Trustees of the British Museum.

5 Samuel Johnson (1709–84), engraved by William Holl, after Joshua Reynolds, and published in *The Gallery of Portraits with Memoirs*, vol. 7 (London: Knight, 1837).

6 Thrale Place, otherwise known as Streatham Place or Streatham Park, drawn and engraved by William Ellis, published 1 August 1792, by Harrison & Co., 18 Paternoster Row, London, *Copperplate Magazine, or Monthly Cabinet of Picturesque Prints, Consisting of Views in Great Britain and Ireland*, 5 vols (Harrison and Co., London, 1792–1802), vol. 1, print 14. 1862,0712.924.
© The Trustees of the British Museum.

7 Hester Lynch Piozzi (née Salusbury, later Mrs Thrale) by unknown Italian artist; oil on canvas 1785–6. NPG 4942. © National Portrait Gallery, London.

8 'Frontispiece for the second edition of Dr Johnson's Letters' by James Sayers; etching, published by Thomas Cornell 7 April 1788. NPG D9898.
© National Portrait Gallery, London.

9 Portrait; half length, seated to left; elbow resting on ledge; wearing hat and cloak tied around neck, vignette. Engraved by Henry Meyer from an original Drawing by John Jackson in 1811. Stipple. A, 2.50. © The Trustees of the British Museum.

10 Brynbella, the Seat of G. Piozzi Esqr., engraved by J. Bluck (fl. 1791–1819; J. Baker, artist, Tremeirchion, Flintshire. National Library of Wales, Aberystwyth.

4

Hester Brewster, or, 'Women have a manifest Advantage over Men in the doing Business'

Southwark adultery and Streatham celebrity were largely funded by porter, a dark-brown or black bitter beer, brewed from partly charred malt, beloved of London porters and manual labourers. According to the historian of eighteenth-century brewing, Peter Mathias, 'Porter had been born in an attempt to undercut other beers (and other brewers)'.[1] London porter established market leadership in price and quality over all other beers. 'Thrale's "entire" porter', so called from its being drawn from an entire butt, retailed throughout London at threepence a quart pot. It was a popular beer, but Thrale lusted after the prospect of its becoming a market-leading brand. Brewing had raised Thrale's father's family from Hertfordshire yeomanry, but just as porter originated in cut-throat competition so Henry Thrale was prey to an obsessively fierce rivalry continually fermenting in the cask of his mind.

In many respects Thrale was in the van of modern brewing science. Encouraged by Johnson's fascination with chemistry,[2] Thrale introduced the use of both the hydrometer and the hydrostatic balance in the Anchor Brewery from 1770, communicating with James Baverstock about the relative specific gravity yield of malts from Burlington and Norfolk, and presenting Baverstock with a silver hydrometer in recognition of his pioneering work.[3] This was advanced stuff, but in Thrale's case it was all dedicated to a single-minded ambition to triumph over his London competitors.

In June 1772 came a lightning bolt – Thrale was facing bankruptcy! The brewery was in debt to the tune of £130,000 (multiply by a hundred for some idea of today's value). Though it was a complete shock, Hester had realised that something was wrong:

> Mr Thrale had for some Time appeared pensive and gloomy—when I asked the Cause, he told me it was something relative to his Business: I grew more inquisitive & he told me that it was the bad Hops he had bought the year before which had spoyl'd all his Beer [. . .] – however bad Beer might be the Pretence to *Me*. well but said I methinks if the Beer is really bad, you should send for Jackson to cook it; he turned from me upon those Words in an Agony I could not then comprehend.
> (*Thraliana*: 1: 312–13)

Hester had touched upon the truth as his agonized look at her mention of Jackson and 'cooking' the beer revealed. In his obsessive determination to outbrew London rivals such as Felix Calvert and Samuel Whitbread, Thrale had involved himself in a ruinous scheme of the chemist Humphrey Jackson to brew beer 'without the *beggarly elements* of malt and hops'. Jackson was to her the biblical 'wicked *Haman*' whose plot, if not foiled, was now at least rumbled by Queen Esther. It is significant that the 'Autobiographical Essays' account of her discovery of this practice upon Thrale, written in old age, and in the immediate context of how her electioneering aid had at least led others to remark, 'how happy Mr. Thrale must be in such a *wonder* of a wife', still represents Jackson not only as arch-deceiver but almost as sexual rival, in 'complete possession' of the secretive Thrale's heart:

> I wondered all the while where his heart lay; but it was found at last, too soon for joy, too late almost for sorrow. A vulgar fellow, by name Humphrey Jackson, had, as the clerks informed me, all in a breath, complete possession of it. He had long practised on poor Thrale's credulity, till, by mixing two cold liquors which produced heat perhaps, or two colourless liquors which produced brilliancy, he had at length prevailed on him to think he could produce beer too, without the *beggarly elements* of malt and hops. (*Autobiography*, 2: 25)

Thrale's attempt to produce 'chemical' beer was undertaken against the advice of John Perkins, his thrifty and responsible chief clerk, and the master brewer, and proved disastrous. Thrale produced a vast output of undrinkable beer, totally beyond 'cooking'. Jackson had also encouraged Thrale to experiment in the production of a wood preservative to safeguard ships' bottoms against marine worms. Hester could scarcely contain her contempt:

> He had persuaded him to build a Copper somewhere in East Smithfield, the very metal of which cost 2000£, wherein this Jackson was to make Experiments and conjure some curious stuff, which should preserve Ships' Bottoms from the Worm; gaining from Government Money to defray these mad Expenses. Twenty enormous Vats, holding 1000 hogsheads each—costly contents!—Ten more holding a *Thousand Barrels* each, were constructed to stew in this pernicious Mess; and afterwards erected, on I forget how much Ground bought for the ruinous Purpose.
> (*Autobiography*, 2: 25–6)

Hester appreciated that their most urgent business problems were of supply: 'We had in the commercial phrase, no beer to start for customers. We had no money to purchase with.' Labour relations suffered: 'Our clerks, insulted long, rebelled and *ratted,* but I held them in' (*Autobiography*, 2: 26). But she also realised that the recent failure in June 1772 of Fordyce's bank had precipitated a financial panic, and she feared that her husband, in his present state of despair, might contemplate suicide. Her philosophical friend Johnson comforted both Hester and her mother:

> 'Fear not the menaces of suicide,' said he; 'the man who has two such females to console him, never yet killed himself, and will not *now*. Of all the bankrupts made this dreadful year,' continued he, 'none have destroyed themselves but married men; who would have risen from the weeds undrowned, had not the women clung about and sunk them, stifling the voice of reason with their cries.' (*Autobiography*, 2: 26)

Johnson realised that the resourceful Hester was a very different sort of woman.

Thus Hester was drawn into taking an active managerial role in the family business by Thrale's increasingly reckless speculation. Johnson rallied round in the counting-house, and Hester tirelessly set about averting the threatened bankruptcy by raising £3,000 from her mother, and placating regular customers and suppliers. This took some doing; Thrale owed £6,400 to his malt-factor Hankin, and £18,000 to his hop-factors. Though heavily pregnant, Hester drove to Brighton to beg £6,000 from a family friend, Charles Scrase. John Perkins was so full of admiration that he repeated to everyone Hester's brief letter to her husband: 'I have done my errand, and you soon shall see returned, whole, as I hope—your heavy but faithful messenger, H.L.T.' (*Autobiography*, 2: 27). In this way, 'Money was raised, the Beer was mended, our whole Conduct in the management of our Trade was changed' (*Thraliana*, 1: 312).

Hester's conciliating gesture to the staff was not 'beer and sandwiches' but genteel tea and cakes, and it certainly impressed Perkins to be invited into her house. She regained the loyalty of a demoralized workforce at the brewery who 'declared they would not live *with Mr Thrale*, but they would do *anything* for *me*' (*Thraliana*, 1: 313). Hester believed not only that their sexuality gave women a special advantage in man management, but also that women get things done: 'Women have a manifest Advantage over Men in the doing Business; every thing smooths down before them, & to be a Female is commonly sufficient to be successful, if She has a little Spirit & a little common Sense'. Her spirit and common sense had saved the brewery, but her eighth child, Penelope, lived only ten hours.

While Thrale was incapacitated by a morose state of bewilderment, Hester and Johnson, schooled in literary collaboration, worked together to restore trade confidence. The burly figure of Johnson inspired confidence at the brewery but in his absence on a trip to Lichfield, the major burden fell upon Hester. His letters at this time are full of references to business matters, to the harvest, the price of malt and of hops. He wrote from Lichfield on 24 October 1772 to stiffen her resolve concerning the regaining of market ground by means of a vigorously economic brewing season:

> The brewhouse must be the scene of action [. . .] The first consequence of our late trouble ought to be, an endeavour to brew at a cheaper rate;

an endeavour not violent and transient, but steady and continual, prosecuted with total contempt of censure or wonder, and animated by resolution not to stop while more can be done. Unless this can be done, nothing can help us; and if this be done, we shall not want help.[4]

He used the first person plural to stress his solidarity, adding that, although the price of malt had risen to 'two pounds eight shillings the quarter', and the price of ale in public houses had risen to an unprecedented 'sixpence a quart', that this constitutes 'an evil which we only share with the whole nation, and which we did not bring upon ourselves'. On 7 November he wrote from Ashbourne to assure her that her advice concerning the reimbursement of a business creditor was sound: 'I think you were quite right in your advice about the thousand pounds for the payment could not have been delayed long; and a short delay would have lessened credit, without advancing interest. In great matters you are hardly ever mistaken.' Two days later Johnson, in expressing his confidence in the gradual financial recovery of the brewery, switched tactfully to the second person plural:

> Mr. Thrale's money, to pay for all, must come from the sale of good beer. I am far from despairing of solid and durable prosperity. Nor will your success exceed my hopes, or my opinion of your state, if, after this tremendous year, you should annually add to your fortune three thousand pounds. This will soon dismiss all incumbrances; and, when no interest is paid, you will begin annually to lay up almost five thousand. This is very splendid; but this, I think, is in your power.[5]

Early March 1773 brought the additional blow that Thrale was embroiled with another chemist, Thomas Alexander, who, together with a certain Mr Eyles, was threatening a lawsuit for fraudulent business practices. Hester was involved in negotiating an out-of-court settlement and, although she followed Johnson's advice to be more imperious, it would seem that she had taken on the transactions alone:[6]

> Your Advice was precisely right, upon my talking in a higher & more fearless Tone my friend Alexander was much disconcerted—apparently so [. . .] [He] profess'd his Confidence in Mr Thrale's honour & Perkins's Honesty, both which he said I had clear'd to him. he then expatiated in praise of my powers of Negotiation.[7]

Johnson now forgot his former pronouncement that Hester was of 'neither Use nor Ornament' to Thrale, and praised her business acumen and her expertise in conciliation and mediation, all achieved while nursing her mother in the cruel last months of a terminal breast cancer. Henry himself should be boiled.

> I shall be glad to see you, for you are much in my head, notwithstanding your negotiations for my master, he has mended his share for one year, you must think of cutting in pieces and boiling him. We will at least keep him out of J—ck—n's copper. You will be at leisure now to think of brewing and negotiating, and a little of, Madam, Your, &c.[8]

When Thrale's 'horrible Stupor' evaporated, one might have expected to find him chastened. But although he had grown more taciturn, his self-confidence was restored and his old ways resumed. John Perkins informed Mrs Thrale in July 1773 that Thrale had 'not done trying Experiments', as he abandoned a cask of sick beer worth £600 when it might have been cured with '50 barrels of good stout porter'.[9]

Amidst all this flurry of mending trade and labour relations, Hester was robbed of her mother, the last link with her Welsh family. The death of Hester Maria Salusbury, which she faced with such courage that she won the deepest respect from Johnson, was an enormous blow to the daughter who had idolized her. Her 'Family Book' entry for the 18 June 1773 records:

> On this day She died, & left me destitute of every real every natural Friend: for Sir Thos. Salusbury has long ago cast me off, & Mr Thrale & Mr Johnson are the mere Acquisitions of Chance; which chance, or change of Behaviour, or Intervention of new Objects or twenty Things

besides Death can rob me of. One solid Good I had & that is Gone—my Mother! (Hyde, p. 65)

She realised, not without a hint of perverse pride, how exceptional was her emotionally myopic focus upon her parent: 'For true Love of one's Mother and real preference of her to all human Kind, I believe I am a singular Example. Johnson says it was not right though' (*Thraliana* 1: 355). A thoughtful modern critic, Mary Hyde, commented: 'Mrs. Thrale was never to have a child who had any such attachment for her' (p. 70). One reason for this was that she had been an only child. But, by this stage of her life as a mother, Hester would have to harden herself – if the high infant mortality of the eighteenth century, even higher for a woman allowed no respite between pregnancies, was not to destroy her sanity. Ralph, her second boy, was born on 8 November but fated only to live for eighteen months; despite the efforts of four physicians, Lucy, 'my lovely Lucy', was to die exactly a fortnight later on 22 November at the age of four years and five months: 'oh what were my Feelings for my Lucy? my Dear, my favourite Girl!' (Hyde, pp. 86, 83).

It was with much relief that Hester bade farewell to the 'accursed Year 1773', which had also seen the death of Sir Thomas Salusbury and the extinguishing of her hopes of being left a fortune, for he had left Offley and his entire estate to his wife. Perkins was coping well at the Anchor, and Hester was gaining strength and for once not pregnant and in the spring of 1774, the Thrales and Johnson decided that a relaxing – if not grand – tour of Italy would raise everyone's spirits. It was finally decided, however, to postpone this trip as various legal problems concerning Hester's inheritance of her mother's estate at Bachegraig required urgent attention. Business and pleasure might be combined, however, by a tour of north Wales instead, and Queeney could accompany them. It was with a mixture of excitement and anguish that Hester anticipated the tour. On the eve of their departure on 5 July, Hester confided her to her 'Family Book' her painful self-doubt concerning the arrangements for the care of her younger children:

had my mother been living perhaps I had done better; perhaps I have lost my Virtue with my Parent: She would not have approved my leaving them & then I should not have gone. I shall now perhaps neglect them more & more—Oh God forbid! and grant us if it be thy blessed will, a happy meeting at my return from Wales. I cannot write for crying tonight, I am so very low spirited. (Hyde, p. 89)

It is impossible having read these words, so full of anxious misgiving, and credit Lawrence Stone's summation of the character of their author: 'Dominant, authoritarian, demanding, possessive and wholly selfish in her pursuit of ego-gratification through her children, as a mother Mrs. Thrale/Piozzi was a total failure'.[10] This was a woman tormented by the immaculate role model presented by a mother who had only one child to worry about, but it is also crystal clear that neither Henry nor Sam shared the burden of her anxieties. They spent their first night at Dunstable and, such was his impatience to show them Lichfield, the two men decided that they should all make a six o'clock start for the journey of more than eighty miles. Although Johnson overslept, they decided to keep to their schedule and Hester was forced to suppress her concern for her daughter, being 'often told how little it signified whether she catch'd cold or no'.[11]

They reached Lichfield at midnight and the following morning Hester was told by Johnson, who obviously wanted to make a grandiose return to his native city, to change her dress 'for one more gay and splendid'. They visited Richard Greene's collection of curiosities, lunched with Erasmus Darwin, founder member of the Lunar Society, and Johnson introduced Hester to his stepdaughter Lucy Porter, who 'received us very kindly and politely'. The cathedral was impressive, but their visit to Johnson's birthplace 'filled my mind with emotion, so tender and so pleasing, that I would have been sorry to quit it for the sake of seeing the Vatican' (Bristow, p, 90). After a few days they proceeded to the magnificent seat of 'the King of Ashbourne', Johnson's close friend, Dr John Taylor, and the party was lavishly entertained amidst charming surroundings. Taylor arranged day trips to Ilam, where the Paradise valley had inspired Johnson's *The History of Rasselas, Prince of Abissinia* (1759); the elegant beauties of Chatsworth House, where the Duke of Devonshire showed them his mechanical fountain, and Kedleston; and the dramatic scenes of Matlock Bath and Dovedale. All would have been well had not her daughter's anticipated cold grown more serious – 'Queeney breaks my heart and my head with her cough' – and been complicated by high fever and an attack of worms. Hester had forgotten to bring a maid, and all the nursing naturally devolved upon her.

Leaving the delights of Ashbourne, they set out for Combermere, going via Buxton, where Hester relaxed in the soothing waters. She thought of the happy times she had known at Combermere Abbey with her uncle Sir Robert Cotton and dreaded Johnson's reaction to the new owners, the embarrassingly rustic Sir Lynch Cotton and his insipid wife. Sure enough, Johnson dismissed him as 'gross', his 'Lady weak and ignorant'. Arriving at Chester on 26 July, Hester became seriously 'out of humour' when the eccentric Johnson insisted keeping her and Queeney up late while he measured the high town walls: 'We walked round the walls which are complete, and contain one Mile, three quarters, and one hundred and one yards' (*Autobiography*, 1: 83).

Two days later, they entered Wales and in the evening arrived at Lleweni Hall near Denbigh, now owned by Sir Lynch's eldest son, her cousin Robert Cotton, 'which struck me extremely as an old family seat of no small dignity' (Bristow, p. 101). Neither Thrale nor Johnson was impressed, they seemed determined not to be; even the mountains were puny compared with those Johnson had seen in Scotland with Boswell. At last they visited the Salusbury mansion of Bachegraig, which Hester was to inherit. Her companions, however, found little to praise, with Johnson noting: 'an old house, built 1567, in an uncommon and incommodious form— My mistress chatted about tiring, but I prevailed upon her to go to the top—The floors have been stolen: the windows are stopped— The house was less than I seemed to expect' (*Autobiography*, 1: 83). Tremeirchion parish church, where Hester's father was buried, was labelled of 'mean fabric' and the journal entry reveals Johnson's dry reaction to a sentimental old clerk who, delighted to see Hester, 'foolishly said that he was now willing to die'. Johnson seemed unsure whether to be to more grumpy at the clerk's flattery or Hester's parsimony: 'The old Clerk had only a crown given him by my mistress' (*Autobiography*, 1: 85).

Some of the outings Hester planned were successful and the Cottons were most hospitable, but any comparison of their respective journal entries reveals a rather jaundiced Johnson and a somewhat harassed, but determined-to-be-happy, Hester. When the party rode to Robert Cotton's summer-house to appreciate the 'fine view of the vale', even Johnson had to admit it 'has a very extensive prospect', but felt bound to remark, 'it is meanly built, and unskilfully disposed'.[12] When they went to Rhuddlan Castle on 4 August, a prosaic Johnson was impressed with this 'very noble ruin' and the massive strength of its six round towers. By contrast, Hester's enthusiastic response was decidedly Romantic: 'Wild in its situation, rude in its appearance, the haunt of screaming gulls and clamorous rooks'. Her mind was filled with poetical 'images of captivity, courage, or desperation': 'Here Danae might have been immured, here Andromeda might have been exposed, and here Alcyone might have breathed her last on the corpse of the faithful Ceyx' (Bristow, p. 105) Whereas her mind expanded, Johnson's response became reductive, Anglocentric, if not condescendingly Cymruphobic, as illustrated by this interchange:

> —Has this BROOK e'er a name?' and received for answer—Why, dear Sir, this is the RIVER Ustrad.—Let us', said he, turning to his friend [Henry Thrale], 'jump over it directly, and shew them how an Englishman should treat a Welch RIVER'.[13]

Hester's repeated attempts to compensate for Johnson's refusal to be charmed by Wales and his rudeness or incivility to her Welsh relatives and friends were themselves subject of Johnsonian criticism:

> 'Madam, let me have no more of this idle commendation of nothing. Why is it that whatever you see, and whoever you see, you are to be so

indiscriminately lavish of praise?' 'Why, I'll tell you, Sir,' said I; 'when I am with you and Mr. Thrale and Queeney, I am obliged to be civil for four!' (*Autobiography*, 1: 86)

In a letter of 16 August 1774 Johnson wrote from Llweni to his friend, the surgeon Robert Levet[t]: 'Wales, so far as I have yet seen of it, is a very beautiful and rich country all enclosed and planted'.[14] Nevertheless Hester's marginal note reads: 'Yet to please Mr Thrale, he Feign'd Abhorrence of it' (*Autobiography*, 1: 88). The perversity of such cruel anti-Cymric 'boys' games' irritated and depressed Hester as they attempted to puncture her enthusiasm for her native land. She was a Welshwoman to the core, and was proud to attribute all those characteristics, which enabled her selflessly to support Samuel Johnson, to what she had imbibed at her Caernarfonshire hearth and home.[15] Hester would subsequently set the record right by publishing, in William Owen Pughe's patriotic *Cambrian Register*, her poem: 'Lines on Bodfel Hall, the Birthplace of Mrs. H. L. Piozzi':

> Nor ye, who, vers'd in critic lore,
> O'er Johnson's *Lives* incessant pore,
> And know how, propp'd with care, the sage
> Prolonged his course another stage,
> Forget—as every page you turn,
> With profit, or with rapture burn,—
>   To Bodfel ye the pleasure owe [. . .]
>
> To Bodfel, then, a grateful song,
> Its woods and meads and streams along.
> Thy aid I supplicate, O Muse,
> Nor thou the supplicated boon refuse;
> So may I haply forth to fame
> The short, but gracious, tale proclaim,—
>   To Bodfel I these pleasures owe.
>   (Stanzas 2 and 6)[16]

On 23 August they went to see Bodfel, Hester's birthplace, but Johnson's journal failed to record the sympathetic interest and tender feelings that had made Hester reluctant to leave his house in Lichfield. Instead, unsparing honesty keeps sensibility at bay: 'This species of pleasure is always melancholy. The walk was cut down, and the pond was dry. Nothing was better. Mrs Thrale visited a house where she had been used to drink milk' (Bristow, pp. 48–9).

Thrale was even more scathing of her memories. Hester remembered Dick Lloyd, a childhood friend who had played 'many a game of romps with me', confessing, 'I was wishing Dick Lloyd alive.' 'What signifies wishing', returned the thick-skinned Thrale, 'if we must wish let it be for our poor Mother who, but for that last cursed illness would have been as able to have taken this journey as yourself' (Bristow, p. 116). The party went on to visit Pwllheli: 'a mean old town', writes Johnson, continuing with a certain irony, 'Here we bought something to remember the place.' Hester's own account is subtly different: 'Mr Johnson would buy something, he said, in memory of his little Mistresses' Market Town.' Hester was grateful for any affection Johnson showed her, in contrast to the distant Thrale: 'he is on every occasion so very kind, feels friendship so acutely and expresses it so delicately that it is wonderfully flattering to me to have his company' (Bristow, pp. 49, 116).

Letters from Streatham had increased her concern about her other children and she has no one to converse with about her anxieties; she baldly and shockingly states: 'Mr Thrale will not be conversed with by *me* on any subject, as a friend, or comforter or adviser.' Her praise of Johnson above might make us think she could turn to him, but it was female friendship she sought: 'My present Companions have too much philosophy for me. One cannot disburthen one's mind to people who are watchful to cavil, or acute to contradict before the sentence is finished' (Bristow, p. 109).

There were some idyllic days as when they were rowed 'in our pretty boat' across to Ynys Môn, admiring the superb situation of Plasnewydd, and the 'mighty pile' of Beaumaris castle, which impressed even Johnson. They were rowed on to Caernarfon where the castle's cannons were announcing the arrival of their friend Pasquale Paoli on his tour of north Wales. On 26 August they set out for the lake of Llyn Peris on a 'party of pleasure' arranged by their hostess, Bridget, wife of Colonel Glyn Wynn MP for Caernarfon Boroughs, and in a cottage by its banks, 'we found a Harper, and Mrs Wynn sang Welch songs to his accompaniment', and had an al fresco lunch. They rowed on the lake, enjoying the magnificent ruin of Dolbadarn Castle, built by Llewellyn the Great in the thirteenth century. Hester drank in the mighty landscape which had been delightfully classicised by Richard Wilson's composition in the manner of Claude Lorrain. It would be powerfully dramatised and Romanticised – exactly a quarter of a century later – by Turner, fascinated by north Wales, its legend of the bardicide Edward I, and the cruel incarceration of Owain Goch. Snowdon towered over the scene and the hills reverberated to 'the blasts from the Copper Mills on the mountain'. As Queeney counted her goats – she had spotted 149, and earned as many pennies, since entering Wales – Hester hoped that her companions would share her love of her homeland: 'Goats frisking on the hills and a cataract playing at a small distance so finished the scene, that nothing, I think, could be wished for' (Bristow, p. 117). Actually, Johnson was distinctly underwhelmed, recording the lake's lack of breadth and the 'great labour' of the climb to the castle: 'I was breathless and harassed.'

On the last leg of their journey home, the party stopped at Gregories in Beaconsfield where they were welcomed by the Whig statesman Edmund Burke, but the news that Parliament had been dissolved provoked some hard drinking in their host and his friends. Hester confided to her journal: 'I had spent three months from home among dunces of all ranks and sorts, but I had never seen a man drunk till I came amongst the Wits' (Bristow, p. 126). Hurrying back to Streatham, Hester was delighted to find her children in good health, but her happiness was overshadowed by the fact that canvassing meant 'that odious dungeon' in Deadman's Place, 'where nobody will come near me, the children are to be sick for want of air *and I am never to see a face but Mr Johnson's*'.

Johnson, however, proved more than useful both in the study and at the stump. He dashed off *The Patriot*, which was published on 12 October 1774, supporting Lord North's ministry against the Wilkites and what he saw as the hypocrisy of opposition groups who proclaimed themselves patriots while siding with American rebellion and the Boston Tea Party. A true patriot, he argued, is not he who attempts 'to change the mode of representation, transmitted by our ancestors'. Johnson ridiculed those who believed in popular sovereignty and who ritually burnt a boot (a rough pun on Lord Bute) or a Scottish bonnet, in their contentious gatherings.[17] But when canvassing he would trade jests with the electors, as Hester recalled:

> A rough fellow one day on such an occasion, a hatter by trade, seeing Mr. Johnson's beaver in a state of decay, seized it suddenly with one hand, and clapping him on the back with the other; Ah, Master Johnson (says he), this is no time to be thinking about *hats*. 'No, no, Sir (replies our Doctor in a cheerful tone), hats are of no use now, as you say, except to throw up in the air and huzza with;' accompanying his words with the true election halloo. (*Anecdotes*, pp. 214–15)

On the 31 October 1774 she recorded in her 'Family Book': 'Mr Thrale is once more elected for Southwark, & his best Friends say he may thank his Wife for his Seat—the truth is, I have been indefatigable' (Hyde, p. 108). But she was being worn down by 'getting Votes all day, & settling Books with Clerks all Night'. In early November she had a serious riding accident when her galloping horse slipped and fell under her: 'the Pommel struck my Side with great Violence, & my Lip was cut almost through: add to this the two black Eyes I had gained, and an immense Swelling at my Jaw, which tho' not broke was greatly injured' (Hyde, p. 108). By the time she was fully recovered another crisis arose: her year-old son, Ralph became severely ill following his inoculation against smallpox. Convinced her baby was dying, she exhausted herself in nursing him: 'Up every Night and all Night long again! – well if this don't kill me & the Child I carry, sure we are made of Iron' (Hyde, p. 110).

In mid-April 1775 the brilliant surgeon Percivall Pott attended her husband to remove a nasal polyp. When Thrale asked him to look at their sickly child Ralph, he bluntly observed: 'This Boy is in a State of Fatuity, either by Accident, or more probably from his birth, you may see he labours under some nervous Complaint that has affected his Intellects; for his Eyes have not the Look of another Child sick or well' (Hyde, p. 115). 'This heaviest of all my Afflictions' had to be borne alone as her husband was in a state of denial about the child's mental impairment. The heavily pregnant Hester dutifully recalled that she ought to be thankful that the rest of her children were well, while revealing a harsh strain of north Welsh Calvinist guilt: 'I shall perhaps have only one Misfortune— may that expiate my criminal pride in my own & my eldest Daughter's Superiority of understanding' (Hyde, p. 117). From Ashbourne, Johnson proffered some distanced comfort: 'I hope occasional bathing, and keeping him about two minutes with his body immersed, may promote the discharge from his head, and set his little brain at liberty' (*SJLetters*, 1: 262). But he was only parroting the advice of Robert Bromfield, without that physician's gentle note of monitory realism: 'while you are trying every Means to preserve the Life of little Master I fear your truest Friends will scarce be able to wish You Success' (Hyde, p. 115).

The 'Iron' lady gave birth to her tenth child at Streatham on 4 May 1775. She was christened Frances Anna, named after Hester's attractive and lively seventeen-year-old niece, Frances Plumbe Rice, now a mother herself, whose company Hester always relished. In May 1773, facing the obdurate resistance of Frances's father, Alderman Samuel Plumbe, the twenty-one-year-old John Rice had eloped with the fifteen-year-old Frances.[18] Hester, delighted with the romanticism of this love-match, wrote supportively from Streatham:

> My Dear Fanny, For so I will continue to call you until Mr. R. lets us know you are no longer *our* Fanny but *his* [. . .] Tell Mr. R that I say *his* father [Morgan Rice, who had accepted the situation] behaves like a *worthy* man, a *wise* man, and a *Welch* man. Of your father's behaviour

the less said the better; but be not uneasy, his violence does his Constitution no harm—He is very well as can be.[19]

Hester's letter to John Rice on the subject of marriage became famous as an elegant, and frequently reprinted, epistle, but first she sent it to Johnson with the instruction: 'Bring it me home at night, and say you like it at least as well as Swift's, which you do *not* like, to the lady' (*SJLetters*, 1: 95). She was humorously seeking her friend's approbation, but displaying remarkable bluestocking ambition in challenging Dean Swift's 'A letter to a very young lady on her marriage', which celebrated a common-sense companionate union: 'yours was a match of prudence and common good-liking, without any mixture of that ridiculous passion, which hath no being but in play-books and romances'.[20]

In her letter 'To a newly-married man' Hester wrote with great wisdom of what she has observed rather than what she has experienced:

> When your present violence of passion subsides however, and a more cool and tranquil affection takes its place, be not hasty to censure yourself as indifferent, or to lament yourself as unhappy; you have lost that only which it was impossible to retain, and it were graceless amid the pleasures of a prosperous summer to regret the blossoms of a transient spring. (*SJLetters*, 1: 97)

But when she spoke of the means of establishing mutuality and enjoying 'a community of pleasure', it became clear that she was gauging the likelihood of their success by the failures of her own attempts. '[N]othing', she argued,

> is so dangerous to wedded love as the possibility of either being happy out of the company of the other; endeavour therefore to cement the present intimacy on every side; let your wife never be kept ignorant of your income, your expences, your friendships, or aversions; let her know your very faults, but make them amiable by your virtues; consider all concealment as a breach of fidelity. (*SJLetters*, 1: 98)

Hester advised him to respect women's sense:

> Listen not to those sages who advise you always to scorn the counsel of a woman, and if you comply with her requests pronounce you to be wife-ridden [. . .] and do not congratulate yourself that your wife is not a learned lady, that she never touches a card, or is wholly ignorant how to make a pudding. Cards, cookery, and learning, are all good in their places, and may all be used with advantage. (*SJLetters*, 1: 99)

However, when published, the letter would incense Mary Wollstonecraft by advising John Rice that 'a woman will pardon an affront to her understanding much sooner than one to her person [. . .] All our attainments, all our arts, are employed to gain and keep the heart of man', and if she feels her attractiveness neglected she will seek 'the attention of others for the slights of her husband!'[21] Wollstonecraft condemns these sentiments as male-identified: 'These are truly masculine sentiments [. . .] Noble morality!' Less conventionally, Hester scotched the notion that materialist acquisition of 'splendid furniture and glittering equipages' would purchase distinction. Modern society was becoming a meritocracy where individuals are respected for their talents and learning:

> The age we live in, pays, I think, peculiar attention to the higher distinctions of wit, knowledge, and virtue, to which we may more safely, more cheaply, and more honourably aspire. The giddy flirt of quality frets at the respect she sees paid to Lady Edgecumbe [a talented harpsichordist], and the gay dunce sits pining for a partner, while [William] Jones the orientalist leads up the ball . . . (*SJLetters*, 1: 99–100)

But Hester repented her own intellectual ambition and recent enjoyment of entering more into society – going to the theatre and attending balls. For early July 1775 saw her at Brighton, desperately consulting doctors as Ralph's condition deteriorated; a letter to Johnson reveals her isolated anguish and misdirected guilt:

> What shall I do? What can I do? has the flattery of my Friends made me too proud of my own Brains? & must these poor Children suffer for my Crime? I can neither go on with this Subject nor quit it [. . .] I opened the Ball last Night — tonight I go to the Play: Oh that there was a Play or a Ball for every hour of the four & twenty![22]

Having briefly returned to Streatham to assure herself of the health of her other children, she was summoned back to Sussex only to find Ralph dead. On post-mortem examination 'the Brain was found almost dissolved in Water, & something amiss in the original Conformation of the Head'. Mary Hyde's tentative diagnosis of hydrancephaly (absence of the cerebral hemispheres, the space in the cranium being filled with cerebrospinal fluid) rather than hydrocephalus (in which enlargement of the skull would be apparent) would seem to be supported by Hester's earlier observations of Ralph's early normality, 'violent fits of Rage', and especially that 'his Muscular Flesh however seemed rather to increase than diminish' (Hyde, p. 125). Filled with a numbed and stoical acceptance, she returned to a Streatham empty but for Johnson's friend, the writer Giuseppe Marc'Antonio Baretti, the Italian tutor of Queeney, who was kindly looking after her five children. She confides to Johnson on 18 July that she was alone with her grief: 'Mr Thrale has been in Town ever since I was gone, but would not come home to me last Night but went to Ranelagh I hear, however I will not be peevish any more, for it torments nobody but myself.' It is Johnson's absence that she laments, ending her letter with a poignant appeal for his return: 'Farewell My Dear sir and let us see you sometime; I think you shall never run away so again: I lost a Child the last Time you were at a distance' (Chapman, 2: 69–70). Johnson replied immediately with some rational sympathy and much affection: but he took a month to return.

5

'Like a Rocket She rises, and leaves us to Stare'

'Notwithstanding the Disgust my last Journey gave me, I have lately been solicitous to undertake another'.[1] Hester began her travel journal by reminding herself how her male companions had taken pleasure in deflating her enthusiasm for her native Wales in their earlier tour. Now, to encourage her excitement, they were making an excursion to France. Henry and his eldest daughter would be as stolid as ever on this second journey, and Dr Johnson, with his poor eyesight and hearing, equally incapable of sharing her delight in scenery and art. Yet Hester could not suppress her eagerness to drink in all the new experiences of a first trip abroad and to enjoy improving her spoken French and Italian, in both of which she was fluent. Dr Johnson preferred to converse in Latin. Hester kept a detailed journal, and saw this as good practice for writing and even publishing a travel book in the future. Earlier that year, Boswell had lent her his manuscript diary of the trip he had made with Johnson to the Hebrides, and that may have prompted her rivalry. She told herself: 'I will relate only what I see – which can hardly fail of being true' (*French Journals*, p. 94).

Hester and Henry, Dr Johnson, Queeney and Queeney's Italian tutor, Baretti, set sail on 17 September 1775 for France, from where they would return on 11 November. A calm crossing of six hours on a neat sloop captained by a school friend of Thrale brought them safe to Calais. A superb dinner at their sumptuous inn, the Hôtel d'Angleterre, was enlivened by the company of a Capuchin friar. The handsome Father Felix had been a soldier, a traveller through Europe and Asia, and was, in Johnson's view, as 'complete a character as could be found in Romance' (*French Journals*, p. 71). He gave them a sight of his 'Convent, Cells, Chapel, & Refectory; the Library was locked, &', remarked Hester, 'I was not sorry, for Mr Johnson would never have come out of it.'

They travelled in style in two coaches and crammed in as much sightseeing as possible, all efficiently organised by the Italian. Both Johnson and Hester were eager to find out all they could about Catholic worship and culture. Johnson's birthday treat on the 18th was an early visit to the Église Notre-Dame, after which Hester was taken by Baretti to a Dominican Convent of British nuns. She was impressed with Miss Gray, the Superior, who possessed the 'Manners & Look of a Woman of high Fashion' despite having been 'immured there 26 years'. Amazingly she was well informed about the very latest London scandal: the clash between Samuel Foote and the bigamist courtier Elizabeth Chudleigh, Duchess of Kingston, whom he had mercilessly satirised as the hypocritical intriguer Lady Kitty Crocodile in his *A Trip to Calais*.

The flamboyant gothic of the cathedrals of Saint-Omer and Arras impressed Hester with their stupendous scale and sumptuous ornament, 'a Silver Crook Seven Feet high, a Crucifix with Diamonds for Nails': 'let us never more talk of English Churches.' At Arras she visited a new Benedictine foundation, noting its library resembling that of All Souls, but met with a reproof from an elderly friar who informed her that their Dormitory was no place for Ladies. The vast space of the nave of Amiens Cathedral, the largest in France, exceeded anything she had yet seen: a Paschal Lamb of white marble on the high altar; and a statue of the Virgin, Notre Dame des Douleurs, with a dagger in her breast. On the road the party counted Calvaries as Queeney had counted Welsh goats on their trip to Wales.

Cecilia Strickland (née Towneley), or 'Stricky', as Hester fondly nicknamed her childhood friend, now widowed, joined the party at Rouen on 22 September. The granddaughter of Henry, the sixth Duke of Norfolk, a 'true Aristocrate and determined Papist' from a Jacobite family, Cecilia had been educated at the convent of Austin nuns in Paris and her daughter was at a convent school in

Rouen. She secured Hester's entrée to more convents and her party's introduction to notable *salonnières*. The following day Hester experienced sharply contrasting examples of female monasticism. The austerity of the English order of Poor Clares made a deep impression: '[They] wore only one Petticoat and that of the very coarsest Stuff, they were bare legged and bare-footed, & had had no Linnen about them except a sort of Band, which was very dirty though I had Reason to think I was expected' (*French Journals*, pp. 79–80). Stricky transported them from such strict and superstitious austerities to the Benedictine Priory of Saint-Louis, 'a Convent of the highest Order', complete with a library and billiard room, and full of Lap Dogs, Cats & Parrots', where the talk was of 'Literature, of Politicks, of Fashions, of everything' (*French Journals*, p. 81). Hester gave Baretti's French translation of Johnson's *Rasselas* to the Abbess, while the Abbé Roffette conversed in fluent Latin with Johnson who delivered an extempore eulogium upon Milton.

Hester's fascination with all-female communities had been nurtured by her reading of Mary Astell's *A Serious Proposal to the Ladies* (1696–7); Samuel Richardson's eponymous hero Sir Charles Grandison's proposal for Protestant convents (1753); and Sarah Scott's utopian novel, *Millenium Hall* (1762), which imagined women sharing their resources and devoting themselves to philanthropy and intellectual pursuits. In France she began to see that even convent life might present a viable alternative to poverty or patriarchal subjection in marriage.

> a Well endowed Convent is of all others the most perfect Refuge from Poverty. With regard to Celibacy—it is for the [most part] uncomfortable in the World [only] because it is a Disgrace, which Objection is lost in a Convent; with Regard to Solitude—few Women live in so much Society as four and twenty or thirty [female] Acquaintance [. . .] Obedience is the most objectible [sic] of all the Vows, & that too seems to be made very easy: their Abbess is of their own chusing, & they elect a new one or the same over again every three Years. (*French Journals*, p. 122)

Apart from the intellectual attractions of the contemplative life, obedience to a democratically elected female might well seem preferable to the patriarchal sway of a husband chosen by her parents, a man whom even Johnson himself habitually termed 'My Master'.

As their two carriages headed for Paris, the countryside surprised Hester with its beauty and burgeoning beneficence, especially as she had been so shocked by the numbers of the French poor everywhere they went:

> [T]he whole country carries an Air of Fertility that is inexpressively delightful: to see Cherries, Apples, Grapes, Asparagas, Lentils & French Beans planted in large portions all around one, & inviting the Traveller to partake the Bounties of the Nation is so perfectly agreeable that one frets to see so many People *beg*, where one is morally certain nobody can starve. (*French Journals*, p. 88)

Their peaceful journey was then shattered by a serious accident which befell the carriage of Thrale, Baretti and Queeney. On the edge of a precipice between Vernon and Saint-Denys its horses burst into a run which threw the postilion: 'the Traces were broken, one of the Horses run over and the Chaise carried forward with a most dangerous Rapidity.' In the following carriage, Johnson continued his monologue toward his captive audience, seemingly oblivious even of Thrale's heroic leap from the carriage in an unsuccessful attempt to stop the horses. The coach was eventually stopped by their servant Sam while his philosophical namesake merely remarked: 'nothing came of it, except that Mr. Thrale leaped out of the carriage into a chalk-pit, and then came up again, looking as *white*!' Hester was deeply shocked both by the accident and by Johnson's unconcern, while Mrs Strickland was furious, 'her Indignation towards him prevailing over her friendship for me' (*French Journals*, p. 89). However, they arrived safely in Paris, recovered from their ordeal in elegant lodgings in Rue Jacob and received reassuring news about the children left at home. The party soon resumed 'running about from Church to Church to see the Splendour of the Romish Religion' (*French Journals*, p. 96). Thrale spent lavishly, they entertained friends and altogether enjoyed a 'Month of extreme Expence, some Pleasure & some Profit' (*French Journals*, p. 149). They attended the theatre where Hester conceded 'the French do beat us at acting Plays' (*French Journals*, p. 137). They went to the races, where they saw the beautiful Queen Marie Antoinette. They visited the historic Gobelin tapestry factory, the Sèvres porcelain works, and the King's museum. Hester met the distinguished woman of letters Anne-Marie Fiquet de Bocages (1710–1802), author of a proto-feminist drama, *Les Amazones* (1749) and translator into French of *Rasselas*. She most of all relished seeing French and Italian art, especially the Orléans collection of paintings at the Palais Royal: 'I half cryed over some of them with mere delight' (*French Journals*, p. 147).

In November the party began to make their way back and had arrived home by the middle of the month. Almost straightaway, the agony of their family life resumed, her baby Frances Anna sickened of influenza and died on 9 December. Hester bravely attempted to school her grief by writing in her 'Children's Book' minute accounts of the four who had been left to her. The apple of his parents' eye was their only son and heir, the outgoing ultra-masculine Harry, who had recently been flogged at school for telling a bawdy story and who was a favourite among the brewery men. Harry had not long celebrated his ninth birthday in February 1776, when the Thrales gave Baretti the go-ahead to arrange another trip abroad, this time to his native Italy. The tour would be quite grand for a bourgeois family as it would last a whole year. All was planned, and Dr Johnson went on a farewell journey to his friends in the Midlands before setting out.

Then in March tragedy struck once more. Hester recorded every detail in her diary of how on the 21st Queeney fell ill and then on the 23rd Harry too developed a fever. Harry's attack was more severe and he doubled up with pain and began vomiting. Hester made him drink a glass of emetic wine, and while waiting for Dr Jebb to arrive she 'plunged Harry into Water as hot as could easily be borne, up to the middle' before laying him in a warm bed. Dr Richard Jebb, the fashionable physician of St George's hospital, tall, thin and sensitive, was a Fellow of the Royal Society and a favourite of George III though a friend of Wilkes. He arrived quickly and proceeded to administer the usual medication of the day – first 'hot wine, Usquebaugh [Irish whiskey], then Daffy's Elixir [senna]' – but within hours the child was dead, probably having suffered like his sister from septicaemia or meningitis (Hyde, pp. 151–3). His death unsurprisingly had such a shattering effect on Queeney, though she was by now improving physically, that Jebb advised 'speedy change of scene' and a journey to Bath was decided upon.

Henry's favourite sister Ann, the six-feet tall kindly widow of Sir John Lade, was on hand to look after the two little girls, Susanna and Sophy, taking them away to Kensington. When Baretti arrived from London, he saw immediately that while the hysterical Hester was the centre of everyone's attention, the effect on Henry of the death of his beloved and only son was a shattering but internalized state of shock: 'Mr Thrale, both his hands in his waistcoat pocket, sat on an arm-chair in a corner of the room with his body so stiffly erect, and with such a ghastly smile on his face, as was quite horrid to behold'.[2]

John Perkins, the capable chief clerk at the brewery, wrote to Johnson to inform him and ask him to return to London, and on 25 March Johnson wrote to Hester: 'This letter will not, I hope, reach you many days before me, in a distress which can be so little relived, nothing remains for a friend but to come and partake it'.[3] On the 30th he counselled: 'Be not solitary, be not idle.' Being childless himself, he could hardly imagine what his friends were going through: 'I know that such a loss is a laceration of the mind. I know that a whole system of hopes and designs and expectations is swept away at once, and nothing left but bottomless vacuity'.[4] Johnson arrived at Streatham just as Hester and Queeney were setting off for Bath where they remained a week. Johnson stayed behind to comfort Henry. However Henry twice had him sent away; the second time the servant told him not to return unless sent for. Then on 5 April Thrale went himself to the old man's house in London and attended church with him that evening. It was when Hester showed Henry the letter Johnson had written from Lichfield that he shed his first tears over Harry (Hyde, p. 156).

In just one year the Thrales had lost three children. They were left only with three girls and no boy to carry on the Thrale name and brewery business. Hester sometimes feared she was being punished for her intellectual vanity, at others that the Thrale blood was tainted. Neither parent would be the same after the death of Harry. Thrale became increasingly morose and, for deliberate distraction from their sorrow, both of them threw themselves into more regular socialising as a couple in London, Streatham, Bath and Brighton. It was not just Henry but his wife too who could not be satisfied with daughters: she longed for a male heir to inherit her own Salusbury estate in Wales. On 1 July she wrote in her diary:

> My three little Girls are all with me, the thin remains of my ruined Family; I find myself with Child again however, & perhaps if God almighty spares me any very great Troubles during Gestation, I may see another Son to live: I shall not remain here long enough to rear him – but no matter, may I but stay till I have seen my Husband without one Debt in the World; my Daughter grown up to Woman's fix'd Estate, a fortune in the Funds ready to portion her – & a Son of my own to inherit my *own* Estate; I shall contentedly leave him, her, and this troublesome World. (Hyde, p. 156)

For the rest of her days Hester would be fixed in this determination to provide Bachegraig with a male heir to carry on the Salusbury line, if not name. However, the baby was merely another female, Cecilia Margaretta, born on 8 February 1777 and named after her women friends: 'Stricky' and her distant cousin the cheerful Margaret 'Peggy' Owen, who had been staying over the winter. Hester had lost confidence in educating her little girls herself. Queeney and Susanna, having inherited their father's taciturn personality, did not share her enthusiasms. Neither did they form such a close relationship with their erstwhile disciplinarian as she had experienced with her own mother. She wrote bitterly of Sophia: 'I will not make her Life miserable as I suppose it will be short [. . .] The instructions I labor'd to give *them* [Harry and Lucy] – what did they end in? the Grave –'.[5] From now on her younger children were taught in school rather than at home. Hester had fallen out with Baretti, specifically over his disapproval of her punishing the children and her insistence on dosing the convalescent Queeney, even when requested not to do so by Dr Jebb. The irascible Italian departed from the household in high dudgeon, furious that the family had cancelled the Italian tour and gone to Bath instead, even though Mr Thrale had presented him with a hundred guineas as compensation for the trouble he had taken with the arrangements. It would be a while before he made it up with the family.

Hester had always been an indefatigable writer – of diaries and journals as well as letters, occasional verses and political squibs. In the 'Children's Book' she had recorded all the family events. On 15 September 1776, she took up a new and much grander journal announcing:

> It is many Years since Doctor Samuel Johnson advised me to get a little Book, and write in it all the little Anecdotes which might come to my Knowledge, all the Observations I might make or hear, all the Verses never likely to be published, and in fine ev'ry thing which struck me at the Time. Mr Thrale has now treated me with a Repository,—and provided it with the pompous Title of Thraliana. (1: 1)

Thrale had been suffering from a painful swollen testicle, either caused by venereal disease or as a result of injury when he jumped from the chaise in France. The 'repository' was a handsome and well-chosen present to reward his wife for her nursing and patience with his ill humour. Henry's gift consisted of six quarto blank books bound in calf each stamped in gold with 'Thraliana'. The Chambers Dictionary of 1728 had defined words with the suffix' -ana' as 'collections of the memorable sayings of persons of learning and wit'. This sort of biographical writing, which the Thrales had noticed was common in France but not Britain, would be at the core of Hester Thrale's writing life from now on and she certainly toyed with the idea of publishing some of it eventually. She began by copying out selected and revised passages from her existing journals, one of which was devoted entirely to Johnson. Hester was not systematic, so Johnson advised that she 'be punctual in annexing the dates'. She also omnivorously collected anecdotes from her reading and from discussion, including occasional verse of her own and her friends. In two years she would have filled the first two volumes. She also contrived opportunities for the conversations which would produce more anecdotes – as she concentrated her formidable energies on becoming a *salonnière* to rival Mrs Montagu, the 'Queen of the Bluestockings'.

Elizabeth Montagu had pioneered parties where men and women conversed on equal terms, and were offered tea and intellectual discussion rather than cards and wine, at her magnificent house in Hill Street, Mayfair. Hester wrote thoughtfully in her journal:

> Mrs Montagu made many polite advances, & desired my Friendship in a Way that flattered my Vanity. She is a very high bred Lady, a very conspicuous Character in the World, and her Conversation flows very freely from a very full Mind. (*Thraliana*, 1: 135)

Elizabeth was a generation older than Hester, but they were both successful authors and *salonnières* and they became firm friends. Some class-conscious critics have declared that Elizabeth's Yorkshire gentry origins indicated that she belonged to a higher social stratum but Hester was confident that her Salusbury parentage closely linked her to ancient Welsh aristocracy. The same restless energy inhabited both women; even as children Elizabeth's family had called her 'Fidget', while Hester's nickname was 'Fiddle'. Both were scholarly and had made marriages of convenience. Each had found herself managing her husband's business – Elizabeth because of Edward's advanced age, and Hester when Henry had experienced a crisis through bad business practice. Much of Edward Montagu's wealth had come from his Newcastle coal mines, which Elizabeth had helped him run and now managed single-handedly since becoming widowed in 1775. Their competitiveness as hostesses partly stemmed from Johnson's ambivalence towards Mrs Montagu. Less deferential to him than Hester, the formidable Elizabeth was also a rival literary critic. Her well-received *Essay on the Writings and Genius of Shakespear* (1769) differed from some of the views expressed in the preface to his Shakespeare edition of three years earlier. Yet Johnson respected Mrs Montagu and said to Hester: 'conversing with her you may find variety in one'.[6] Elizabeth

Montagu appreciated that membership of the Thrale coterie betokened social and cultural arrival, and the rival 'Queen' blue became a frequent dinner guest at Streatham.

When the Thrales were staying at Brighton in Autumn 1776 they were honoured with a poem on their wedding anniversary, by William Weller Pepys, one of the Masters of Chancery, citing their marriage as proof that intellectual women could make loving wives.[7] Pepys had been nicknamed 'Mrs Montagu's Prime Minister', for he, together with his brother Dr Lucas Pepys, presided over the bluestocking set whose meetings were rather more formal than other such gatherings hosted by Frances Boscawen or Elizabeth Vesey (Hyde, p. 169). Hester was accepted as one of the metropolitan *bon-ton*, attending Court for the first time in 1777. Her vivaciousness, Henry's money and the draw of Dr Johnson continued to render Streatham Park the most delightful salon. Everyone wanted to be invited there for a country house weekend where they could study as well as talk, walk around the grounds to view the recently constructed lake, inspect the magnificent hothouses and ornamental poultry, or muse in the summerhouse before joining the company for gastronomic cuisine

Hester had invited Dr Johnson's old friend, the musician Charles Burney to teach Queeney music once a week at Streatham and, already a member of Johnson's Literary Club, he too became a favourite with the Thrales. He was beginning to publish his *A General History of Music*, which by 1789 had extended to four volumes and for which Johnson wrote the dedicatory preface: 'Such was the fertility of his Mind, and the extent of his knowledge; such the Goodness of his Heart and Suavity of his Manners that we began in good earnest to solicit his Company, and gain his Friendship' (*Thraliana*, 1: 137).

Hester began to collect Burney's bon mots in *Thraliana*, and she was particularly grateful to him for relieving her in staying up late drinking tea with Johnson, who hated to go to bed. In 1778 the musician's daughter, Frances, visited the Thrales for the first time. Though the young woman was herself a literary lion, having recently been revealed to her own father and the rest of the world as the anonymous author of the delightful comic novel *Evelina or, A Young Lady's Entrance into the World* (1778) – she was quite overwhelmed: 'August – I have now to write an account of the most consequential day I have spent since my birth, my visit'.[8] The critical acclaim of her novel secured her entrée into what had earlier been an almost exclusively male preserve. Hester was sensitive to Fanny's extreme shyness and took her away to the library, away from the other guests, to tell her how much Dr Johnson had enjoyed the novel and to laugh at herself for unwittingly recommending Dr Burney to read it. She privately confided to *Thraliana* that she thought *Evelina* 'pretty enough' but 'flimzy' (1: 329). 'Little Burney', however, became a favourite, especially of Johnson's, and gradually became a semi-permanent house guest. Fanny tried her hand at a comedy satirizing the bluestockings, entitled 'The Witlings', but her family declared it should never see the light of day, lest it should offend them, and Hester was glad, for fear 'it may bear hard upon some Respectable Characters' (*Thraliana*, 1: 401).

In 1778 the delightful seclusion of *Thraliana* allowed Hester to rate her friends and acquaintances for their moral qualities, social and intellectual gifts and abilities. Johnson scored a perfect 20 for religion and morality but nought for person and manner, as we might expect. Garrick came top for wit and the handsome Henry was highest for person and voice. For the women, Hannah More and Sophie Streatfeild were placed first for 'worth of heart' with the former also scoring most highly for useful knowledge and the latter for good humour. Elizabeth Montagu topped the table for conversational powers over high-scoring bluestockings such as Frances Boscawen, Elizabeth Carter and Hester Chapone. Indeed Elizabeth Montagu came out the highest-rated woman overall. Hester also composed an honest self-portrait in *Thraliana*, where she commented that people who did not know her, thought her foreign because of her Celtic theatricality in company:

> The first Question is when She quits the Room,—does not that Lady come from abroad pray?—& I fear the Answer is too often—*no doubt on't*; do not you see how She is painted? The Character of her Mind

however is almost wholly Italian, or rather Welch perhaps;—for her Temper is warm even to Irascibility; Affectionate and tender, but claiming such returns to her Tenderness & Affection, as busy People have no Time to pay, and coarse people have no pleasure in paying: She is a diligent & active friend, who spares neither Money nor Pains to oblige, but who is soon disgusted if the Person obliged does not express the Sense of Obligation—by Nature a rancorous and revengeful Enemy.
(*Thraliana*, 1: 321)

These were glittering years for the wealthy Thrales, and Henry decided that, now that his library at Streatham Park was complete, he would commission Joshua Reynolds to provide 13 paintings of their intimates to hang there. A double portrait of Hester and Queeney was set over the mantelpiece, the only females. Henry Thrale hung over the door to his study, then around the walls were placed portraits of Edwin, Lord Sandys, Lord Westcote (William Henry Lyttelton, colonial governor), Arthur Murphy, Goldsmith, Robert Chambers (jurist and judge), Garrick, Baretti, Burney, Burke, Johnson and the artist himself.[9] In the years to come, Hester would compose a shrewd critique in octosyllabic verse for each. Deprecating her own portrait for lack of likeness, she wrote:

> In features so placid, so smooth, so serene
> What Trace of the Wit – or the Welch-woman's seen?
> Of the Temper sarcastic, the flattering Tongue,
> The Sentiment right – with th'Occasion still wrong.
> What Trace of the tender, the rough, the refin'd,
> The Soul in which all Contrarieties join'd?
> Where tho' merriment loves over Method to rule,
> Religion resides, and the Virtues keep School;
> Till when tired we condemn her dogmatical Air,
> Like a Rocket She rises, and leaves us to Stare.
> (*Thraliana*, 1: 471)

In 1778, Mrs Montagu had become enough of an intimate that she was chosen godmother to Mrs Thrale's twelfth child, Henrietta Sophia.[10] When Thrale was struck again by depression and money worries, and Johnson was absorbed in writing his *Lives of the Poets*, Hester sought distraction for her husband in socialising together with health-giving spa treatment at Tunbridge. She made two very good friends there, both named Sophia: the beautiful young classicist, Sophia Streatfeild, whose party trick was to weep at will and with whom Henry flirted, and Sophia Byron, wife of the Admiral nicknamed 'Foulweather Jack' on account of his bad luck at sea, whose grandson became the celebrated poet. Hester also amused herself by sending some political verses to the *Public Advertiser* that November. They were addressed to a close friend, Sir Philip Jennings-Clerke, MP for Totnes, an opposition member who objected to the American war. Her loyalist broadside developed the metaphor of a huntsman's unruly pack of hounds for those politicians whose allegiance had been transferred to the new republic following the revolt of 1776.[11]

Henry's depression lifted, but this was to be a short-lived interlude. In June 1779 he suffered a minor stroke, and though he quickly recovered, it was to prove the beginning of a sharp decline in both his mental and physical health. The seizure happened whilst he discussed the will of his late brother-in-law, the businessman Arnold Nesbitt, and realised that the latter was insolvent. Thrale was Nesbitt's executor and had stood security for Nesbitt in speculative ventures nineteen years earlier. The possibility was now pointed out to Henry that a claim could be made for £220,000.[12] That never came to pass, but the porter business was suffering a slump owing to the American war. Depression and ill health exacerbated Thrale's existing irascibility and sullen taciturnity.

'Oh Lord have mercy on us!' cried Hester. 'Five little girls, & breeding again, & Fool enough to be proud of it' (*Thraliana*, 1: 389). That July found the thirty-eight year-old Hester experiencing a tricky pregnancy which demanded she rest as much as possible. Yet Thrale's incapacity meant she needed to attend the counting-house, and she went systematically through the accounts at the brewery, comparing the present low takings with those of the previous year, which had been so much higher. On 10 August, though she was near term, Henry insisted she travel from Streatham to Southwark to exert her authority and charm on the unruly clerks, and, – ever the Master, he obstinately refused to let her return straight away in spite of her worsening state as she waited:

> So I lay along in the Coach all the way from London to Streatham in a State not to be described, nor endured;—*but by me;*—and being carried to my Chamber the Instant I got home, miscarried in the utmost Agony before they could get me into Bed, after fainting five times. (*Thraliana*, 1: 401)

The men thought Thrale was 'under ye Influence of his Disorder' and Perkins described him as 'planet-struck'. He did not seem to be much affected by the tragic birth of a dead baby boy, apparently perfect, or by Hester's own danger. His wife aided her recovery from the trauma by writing – first the bitter account in *Thraliana*, and then three sparkling dialogues in a Swiftian mode, imagining all their friends discussing her death. She particularly prided herself on 'the perfect & finished Resemblance every Speaker's Speech & Phrase has to the person speaking'. The best dialogue was the first, where the grieving Dr Johnson is irritated by the casual mention of his deceased friend and frightens the timorous scholar William Weller Pepys, who goes straight to his patroness to complain:

> PEPYS. Why the oddest Thing in the World—I meant to please him & mentioned Mrs Thrale's name, but he flew out so fiercely—It put me in mind of a Thing—
>
> MRS MONTAGU. Ay! Flew out—did not he—we heard him quite across the Room; why he burst in your hand like an overcharged Musket, & you seem a little shattered by the Recoil too I protest—but he has had a Loss you'll allow—Mrs Thrale, among her other Qualifications, had prodigious strong Nerves—and that's an admirable Quality for a Friend of Dr Johnson's.[13]

We may compare this dialogue of Hester's with the actual spat between Dr Johnson and the clique of Elizabeth Montagu in 1781 over Johnson's cool treatment of their friend Lord Lyttelton in *Lives of the Poets*. Fanny Burney recorded the row:

Never have I seen Dr Johnson speak with so much passion. 'Mr Pepys,' he cried, in a voice the most enraged, 'I understand you are offended by my "Life of Lord Lyttelton." What is it you have to say against it? Come forth, man! Here I am ready to answer any charge you can bring!' ... Afterwards Mr Pepys came and said,—'Just what I had so much wanted to avoid! I have been crushed in the very onset'.[14]

That Autumn, visits to Tunbridge and Brighton failed to rouse Thrale, who had presumably suffered brain damage, as he began to wander in his conversation. In December he 'got a Fit of the horrors again', worrying that the beer would turn out bad (*Thraliana*, 1: 414). He had made his will in Brighton and asked Hester whom she would appoint joint executers with herself. She named Johnson, the MP and wealthy property developer John Cator and Pepys. She had become more appreciative of the latter's kindness and genuine concern for her predicament, and rather repented mocking him in her Dialogues. By January 1780, the Thrales had to reside at Southwark because the business, if not the beer, was 'in a cloudy condition'. Thrale was now afflicted by heart and lung troubles (*Thraliana*, 1: 416), and Johnson, Perkins and Hester managed the business together for the rest of his life. Hester noted: 'we shall brew but Sixty Thousand Barrels of Beer this Year! [. . .] the Year before last we brew'd 96,000 Barrels—last Year only 76,000 [. . .] So horribly is the Consumption lessened by the War' (*Thraliana*, 1: 423). She was gratified to be visited by *bon-ton* ladies in the gloomy Southwark house abutting the brewery. But she was bitter that some of her woods in Wales had been felled to contribute to the family finances.

Henry declined further, suffering another stroke on 21 February, but assisted in his recovery by Dr Jebb's skilful treatment. His sisters and eldest daughter alternated in sitting up with him at night, but he was his usual distant silent self. By 28 March he was well enough to travel to Bath accompanied by Hester, Queeney and Fanny Burney. Fanny remarked in her diary that in the inn at Devizes they had been struck by the 'amazing' talent for drawing of their landlady's ten-year-old son, Thomas Lawrence, who would soon become known as an artistic prodigy.[15] Sir Philip Jennings-Clerke, Mrs Montagu and Mrs Byron were at Bath, and Hester made new friends, too, such as the dilettante clergyman and poet Thomas Sedgwick Whalley, and the philanthropist Thomas Bowdler and his sister, Henrietta Maria, who collaborated on *The Family Shakespeare* while resident in Bath and Oystermouth. They stayed in good lodgings in the South Parade and Henry treated his wife, daughter and Fanny to handsome gifts of millinery. Hester diverted herself from all her cares and responsibility for her daughters, the business and her invalid spouse by losing herself in the theatrical games of witty conversation, and especially in competing with Elizabeth Montagu. Fanny (with Hester looking over her shoulder) wrote of Elizabeth: 'She is always reasonable and sensible, and sometimes instructive and entertaining; and I think of our Mrs Thrale, we may say the very reverse, for she is always entertaining and instructive, and sometimes reasonable and sensible'.[16] Hester herself provided a more graphic image in *Thraliana*: 'If I am like the Rattlesnake, Mrs Montagu is like the Peccary; who when it hears the Serpent's Approach which fills every other Tenant of the Desart with Fear, runs and devours it' (1: 430).

Whilst they were there, an election was announced and, despite his deteriorating health, Henry obstinately insisted on standing for Southwark. Johnson suggested that Hester come to London to campaign on his behalf but cautioned her not to let the electors see Henry, as the sight of him would scotch his chances. In May she left Bath for ten days, taking with her William Devaynes, a director of the East India Company and Sir Philip Jennings-Clerke: 'the boro' folks called them my two-edged Swords, as they cut upon Sir Richard Hotham both ways, the first as connected with the India house, the other as attached to the patriots.' Johnson wrote admiringly to Queeney that Hester had 'run about the Borough like a Tigress seizing upon every thing that she found in her way' (*Thraliana*, 1: 436).

She had not long returned to Bath when all the gay company was dispersed in panic by the outbreak of what was the nearest thing to a revolution that Georgian Britain would experience – the anti-Catholic Gordon riots. Bath itself experienced rioting, and a new Roman Catholic chapel was burned down. In the Bath newspaper the Thrales read assertions that the brewer was a papist, and they set off realising that both Streatham Park and the Southwark brewery would be under attack.

On 2 June the charismatic though unbalanced leader of the Protestant Association, Lord George Gordon, had led a march of 60,000 followers from St George's Fields in Southwark to the House of Commons, calling for the repeal of the Catholic Relief Act (1778) which permitted Catholics to open schools and own land, and released them from Anglican oaths of allegiance to be sworn before joining the army. These concessions (Catholics still could not attend university or hold public office) roused the passions of bigoted mobs fired up by the American revolution, and the dying embers of seventeenth-century sectarianism. They burned down the houses and businesses of known Catholics and those who had supported the Act, such as Lord Mansfield, and they went after Thrale too. In what Dr Johnson described as this 'time of terrour', when the King called 15,000 troops to restore order, the rioters arrived at Southwark on 6 June. They had already attacked the Bank of England and released prisoners from Newgate and other gaols, and were dragging the chains as spoils. Perkins greeted them insouciantly with an invitation to drink porter: 'nothing but the astonishing Presence of Mind shewed by Perkins in amusing the Mob with Meat and Drink & Huzzas, till Sir Philip Jennings-Clerke could get the Troops & pack up the Counting House Bills Bonds &c: —could have secured us from actual Undoing,' wrote Hester. 'The Villains *had* broke in, & our Brewhouse would have blazed in ten Minutes; when a property of 150,000£ would have been utterly lost, & its once flourishing possessors quite undone' (*Thraliana*, 1: 437).

Leaving Henry at their own house in Brighton and making arrangements for the rescue of the children and for the removal of the furniture from Streatham Park, Hester went to Southwark: 'we have now got Arms, & mean to defend ourselves by Force, if further Violence is intended.' Henry had authorised her to present Perkins with a hundred guineas but she doubled this amount and gave his wife a silver urn engraved 'Mollis responsio, Iram avertit' ('A soft answer turns away wrath'). Over 200 people had been shot and killed before order was restored, and Lord George Gordon was imprisoned in the Tower to be tried for treason.

Hester then returned to Brighton for summer sea-bathing with Henry, Queeney and her little girls, Susanna and Sophia. One day at a bookshop she spotted the talented Italian singer and composer, Gabriel Piozzi, whom she had heard perform at the house of his friend, Dr Burney – and had been reproved by her host for mimicking behind his back. She now asked him in Italian if he would give her daughters music lessons whilst they were at Brighton, but he was proud and coldly refused at first. Then, after finding out she was the rich brewer's wife, he readily agreed.[17] She was soon confessing to her journal:

> Piozzi is become a prodigious Favourite with me; he is so intelligent a Creature, so discerning, one can't help wishing for his good Opinion: his Singing surpasses every body's for Taste, Tenderness, and true Elegance; his Hand on the Forte Piano too is so soft, so sweet, so delicate, every Tone goes to one's heart I think; and fills the Mind with Emotions one would not be without, though inconvenient sometimes. (*Thraliana* 1: 452)

Hester's life had hitherto been devoid of the inconvenient emotion of romantic love but that situation was not to last.

In September Parliament was dissolved and, despite coming near to another stroke, Henry insisted on canvassing in person, so they departed for London. In Hanoverian England, public opinion was an important part of the political process. Electoral rituals were highly visible and prolonged affairs, involving noisy marching to the hustings, 'treating' of the voters to dinners and intense interaction with rowdy crowds.[18] Husband and wife campaigned together so strenuously that Hester lost her voice for a week, but then at St George's Church she 'had the Mortification to see him seized with such Illness as made him look a perfect Corpse in full view of an immense Congregation' (*Thraliana*, 1: 453). Thrale was too ill to continue and eventually came last in the polls.

All could see that Thrale's days were numbered but he was restless for continual change and seized by an abnormal appetite which caused him to gorge and drink 'Strong Beer in *such* Quantities!' (*Thraliana,* 1: 489). (This might possibly have been caused by untreated diabetes.) He also spent money so prodigiously that the question of legal restraint was raised by Dr Pepys, though Hester would not hear of it. Henry even took a house 'at the flashy End of the Town' (*Thraliana,* 1: 478) in January 1781 and allowed Perkins to occupy the house at Deadman's Place next to the brewery. Hester boasted to Fanny Burney that she had held a *conversatione* where 'Mrs Montagu was brilliant in diamonds, solid in judgement, critical in talk. Sophy [Sophia Weston] smiled, Piozzi sung, Pepys panted with admiration, Johnson was good-humoured, Lord John Clinton attentive, Dr Bowdler lame, and my master not asleep'.[19] Hester went to Court dressed in a spectacular satin gown whose pattern was copied from material 'torn from the back of the Indian who killed Cap^n Cook with his club' (*Thraliana*, 1: 481) and this 'Tahitian' fashion made the newspapers.

Full of a newly intensified love of music, Hester employed the handsome Piozzi to sing for her bluestocking guests and teach the girls music, 'pleased to show my fondness for Piozzi, and my Desire of producing him every possible Advantage' (*Thraliana*, 1: 479). But when she went to present him with the £35 she had collected in a benefit concert, she found herself unaccountably bursting into tears,

> saying I was sure Mr Thrale would dye. The tenderhearted Italian was affected, bid me not despair so, but recollect some precepts he had heard Dr Johnson give me one day; & then turn'd to me with a good deal of Expression in his Manner, rather too much—it affected me.—and sung Rasserena, il tuo bel Ciglio &c &c. (*Thraliana*, 1: 489)

Hester later added a note to her account: 'I suppose (says Mrs Byron who saw and heard him) that you *know* that Man is in Love with You. I am, replied I, too *miserable* to care *who* is in Love with me. *She remembers it*' (*Thraliana*, 1: 489).

Thrale died not long afterwards, at six o'clock on the morning of 4 April 1781, aged fifty-two, following a series of apoplectic fits.

Hester ran away to Brighton 'to collect her scattered thoughts'. She did not attend the funeral, as was the custom for women at the time. She determined 'to revise my past life, & resolve upon a new one' (*Thraliana*, 1: 490). Thrale had made a second will which left his wife Streatham Park for her lifetime, after which it would pass to her daughters, and £2,000 p.a. out of the brewery profits, as well as maintenance for the children. If the brewery was sold, she was to receive £30,000 with the remainder held in trust for her daughters, who were made wards of the Court of Chancery. The executors – Johnson, Hester, John Cator, Jeremiah Crutchley (believed by Hester to be Henry's natural son) and Henry's cousin Henry Smith – were appointed guardians of the children. John Perkins was left £1,000 and the chief brewer, John Townsend an annuity of £100 (Hyde, p. 227).

With Elizabeth Montagu's encouragement and Dr Johnson's help, Hester continued to run the business and devoted three days a week to the counting-house. Heady with the new-found independence of a widow she wrote:

> If an Angel from Heaven had told me 20 years ago that the man I knew by the Name of *Dictionary Johnson* should one Day become partner with me in a great Trade, & that we should jointly or separately sign Notes, Draughts &c for 3 or 4 Thousand Pounds of a Morning, how unlikely it would have seemed ever to happen! (*Thraliana*, 1: 492)

She could not, however, rid herself of a genteel contempt for commerce and also worried that, should the business fail, she might compromise the inheritance of the girls. On 3 June she proclaimed triumphantly to her journal that she had completed: 'The greatest Event of my Life:—I have sold my Brewhouse to Barclay the rich Quaker for 135000£' (*Thraliana*, 1: 498) to be paid over four years. Perkins and his brother-in-law had each taken quarter shares to match those of bankers David and Robert Barclay. Hester's generosity showed itself in the fact that she loaned Perkins part of his share, and gifted him and his wife the furniture in the Southwark house.

That Summer, when Piozzi returned to Italy to see his family, Hester was miserable and uneasy when she did not hear from him, until in November she could write: 'I have got my Piozzi home at Last' (*Thraliana*, 1: 519). The New Year of 1782 found her resolving to wait four years before setting out for a journey to his homeland: 'I would make it worth his while; & we should live happily together' (*Thraliana* 1: 525). She intended to take the girls, and the unsuspecting Queeney agreed to the scheme. But by August of that year Hester was already making arrangements to let Streatham to Lord Shelburne, declaring: 'After having long intended to go to Italy for Pleasure, we are now settling to go thither for Convenience' (*Thraliana* 1: 540). It was proving impossible to run Streatham Park on her reduced income. The situation was exacerbated by a Chancery suit instituted by Lady Salusbury (Hester's aunt by marriage) on account of 'a long-forgotten mortgage made in favour of her husband by John Salusbury, Mrs Thrale's father, on the security of his Welsh property'. She now demanded payment of the bond and Hester 'agreed to pay a composition of £7,500' for Bachegraig.[20] The ailing, elderly Johnson had declared he would not go to Italy even if he was asked, and Hester unreasonably felt offended: 'I begin to see [. . .] that Johnson's Connection with me is merely an interested one—he *loved* Mr Thrale I believe, but only wish'd to find in me a careful Nurse & humble Friend for his sick and his lounging hours' (*Thraliana* 1: 541).

By September Hester knew she was in love with Gabriel Piozzi and debated with herself whether or not to marry him, at first in *Thraliana*, then confessing her dilemma to Queeney and Fanny Burney. At first Queeney still planned to accompany her mother to Italy, so Hester gave Gabriel encouragement to hope. But as 1781 came to an end, the growing disapproval of all her family and friends gave the girl pause for thought. By January 1783 the gossip mill frightened the Thrale daughters who now begged Hester to stay and abandon thoughts of Piozzi. The cool Queeney explained to Gabriel how scandal would damage the honour of Hester herself and thus her unmarried daughters. Chivalrously he renounced the marriage, went home, brought all his love letters from her mother and delivered them to the nineteen-year-old Queeney. What was more, he arranged his affairs in order to leave London and return to Italy, presenting Hester with £1,000 of his savings to show he was no fortune hunter. 'God give me Strength to part with him courageously,' she declared (*Thraliana* 1: 561).

That spring Hester took little interest in sea-bathing at Weymouth, and then decided to retire to Bath where she determined to live on £1,000 p.a. to 'pay my debts and fly to the man of my Heart' (*Thraliana* 1: 562). She was summoned back to Streatham by the news that her two youngest children were seriously ill, Cecilia with whooping cough and Henrietta (Harriett) with swollen glands, measles and whooping cough. The former had recovered by the time she arrived, but the four-year-old Harriett died that Easter and was buried at St Leonard's Church, Streatham. Then in June Dr Johnson suffered a stroke and was devastated when his dear Mistress did not rush to his side. Uncharacteristically the usually buoyant Hester was sunk into depression throughout the summer, rancorously bitter at her elder daughters for standing in her way. She also began to suspect that Fanny Burney was siding with Queeney behind her back. Only the serious illness of Sophia that November with 'Fits, sudden, unaccountable' (*Thraliana*, 1: 580) roused her mother out of her lethargy. 'I rubbed her while just expiring, so as to keep the heart in Motion: She knew me instantly, & said you warm *me* but you are killing *yourself*—I actually was in a burning Fever from exertion.' As soon as the girl was out of danger her mother collapsed entirely. At last Queeney gave way and Hester was allowed to summon Gabriel back to England.

6

'To revise my past Life, & resolve upon a new one'

Having 'married the first Time to please my Mother', Hester came close to cancelling her second marriage to placate her starchy daughter, Queeney. Eventually, however, she determined to brave society's prejudice against an Italian, Roman Catholic and professional singer. It is difficult from a twenty-first-century vantage point to understand the outrage that this match generated. The couple were both unattached and of the same age; neither had loose morals; Hester had money enough for both. Nevertheless, the newspapers were full of salacious jibes that the widow had been captivated by the musician's 'instrument'. Even more hurtful was the vitriol of Hester's most intimate friends. Dr Johnson, stung by jealousy, wrote furiously: 'Madam, if I interpret your letter right, you are ignominiously married' (*Autobiography*, 1: 239). Mrs Montagu, who, in her own widowhood, relished the unfettered freedom of sole management of her wealth and coalmines, confided to Mrs Vesey:

> I am myself convinced that the poor Woman is mad, and indeed have long suspected her mind was disordered. She was the best Mother, the best Wife, the best friend, the most amiable member of Society. She gave the most prudent attentions to her Husband's business during his long state of imbecility and after his death, till she had an opportunity of disposing well of the great Brewery. I bring in my verdict lunacy in this affair. (Blunt, *Mrs Montagu*, 2: 274–5)

Frances Burney refused to congratulate the couple. For Gabriel was a mere musician, whereas the wealthy widow was descended from a distinguished Welsh family with aristocratic connections. Their union inverted patriarchal norms in which the husband's social standing determined the rank of his spouse. Bystanders also assumed a wife would convert to her husband's religion, in which the children of the marriage would be brought up. A 'mixed marriage' was anathema: it was only four years since the Gordon mob had branded all Catholics traitors and attacked Thrale's brewery under the mistaken impression that the proprietor was a papist. Nevertheless, the couple were married in London by a Catholic priest on 23 July, and two days later in an Anglican service at St James's, Bath. Hester confided to her journal 'I have always been partial to *Peter* as elder Brother' (*Thraliana*, 2: 637), even though staunch Protestantism was the backbone of her patriotism, as it was for the majority of the population. In years to come, it was Gabriel who would eventually adopt Anglicanism in tandem with the life of a Welsh country squire.

When Hester failed to reappear after a month honeymooning in her new husband's native country, rumours circulated in Britain that Gabriel had 'sold my Joynture and shut me in a convent!' (*Thraliana*, 2: 627). The Piozzis, however, were blissfully happy and in no hurry to return. They travelled in a specially commissioned carriage with room for Gabriel's portable harpsichord, and planned not only to view the peninsula's picturesque countryside and renowned art and architecture but to make music and improvise occasional verse with friends new and old, of different nationalities. By embarking on a full-scale Grand Tour of Italy in addition to visiting France, Switzerland and Germany, from September 1784 to March 1787, Hester Piozzi proclaimed a cosmopolitanism greater than that of older generation Bluestockings such as Elizabeth Montagu and Elizabeth Carter, whose visits to the continent were relatively brief and confined to France, Germany and the Low Countries. From her girlhood, she had loved learning languages – especially French, and the romance tongues of Italian and Spanish. Like her mentor, Dr Johnson, Hester was fascinated by etymology and language variation. It is clear from the outset that she had a travel book in mind, as she kept meticulous accounts of the journey in notebooks labelled 'Italian Journey' and 'German Journey' in addition to more personal jottings in *Thraliana*. Indeed, Hester soon felt so well travelled that she declared she was 'half amphibious grown'.

Hester Lynch Piozzi had begun a new life in 1784. In love for the first time, she had put her maternal role aside and not only secured personal happiness but also freed herself from the inhibiting presence of Johnson. The Great Cham's ill health had increased both his self-absorption and the violence of his opposition to Hester's marriage. Responding to Frances Burney's half-innocent question whether he had heard from from Mrs Piozzi, he burst out in rage:

> 'No,' cried he, 'nor write to her. I drive her quite from my mind. She has disgraced herself, disgraced her friends & connections, disgraced her sex, & disgraced all the expectations of mankind! If meet with one of her letters, I burn it instantly. I have burnt all I can find. I never speak of her, and I desire never to hear of her more. I drive her, as I said, wholly from my mind'.[1]

Hester's letter of 4 July 1784 represents a model of restrained reproof and dignified forgiveness:

> [T]o hear that I have forfeited my Fame is the greatest Insult I ever yet received, my Fame is as unsullied as Snow, or I should think it unworthy of him who must henceforward protect it [. . .]
>
> You have always commanded my Esteem, and long enjoyed the Fruits of a Friendship never infringed by one harsh Expression on my Part, during twenty Years of familiar Talk. Never did I oppose your Will, or controal your Wish: nor can your unmerited Severity itself lessen *my* Regard—but till you have changed your Opinion of Mr. Piozzi—let us converse no more. God bless you![2]

Only after his death, on 13 December, 1784, did she gain the confidence to publish her writing, for 'in Johnson's intellect mine was swallowed up and lost' (*Autobiography*, 1: 306). Initially, her major publications would be forms of life writing, while her poetry, dramatic prologues and political pieces were mostly called forth by specific occasions in the here and now. Her first spell of literary creativity was generated not so much by contentment as by determination to answer the malicious reports circulating at home, and to establish 'that I was not *lost* to the world'. She first intended to adopt a long-considered plan to write a multi-volume biography of her mentor, Johnson, drawing on his many letters to her and some unpublished poems, which were left behind in London. As the closest female friend of the last twenty years of his life, no one alive knew Johnson better than she. However, she was so keen to be first out of the blocks that she could not wait until her return to England; she knew other biographers were waiting in the wings. Rather than have the letters sent to her in Italy, she decided to write one volume of anecdotes to be published straight away, stealing the thunder of rivals Sir John Hawkins or James Boswell. At the very same time, the publisher Charles Dilly approached James Boswell to see if he had a biography ready. No one could match Mrs Piozzi's long and intimate relationship with the great man, but Boswell had spent 101 days with him during their Scottish expedition, and had recorded their conversation in the greatest detail. With the help of the Shakespearean scholar Edmond Malone, Boswell composed and published his *Journal of a Tour to the Hebrides* in September 1785, which, though it shocked readers by its extremely detailed record of the scholar's private life and conversation, was received with great acclaim. This inspired Boswell to work with Malone on a massive biography of the lexicographer, which would not appear until 1791.

Without being able to draw on her correspondence, and with only *Thraliana* to check her facts, *Anecdotes* could not aspire to the scholarly authority which Boswell assumed by virtue of the care and time he and Malone devoted to the task. So Hester made a virtue out of necessity by addressing the reader directly in an informal, indeed intimate and conversational style that also startled contemporary critics. She also deliberately created a feminine authorial persona, based on her role of bluestocking hostess. This would contrast completely with that of Boswell's man about town. The preface of her 'little book', *Anecdotes of the Late Samuel Johnson*,

LL.D. during the Last Twenty Years of His Life, she compared with 'the portico before a house', 'contrived, so as to catch, but not detain the attention of those who desire admission to the family within, or leave to look over the collection of pictures made by one whose opportunities of obtaining them we know to have been not infrequent'.[3] The authorial lady of the house did not present herself as the organiser of brilliant parties and the superb conversationalist she was, but as the motherly nurturer of male genius. Hester's close friends had come chiefly to visit her literary lion house guest performing in his inner circle beneath the mirrored brilliance of Reynolds's Streatham Portraits. Now her readers were being offered an intimate entrée to the 'collection of pictures', revealing the manners and sentiments of the 'Great Cham' of literature to a substantially wider audience. Hester anticipated the shock that readers would feel at her breaking the convention of not speaking ill of the dead, by honestly describing Johnson's rough manners. Accordingly she declared 'his superiority to the common forms of common life' (*Anecdotes*, p. vi). Johnson needed no excuses or prevarication. He was a proud lone oak, symbol of British heritage, a Trajan's column testifying to the civilising mission of his country's empire. It was because she was delineating the character of an extraordinary genius that Piozzi could so frankly disclose Johnson's quarrelsomeness, rudeness and, towards the close of the book, categorically state the difficulties of living with him after the death of Henry Thrale.

Biography was a genre in its infancy, and Hester Piozzi was following in Johnson's own footsteps in attempting it, but she outdid Boswell by showing her subject at home, not in his public persona, and yet was even more pioneering than him by virtue of her lack of sentimentality. She tells us something of her methods. Though occasionally she had asked Samuel Johnson for permission to note down a particular opinion he had voiced in conversation, and sometimes he voluntarily dictated to her anecdotes for her commonplace book, she distanced herself from other acquaintances who made a habit of actually taking notes in company. To her, talk was 'a kind of game' (*Anecdotes*, p. 45) where one should abide by the rules. In his old age, and with poor eyesight and hearing, talking was her friend's greatest pleasure, and her primary role had been to generate conversation, rather than passively record it. 'Mr. Johnson indeed, as he was a very talking man himself, had an idea that nothing promoted happiness so much as conversation' (*Anecdotes*, p. 207). He was not a holder-forth but liked to respond to others and had no time for silent companions. She cites him as saying: 'There is in this world no real delight (excepting those of sensuality), but exchange of ideas in conversation; and whoever has once experienced the full flow of London talk, when he retires to country friendships and rural sports, must either be contented to turn baby again and play with the rattle, or he will pine away like a great fish in a little pond, and die for want of his usual food' (*Anecdotes*, pp. 266–7). Of course Mrs Piozzi had regularly made notes of Johnson's conversation from memory in her commonplace book, *Thraliana*. Both she and Johnson knew she would attempt his biography after his death. They had discussed who would be his chosen candidate, and she quoted him declaring: 'I intend, however, to disappoint the rogues, and either make you write the life, with Taylor's intelligence [his old friend, Dr. Taylor of Ashbourne]; or, which is better, do it myself, after outliving you all' (*Anecdotes*, p. 32).

She conceded that because she knew Johnson in the later stages of his life and in a domestic setting, her collection of anecdotes could only be a 'piece of motley Mosaic work' or a *'candle-light* picture of his latter days' (*Anecdotes*, pp. 240, 244). Yet *Anecdotes* recounts Johnson's remembrances of childhood, his touching love for her own brood of children and his intense interest in their education and upbringing when he lived with the Thrales. But there is little on his early years of poverty and struggle. As a genius, Johnson is portrayed as having from his youth possessed the 'facility of writing' yet the 'dilatoriness ever to write'; the *Rambler* on 'Procrastination' being composed 'while the boy waited to carry it to press' (*Anecdotes*, pp. 47–8). He relied less on painstaking research than on his fine retentive memory and his wits. Yet he was not carefree, but was plagued by melancholy – traditionally linked to unusual intellectual gifts – and Mrs Piozzi records some instances of his weeping in company.

The chief strength of *Anecdotes* lies in character study, and especially its revelation of the psychological basis of Johnson's dependence upon the Thrales. Though he was pious, generous to the poor and a stern moralist, Johnson was racked by guilt and fears concerning his Christianity. He confided in Hester that at the age of ten he had experienced doubts about the afterlife, which had inspired him to educate himself sufficiently to understand theological books whose arguments eventually convinced him of the soul's immortality. Hester responded that, though they were so very different, he reminded her, in his morbid sensitivity, of that other great tormented genius of the age, Jean-Jacques Rousseau. By 1766 Dr Johnson had experienced a complete nervous breakdown, unable to leave his house for months and wildly imploring the prayers of the doctor, perhaps experiencing suicidal thoughts and doubtless fearing impending insanity. Henry Thrale had then instructed Hester to persuade Johnson to move to Streatham, 'where I undertook the care of his health, and had the honour and happiness of contributing to its restoration' (*Anecdotes*, p. 128).

Writing *Anecdotes* was not merely an opportunity to answer those who criticized her later 'abandonment' of Dr Johnson after Thrale's death; it gave her the opportunity for cathartic reassessment of the social expectation that not only should she remain a widow but one bound by duty to continue to nurse her first husband's aged friend, rather than marry again. So strong was this that there had been jocular speculation in the press that Hester would actually marry Johnson:

> Veneration for his virtue, reverence for his talents, delight in his conversation, and habitual endurance of a yoke my husband first put upon me, and of which he contentedly bore his share for sixteen or seventeen years, made me go on so long with Mr. Johnson; but the perpetual confinement I will own to have been terrifying in the first years of our friendship, and irksome in the last; nor could I pretend to support it without help, when my coadjutor was no more. To the assistance we gave him, the shelter our house afforded to his uneasy fancies, and

to the pains we took to sooth or repress them, the world perhaps is indebted for the three political pamphlets, the new edition and correction of his Dictionary, and for the Poets Lives, which he would scarce have lived, I think, and kept his faculties entire, to have written, had not incessant care been exerted at the time of his first coming to be our constant guest in the country; and several times after that when he found himself particularly oppressed with diseases incident to the most vivid and fervent imaginations. (*Anecdotes*, pp. 293–4)

Mrs Piozzi sent off the manuscript from Italy to her friend, the young antiquary Samuel Lysons, who would see it through the press for her in London. Checking through the printed sheets, he noticed she had briefly attacked Boswell for an anonymous piece in the *St James's Chronicle* which praised *Journal of a Tour to the Hebrides*, while ridiculing Mrs Thrale's marriage to 'an obscure and penniless fiddler'. This Lysons judged (correctly) not to be authored by her rival. It had actually been written by Edmond Malone's colleague, the Shakespearean critic George Steevens. Lysons removed the accusation from *Anecdotes* to save Piozzi from embarrassment.[4] Another friend, the physician Sir Lucas Pepys, thinking to forestall hostility from Bluestocking circles, suggested she write a postscript to *Anecdotes*, responding to Boswell's report in *Journal of a Tour to the Hebrides* that Johnson had declared that neither he nor Mrs Thrale had been able to finish Mrs Montagu's *Essay on the Writings and Genius of Shakespear* (1769). Pressurized, Mrs Piozzi agreed he could add a note declaring, on the contrary, her high regard for the *Essay* and her certainty of Johnson's respect for Montagu's intellect. Although she was saved from embarrassment, this public contradiction of Boswell was bound to provoke his ire.

Tittle-tattle about the breakdown of Hester's relationship with Johnson and the notoriety of the Piozzi marriage had stoked the already intense anticipation concerning all accounts of Johnson's life, and *Anecdotes* became an instant bestseller when it was published on 25 March 1786. Even the King was not able to obtain it on the first day of publication, and the publisher Thomas Cadell had to send him his personal copy. By 5 May the public was demanding a fourth edition. It is calculated that about 3,500 copies were sold in these few months. The *Critical Review* conceded that the book was 'very entertaining, written in a pleasing manner' despite some 'colloquial barbarisms'. Charles Burney, in the *Monthly Review,* was much more censorious of his friend's 'egotisms' and voiced many readers' shock at her inclusion of 'much that ought to have been suppressed'.[5] To add to the controversy over revelations of Johnson's private life, the public was hugely entertained by the quarrel erupting between the two rival biographers respecting Boswell's resentment at Mrs Piozzi's contradicting his anecdote about Johnson's alleged claim that 'neither I, nor [Topham] Beauclerk, nor Mrs Thrale, could get through' Mrs Montagu's *Essay on Shakespeare.*[6] Elizabeth Montagu had written her erstwhile friend a pleasant letter in response to the postscript, reassuring her that she never gave too much credence to what Boswell wrote, as he was so seldom sober. Boswell himself now took to the *London Chronicle,* pointing out that Hester had seen his journal in manuscript, and had not objected to the anecdote at the time. Of course, he did not contemplate the possibility that Hester lacked the confidence to contradict the great scholar. His riposte was followed, on the same page, with his pseudonymous publication of some ribald 'Piozzian Rhimes by Old Salusbury Briar'.[7] Privately, he and Malone conceded that her *Anecdotes* contained 'a great deal of valuable memorabilia'.[8]

The *English Review* judged Mrs Piozzi's the best 'of the *nine lives* of this giant in learning' (6 (1786), 255), although some contemporary critics accused her of a self-justifying stress upon Johnson's foibles and failings. Hannah More commented ambivalently but correctly that this was 'new-fashioned biography'. Luckily, until her return, Mrs Piozzi was blissfully unaware of the many caricatures and skits her book had inspired, such as *Anecdotes of the Learned Pig* (1786),[9] 'How to Write the Biography of a Friend' (1791), and Peter Pindar (John Wolcot)'s, *Bozzy and Piozzi, or The British Biographers, A Town Eclogue* (1786). In the latter, she is depicted robustly scorning the Scot's sentimentality towards his subject:

> Good me! You've grown at once confounded *tender* –
> Of Doctor Johnson's fame a *fierce defender!*
> ... *Now* for a *saint* upon us you would palm him –
> First *murder* the poor man, and then *embalm him!*

Hester Lynch Piozzi's literary career had begun and she remained in the limelight for the rest of the eighties. In five years she would have edited and contributed to an influential Anglo-Italian poetry collection: *The Florence Miscellany* (1785); followed up her candid biography of her former mentor, *Anecdotes of the Late Samuel Johnson* (1786), with an edition of about a quarter of his known correspondence in *Letters to and from the Late Samuel Johnson* (1788); and introduced a new intimacy of tone to travel writing with her popular *Observations and Reflections made in the Course of a Journey through France, Italy, and Germany* (1789). These golden years of literary creativity reflected not just a personal coming of age but also the flowering of her whole generation. Female poets such as Hester's friends, Helen Maria Williams and Anna Seward, and dramatists such as Hannah Cowley and Hannah More, as well as novelists such as Frances Burney, Charlotte Smith and Sophia Lee, were not only boldly publishing their work but now actually dominating the literary market.

The next decade would see ideological divisions separate these women writers in the wake of the French Revolution, when the Jacobins rejected the British model of constitutional reform and instituted a secular republic, embracing first state terrorism and then military aggrandisement. Hester's 1790s political pamphleteering would leave no one in doubt of her anti-Jacobinism, as we shall see in the next chapter. Therefore it is interesting to reflect on her self-presentation when she first went into print in the 1780s, defining herself specifically as a British traveller writing home to her compatriots, yet not as Jane Bull. The Italian-speaking Mrs Piozzi could adopt a mediating position from which to compare each country's mores. Highlighting her own Welsh-British identity was what particularly enabled her to celebrate cultural diversity both at home and abroad.

Ironically, she would herself become a target for 1790s Juvenalian anti-Jacobin satire, because of the leading role she had taken in publishing *The Florence Miscellany*, whose stylised sentimental verse articulated the early stirrings of Tuscan patriotism. The book was a handsome, privately printed collection of Anglo-Italian poetry and music, to which both Piozzis contributed, together with young English and Italian friends they met while sojourning at Florence. The well-connected Bertie Greatheed and dashing gambler Robert Merry, who had both been travelling in Europe for some years, together with the enthusiastic William Parsons, all shared liberal political views and were enthusiastic amateur poets. In contrast, the Marquis Ippolito Pindemonte (whom Mrs Piozzi found 'accomplished and highly cultivated' (*Thraliana*, 2: 654), Lorenzo Pignotti (with a 'taste for elegant poetry'), Abate Giuseppe Parini and Conte Angelo D'Elci (erudite but 'odious') were established writers. Hester, who presumably bankrolled the production, wrote the prose preface and verse conclusion, translated two of the Italian contributions into English and imitated three more, but contributed only a few short lyrics of her own. In spite of being privately printed and distributed, the book became quite well known, especially during the controversy over *Anecdotes*. Mrs Piozzi's preface was reprinted in the *Gentleman's Magazine* in 1787 and many of the poems from the volume found their way into the *European Magazine* and the *London Chronicle*.

However, both Parsons, who wrote the dedication, and Hester in her Preface made clear they invited no attention from patrons or critics, characterising their verse as a dilettante coterie production, an inoffensive and ephemeral memento 'to preserve Friendship from decay'. She characterised their effusions as 'The waters of a universal spring which sparkle in the glass, and exhilarate the spirits of those who drink them on the spot, grow vapid and tasteless by carriage and keeping'.[10]

Certainly there was occasional verse exchanged by aristocratic friends, encouraging a creative ambience and cementing close relationships. The opening of Piozzi's song 'To William Parsons' celebrates the inspiration of the dedicatee, Robert Merry, who 'can mount on the eagle's wide wing, / Or melt in the nightingale's lays', and Bertie Greatheed 'Dividing his hours and varying his theme / With Philosophy, Friendship and Love'. The second stanza, however, reflects on her own memories of the hostility experienced in England as she laments the inability of natural or artistic beauty to arouse her spirits and determines to abandon her pursuit of 'the charms of celebrity':

> In vain all the beauties of Nature or Art,
>   To rouze my tranquillity tried;
>   With reciprocal tenderness blest;
> No more will I pant for poetical flights,
>   Or let vanity rob me of rest.
>   ('To Wm. Parsons Esqr.', ll. 9–16)

She acknowledges the soothing and 'seducing delights' of music in the shape of Gabriel and the soft harmonies of their 'reciprocal tenderness' which fulfil a central objective of her Della Cruscan coterie: 'to divert ourselves and to say kind things of each other'. The encouraging response of William Parsons, 'To Mrs. Piozzi in Reply, Written on the Anniversary of Her Wedding, 25 July 1785', assures her that her marital bliss 'cannot impede her poetical flights', championing the power of collective support:

> Then sitting so gaily your table around.
>   Let us all with glad sympathy view
> What joys in this fortunate union abound,
>   This union of Wit and Virtû! [. . .]
>
> Nor fear that your fertile strong Genius can fail,
>   All thoughts of "stagnation" dispel,
> The Fame which so long has attended a THRALE
>   A PIOZZI alone can excel!
>   ('To Mrs. Piozzi in Reply', ll. 5–8; 13–16)

On the other hand, the *Miscellany* did not neglect the poetry of politics. There was also a clear Italophile theme with tributes to the precursor of the Risorgimento, Count Vittorio Alfieri, praise and imitations of Petrarch and the Tuscan immortals, as well as sentimental effusions on the peninsula's past greatness and present beauty. Parsons's and Piozzi's disclaimers were meant to disarm the censor, for resentment at Austrian rule of Tuscany laced this romanticisation. Gaps were left in passages criticising the 'reforms' of Grand Duke Leopold (1747–92), where pre-printed slips containing the incendiary material could be pasted in. Bertie Greathead's 'Ode on Apathy' besought:

> O! would the sons of Italy arise!
> And shake the leaden slumbers from their eyes. (ll. 23–4)

Some commentators have assumed Hester was too naïve to notice the subtext of the *Miscellany*. In fact, she translated Pindemonte's 'Hymn to Calliope', one of the most openly political of the contributions. It was addressed to 'Britain, the generous, brave and wise!' and was excerpted from his epic *Gibilterra Savata* which celebrated the successful British defence of Gibraltar against Spain and France under General Elliot. Britain was mythologised as a bastion of freedom while ruling the waves and controlling her colonies. This would appeal to readers back home. In the Italian context, the poem implied dissatisfaction with the fact that the French had supplanted British influence in the peninsula after the Seven Years War, and allied themselves with the Austrian rule of the Habsburg dominions. Even Hester's 'On an Air Balloon' was not so light a bubble as it appeared: it critiques imperial strife for dominion over the globe. As Steve Clark has pointed out, Montgolfier's original purpose in inventing the air balloon was military, and specifically to intervene in the siege of Gibraltar.[11] Hester Piozzi and her friends implicitly juxtaposed British liberal values with French and Austrian absolutism.

Historians today point out that the much-resented regulation of Tuscan religious and civic practices introduced by the Grand Duke Leopold was rational modernization, and that this coterie of aristocrats and staunch Catholics, who resented interference with local customs, were backward-looking in their romanticisation of the Italian past and picturesque present. Nevertheless, it had been an incendiary move when the Grand Duke abolished the Accademia della Crusca, which had been established in 1582 to purify the Tuscan language in accord with the usage of Dante, Petrarch and Boccaccio: this was undoubtedly because the Accademia stirred up patriotic sentiments and discontent with the region's lack of autonomy. When Leopold gave Robert Merry membership of his newly founded Accademia Fiorentina, which replaced it, this was intended both to placate him and to keep him under scrutiny. Merry was actually conducting an affair with Leopold's mistress, Lady Cowper, when not fomenting resentment of Austrian rule. Mrs Piozzi and William Parsons certainly took the lead in *The Florence Miscellany* (rather than Merry, who would become more famous for erotic poetic exchanges with Hannah Cowley and Mary Robinson in the British periodicals on his return to England). *The Florence Miscellany* introduced a newly sympathetic and nostalgic view of the peninsula, in place of traditional Protestant prejudice against enslaved Catholics. This, rather than its poetic quality, is what gives the book its significance in literary history. The sentimental depiction of Italy would become a central theme in the Romantic movement. Madame de Staël would follow in Hester's Italophile footsteps with her travelogue-novel, *Corinne, or Italy* (1807). However, it would be a generation and more before nostalgic romantic patriotism turned into active revolt in Italy.

Hester's own travel book, *Observations and Reflections Made in the Course of a Journey through France, Italy and Germany* (1789) would not be published until she was back in Britain, as she had put off the task of revising and compiling extracts from her travel diary until after she had responded in print to the death of Dr Johnson, first with a biography and then an edition of his letters to her and to others. But she could afford to take more time with her travel book, and in this, perhaps her most successful publication, she developed further her fondness for regional particularity and local customs. 'She noticed how little did one state of Italy connect with another: The manners differ entirely' (*Observations*, 2: 123). She alluded to her own 'republican spirit' (*Observations*, 1: 23), by which she meant an aversion to the rigidity of Italian class distinctions (*Observations*, 1: 86) and approval of a constitutional monarchy over the absolutism she observed in Austrian rule over Tuscany. 'Here almost every thing is hereditary, as in England almost every thing is elective' (*Observations*, 1: 216). Mrs Piozzi asserted that her Italian and Italophile friends' continual lamentations about the lack of liberty in the peninsula became tedious, implying she would be even-handed in the matter, as an Enlightenment travel writer should. She certainly did not indulge in a Protestant knee-jerk reaction to the Grand Duke's closing-down of religious houses. Hester had visited several Catholic nunneries in her first visit to France and had conversed with the English female inhabitants at length, finding the life a civilised alternative for unmarried gentlewomen.

She now pronounced that Italian monasteries were a necessary refuge in a country lacking commercial or martial employment for men (*Observations*, 2: 139). On the other hand, she could only see emancipation in the Austrian edict that prayers must be in the vernacular rather than Latin (*Observations*, 1: 301). On balance, she felt an aversion to 'such sudden and rough reforms' in the name of utility (*Observations*, 2: 204), and questioned sceptically why the people did not find these same 'hasty innovators erecting public schools for the instruction of the poor' or providing Bibles in the local dialects as they surely would if they were truly inspired by religious reform (*Observations*, 2: 205). She drily conceded that the streets in Milan were cleaner at the end of her tour than when she arrived, and after visiting Vienna, she could not question the devotion to duty of the Holy Roman Emperor and ruler of the Habsburg Empire, Joseph II. Nevertheless, Mrs Piozzi judged that his reputation would not be unblemished in the eyes of posterity (*Observations*, 2: 298). In her private journal she noted: 'these Austrian rulers are very tyrannical indeed' (*Thraliana*, 2: 635).

While her mediating approach to political and religious differences was calculated to disarm her readers, Mrs Piozzi outraged the critics with her improvisatory conversational style which the

Critical Review likened to a 'loose negligent undress' (*CR*, 68 (1789), 103) and the *Monthly Review* dubbed 'vulgar and provincial' (*MR*, 1 (1790), 193). 'I will tell nothing that I did not *see*' (*Observations*, 1: 18) claimed the author, who transposed passages from her journal without first crafting them into the more formal genre of letters. Because she could speak the language and was accompanied by her Italian husband, Mrs Piozzi could dispense with printed authorities and communicate the spontaneous flavour of life on the streets: 'One may chance to gain that insight into every day behaviour and common occurrences, which can alone be called knowing something of a country' (*Observations*, 1: 66).

She assures her audience back home that the English consul at Genoa was cheered on the streets 'wherever he went, and [the populace] 'crying *viva il General ELLIOTT*' (*Observations*, 1: 61). Sometimes, though, she would deliberately confound her readers' prejudices by asserting the high status of Italian women, the warmth of Italian hospitality to guests, and detailing the considerate treatment of servants she experienced in Italian homes. At other times, she would satisfy her Protestant readers' prurient curiosity about customs such as cicisbeism and traditional religious practices while refraining from outright criticism: 'These dear people too at Rome and Naples do live so in the very hulk of shipwrecked or rather foundered paganism' (*Observations*, 2: 86). Rather than maintaining a stance of superiority over the superstitious, she uses empathy. After observing poor people asking the Pope's blessing as he passes in his carriage, Hester remembers a poor tenant travelling from the Welsh mountains to be blessed by the bishop of St Asaph in the hope that it would cure his rheumatism (*Observations*, 2: 105). When in Loreto she marvelled that accounts of the miracle of Santa Casa were given in twelve languages, including Welsh, for 'pilgrims from the Vale of Llwydd [Clwyd] visited not unfrequently and told of the wonders of their own holy well' (*Observations*, 2: 161). This delight in regional particularity was presumably what the *Monthly Review* found 'provincial'.

As a Welshwoman, Mrs Piozzi knew how to value the traditional way of life of peoples vanquished long ago and remote from modern centres of empire. Wales in the eighteenth century had no capital or civil institutions and 90 per cent of its half-million inhabitants spoke only Welsh. It often featured as a Rousseauistic pastoral Eden in fiction of the time, and its indigenous population were mythologised for their independent spirit. Mrs Piozzi, too, inverted the usual notion of conquered people having degenerated in comparison with their overlords, by asserting that 'the warm and generous Briton of ancient days may be produced and happily bred *down,* (to make) the clay-cold coxcomb of St James-Street' (*Observations*, 1: 292). In Italy, she especially relishes the independence of the folk, such as the Milanese friars who have 'that intelligent shrewdness and arch penetration so visible in the countenances of our Welch farmers and curates of country villages in Flintshire, Caernarvonshire etc.' (*Observations*, 1: 81). 'Tis astonishing how like these Lombards are to our Welch people! The low ones in particular', she noted in her journal (*Thraliana*, 2: 618). She noted the Milanese took pride in their dialect 'which they are not ashamed of as we' (*Thraliana* 2:620). Until they arrived in Florence, where the purest Tuscan is spoken, 'all is dialect' she observes (*Observations*, 1: 328), for the Italian regions have evolved different linguistic usages.

Hester was not afraid to risk ridicule by comparing the famously picturesque countryside of Italy with that of Wales, for example the Alps and the Appenines with Snowdonia (*Observations*, 1: 66, 1: 270); and she even compared the Ponte della Santa Trinità in Florence with 'the fine arch thrown over the Conway at Llanwrst' (*Observations*, 1: 271).

> Had I told my companions of yesterday perhaps, that the view from *Madonna del Monte* reminded me of Chirk Castle Hill in North Wales, they would have laughed; yet from that extraordinary spot are to be distinctly seen several fertile counties . . . I think that view has scarce its equal anywhere; and if anywhere, it is here in the vicinity of Varese. (*Observations*, 2: 228)

She declared with the enthusiastic confidence of an inveterate bather:

> Were I to affirm that the sea is of a more peculiar transparent brightness upon the coast of North Wales than elsewhere, it would seem prejudice perhaps, yet it is strictly true: I am not less persuaded that the sky appears of a finer tint in Tuscany than any country I have visited. (*Observations*, 1: 310)

Between them, she and Gabriel could lay claim to the most beautiful views in Europe. But Hester even declared that Italian prospects have 'too great perfection' in comparison with British interplay of light and shade. The scenery 'round Conway castle . . . with a thunder storm rolling over the mountain exhibits a variety difficult to equal anywhere' (*Observations*, 2: 269).

Mrs Piozzi particularly admired the Italian 'Improvisatori' who recited stories and verses to entertain the populace, and especially the famous poetess Maria Maddalena Morelli, known as Corilla. The story of Corilla being crowned as poet laureate in 1776 would go on to inspire de Staël's *künstlerroman*, *Corinne*, one of the most influential texts on women's writing in the nineteenth century. Hester argued that such entertainment as improvising verse would never be tolerated in a capital city such as London or Paris, where wit is valued over sentiment. One would have to travel to the Principality where:

> Our Welch people can make the harper sit down in the church-yard after service is over; and placing themselves round him, command the instrument to go over some old song tune; when having listened a while, one of the company forms a stanza of verses, which run to it in well-adapted measure; and as he ends another begins: continuing the tale, or retorting the satire, according to the style in which the first began it. All this too in a language less perhaps than any other melodious to the ear, though Howell [James Howell *c*.1593–1666] found out a resemblance between their prosody and that of the Italian writers in early days, when they held agnominations [alliteration or assonance], or the inforcement of consonant words and syllables one upon the other, to be elegant in a more eminent degree than they do now. For example, in Welch, *Tewgris, todyrris, ty'r derrin, gwillt* etc. In Italian, *Donne, O danno che felo affronto affronta: in selva salvo a me*, with a thousand more. The whole secret of improvisation, however, seems to consist in this: that extempore verses are never written down. (*Observations* 1: 239)

Hester's romanticisation of spontaneous composition, which we saw in the aristocratic coterie production of occasional verse like *The Florence Miscellany*, also sought to capture the flavour of peasant oral culture before it vanished. The same nostalgia enthused collectors of popular ballads in Scotland and Ireland; back in Wales it would stimulate the revival of the *Eisteddfod*.

The Piozzis had returned to London on 10 March 1787, and, before even renting a house, Hester was already negotiating with Cadell, who agreed to pay her 500 guineas for an edition of Johnson's correspondence. She also requested that the faithful Samuel Lysons would help her with the task. Meanwhile, she and Gabriel put their finances in order, pleased to find out that they had actually saved money whilst on their travels. They greeted Hester's daughters and took the youngest, ten-year-old Cecilia, out of school to live with them. Though amicable, the elder daughters kept their distance from the Piozzis to show their continued disapproval of the match, and Queeney shocked even the straight-laced Frances Burney by suggesting that her mother should not be allowed to take care of Cecilia. In May the couple held a lavish party comprised of those old friends still loyal to Mrs Piozzi, and new ones made on the continent. Then they departed for the Midlands to visit the Greatheeds. Next, it was on to Lichfield to attempt to procure more of Johnson's letters for the edition, especially after Queeney refused to add those addressed to her to her mother's collection. There Hester met and took a liking to the formidable poet Anna Seward, who promised her help in obtaining letters which had been written to Miss Hill Boothby, even though they had already been promised to Boswell. That would be a coup!

Hester was still worried that there would not be enough Johnson letters for the projected two volumes, but, before she returned to undertake the work, treated herself to a short trip to show her new husband her native country:

> Well! My Journey to Wales was exquisitely delightful indeed, and I hope the Gratitude of my Heart was acceptable to that God who has protected & conducted me to my own Country again – such a

> *sweet* Country as it is too! And Dear Piozzi so pleased with it! . . . Our Caernarvonshire Hills looked very respectable after seeing both Alps & Appenines; we agreed that Penmanmawr [sic] was about the size of Vesuvius, & looked not unlike it one Evening from Bangor Ferry when I shewed it Cæcilia as a light Cloud covered its Top, & told her that it represented the Smoke issuing out of the Crater cleverly enough, & so it did. (*Thraliana*, 2: 691)

When she had toured Wales with Thrale and Johnson, the men had enjoyed deflating her enthusiasm for the picturesque scenery of the Principality, but Gabriel was so taken with Wales, and especially with the beautiful village of Tremeirchion, that the couple thought of building a 'cottage' there. Hester showed him all the gentry houses in the locality as well as introducing him to her own properties, in which she anticipated his taking a close interest. He was to prove an economical and methodical manager of her business interests, and she fantasised about his discovering lead or copper in the mountain, for mining and industry were booming in north Wales as the Industrial Revolution took hold.

Once returned to the capital, Mrs Piozzi set to work on editing Johnson's letters to her and, to swell the number, she decided to include some of her own to Johnson which she could argue would help the reader contextualise their dialogue. By November the work was ready to be consigned to the press. Cadell hung fire until the spectacular early sessions of the Warren Hastings impeachment were concluded, as they were engrossing everyone's attention, so it was not until March 1788 that the public first saw the two volumes entitled *Letters to and from the Late Samuel Johnson, to which are added some Poems never before Printed. Published from the Original MSS. in Her Possession by Hester Lynch Piozzi*. As the title makes clear, Mrs Piozzi intended to dispense with the traditional proprieties. The eighteenth- and even nineteenth-century custom was to destroy private correspondence in order to protect the reputations of both the dead author and his acquaintances, or at the most to print a heavily redacted and sanitised version. But Hester Piozzi reverenced and wished to preserve the relics of an original genius: her preface declared: 'the letters remain just as he wrote them' (p. iii). Secondly, as a woman, she would champion the genre of the private letter, citing for precedent 'Sévigné's tenderness and Maintenon's piety', though in the eighteenth century family papers were assumed not sufficiently serious to have literary merit. While warning that 'none but domestick and familiar events can be expected from a private correspondence' (p. ii), Mrs Piozzi suggested that readers might 'prefer the native thought and unstudied phrases scattered over these pages, to the more laboured elegance of his other works' (pp. iv–v).

Contemporary readers were divided on the ethical question of whether one should publish missives intended by the author to be private. While Elizabeth Montagu admired Piozzi's scholarly approach ('She writes like a Woman of Parts'),[12] Hannah More pronounced scornfully on the letters' mundanity: 'They are such letters as ought to have been *written* but ought never to have been *printed.*' She went on to quote Burke's contemptuous comment on Johnson's editors and biographers: 'How many maggots have crawled out of that great body!'[13] Frances Burney was even more shocked: 'She has given all – every word – and thinks that perhaps, a justice to Dr. Johnson, which, in fact, is the greatest injury to his memory'.[14] Ironically, contemporary scholars have found fault with Hester Piozzi for precisely the opposite reason: she was not as scrupulous as a modern editor would be. According to today's editors of Johnson's letters, she abridged letters without acknowledgements in order to excise some passages relating to potentially embarrassing medical details of Johnson's illnesses and Thrale's business practices, as well as to minimise the importance of the friendship with Boswell. Today's editors wince when reading her letters to Lysons: 'Pray take care to scratch the names out, in other words permanently *'expunge* with salt of Lemons' (Clifford, pp. 296–8). This, however, was the standard practice of the times. In the main, Mrs Piozzi respected the integrity of Johnson's letters. But she felt differently about her own, which she entirely recrafted, especially that about the 1775 regatta and one giving advice to a young man on marriage: these became mini-essays in order to display her literary talent.[15]

Letters to and from the Late Samuel Johnson deservedly became a literary classic for very many years, until it was eventually superseded by modern complete collections of Johnson correspondence. Even now, as the record of a close and unusual friendship, it has an unparalleled unity and can be read like an epistolary novel. As early as 20 July 1767, Johnson was calling Streatham 'home'. When he was away on boring summer visits to family in Lichfield or staying in the country with his agriculturally minded friend Dr Taylor, he constructed something out of nothing in ironically announcing snippets of rural news: 'I have seen the great Bull, and very great he is' (*SJLetters*, 1: 33) before concluding his missive with an equally ironic courtly compliment to his 'true Mistress'. His letters are carefully composed though fairly short and to the point. Like sonnets, they conjure up a space for intimacy out of the fact of the couple's being parted. The *Gentleman's Magazine* commented that Johnson lays aside 'the sternness of his philosophy' as expressed in *The Rambler*, 'and appears in the character of a polite, elegant gentleman'.[16] This, of course, was much in contrast to the revelations in *Anecdotes* of Johnson's rough manners in person. In giving a sample from the edition, the reviewer pronounced: 'We may imagine he would not have taken much more pains had he been writing it for the press.' The modern editor of Johnson's letters, Bruce Redford, singles out those written to Mrs Thrale for their 'high literary standard, varied subject matter, and technical inventiveness', especially pointing out Johnson's experiments with 'the pyrotechnics of compliment'.[17] In later more querulous letters, the older man might detail his ailments and express his longing for the comfort of being nursed by Mrs Thrale. Johnson also sprinkled them with fond messages to all the children and their pet poultry ('infantine' sneered the *Critical Review*, 65 (1788), 258), and threw out excited plans for resuming their chemistry experiments on his return. When parted from the family during Mrs Thrale's numerous confinements, or when her mother, Mrs Salusbury, was dying of cancer, the relationship was sustained by frequent concerned messages. Yet often the friends wrote just for the sheer pleasure of it. On 4 November 1772 Johnson confessed: 'We keep writing to each other when, by the confession of both, there is nothing to be said, but, on my part, I find it very pleasing to write' (*SJLetters*, 1: 62). Frequent topics in the letters are Johnson's electioneering for Henry Thrale; his detailed advice and reassurance over Hester's worries about Thrale's conduct of the brewery; discussion of all the latest literary and theatrical productions, his own literary work, his own health; and news of all their friends and acquaintances. There are also letters from the 1770s which are painful to read, responding to the hammer-blow deaths of Lucy, Anna, Ralph and Harry Thrale. Sometimes Johnson writes intimately and at length on death and mourning, at other times more breezily, counselling stoicism and keeping busy.

Of great interest to contemporary readers were the long letters Johnson wrote to Hester during his trip with Boswell from London to Scotland: the equivalent of a travel journal and fascinating to compare with Boswell's published *Journal of a Tour to the Hebrides*. Boswell must have been chagrined to find the great man in a jaundiced frame of mind at the beginning: 'You have often heard me complain of finding myself disappointed by books of travel. I am afraid travel itself will end likewise in disappointment' (*SJLetters*, 1: 101). Johnson gave Mrs Thrale a detailed account of all the towns, churches and people he met in the north of England, Edinburgh and Aberdeen, but it was when he saw the wild landscapes of the isle of Skye and witnessed the hard struggle of life in the Highlands that the tone changes and both ennui and matter-of-fact note-taking vanishes: 'I have now the pleasure of going where nobody goes, and seeing what nobody sees' (*SJLetters*, 1: 120). In October 1773, despite seasickness and lack of home comforts, he was nourished by much food for thought: 'The use of travelling is to regulate imagination by reality, and instead of thinking how things may be, to see them as they are' (*SJLetters*, 1: 139). Having visited Mull, Inverary, Ulva, the Hebrides and Glasgow, he could boast: 'I am grown very much superior to wind and rain; and am too well acquainted both with mire and with rocks to be afraid of a Welch journey. I had rather have Bardsey than Macleod's island' (*SJLetters* 1: 198). By 12 November 1773 the old man had had enough, writing: 'I long to come under your care, but for some days cannot decently get away' (*SJLetters*, 1: 202). Two years later, on 11 June 1775, Johnson wrote to ask Hester how she had enjoyed reading Boswell's own meticulous travel diary: 'You never told me, and I omitted to enquire, how you were entertained by Boswell's journal. One would think the man had been hired to be a spy upon me' (*SJLetters* 1: 233).

In the second volume, readers were able to follow the decline and death of Henry Thrale as recorded in the correspondence, as well as to notice the growing querulousness of the elderly Johnson, especially following his paralytic stroke. Mrs Piozzi included the letter she had sent him, after the event, to inform him of the second marriage she knew he would resent: 'Indeed, my dear Sir, it was concealed only to save us both needless pain; I could not have borne to reject that counsel it would have killed me to take' (*SJLetters*, 2: 375). She also included the more measured response which had followed his first intemperate outburst:

> I wish that God may grant you every blessing, that you may be happy in this world for its short continuance, and eternally happy in a better state; and whatever I can contribute to your happiness I am very ready to repay, for that kindness which soothed twenty years of a life radically wretched. (*SJLetters*, 2: 376)

Letters to and from the Late Samuel Johnson sold well, attracting some justified abuse from Boswell, who detected some manipulative editing, and less deserved rancour from the disgruntled Baretti who published an anonymous play satirising Hester as Lady Fantasma Tunskull whose daughters' tutor is Signor Squalici.[18] Arthur Murphy wisely praised the *Letters* for revealing Johnson 'behind the curtain, and not preparing to figure on the stage', for privileging us to see him 'in the undress of his mind' (*Monthly Review*, 78 (1778), 326). Many contemporary readers disapproved of the hostess turning editor. Johnson's ghost was imagined by the caricaturist James Sayer looking down in horror at Mrs Piozzi's publications and declaiming:

> When <u>Streatham</u> spread its pleasant board,
> I opened learning's valued hoard,
>   And as I feasted, prosed.
> Good things I said, good things I eat
> I gave you knowledge for your meat,
>   And thought th' account was closed.
>
> If obligations I still owed,
> You sold each item to the crowd,
>   I suffered by the tale.
> For God's sake, Madam, let me rest,
> No longer vex your *quondam* guest:
>   I'll pay you for your ale.
>   (*Autobiography*, 1: 320)

Having been satirised as a diminutive creature riding to literary acclaim on the gigantic shoulders of Johnsonian erudition, Hester Piozzi finally emerged out of Johnson's shadow when she eventually published her important travelogue, *Observations and Reflections made in the Course of a Journey through France, Italy, and Germany*. Reviewing it at length for the *Analytical Review*, the young Mary Wollstonecraft appreciated that 'The shade of Dr. Johnson frequently flitted before us [. . .] but Mrs. P. evidently did not catch his growling petulance or propensity to contradict, for she is ever in the highest good humour, and inclined to turn her eyes on the smooth and fairest side of things.' She charged Piozzi with lack of courage to be critical – presumably of the Austrian government of Tuscany: 'They who are very scrupulous not to say any thing the world at large will not approve of, seldom think for themselves' (*Analytical Review*, 4 (1789), 143–5). While the reader would find 'some information and much amusement' in the book, s/he would also be repelled by 'all the childish feminine terms, which occur in common novels and thoughtless chat, *sweet, lovely,* dear dear, and many other pretty epithets and exclamations' (*Analytical Review*, 4 (1789, 301–4). On 15 July, Fanny Burney, now a courtier, was having to praise her erstwhile friend's talent, for the Queen herself took the lead:

The Queen is reading Mrs Piozzi's *Tour* to me, instead of my reading it to her. She loves reading aloud, and in this work finds me an able commentator. How like herself, how characteristic is every line! Wild, entertaining, flighty, inconsistent, and clever!'[19]

This characterisation of wild, mercurial and somewhat meretricious charm draws on stereotypical 'Celtic' characteristics – the opposite of the rational English – which the Welshwoman had seemingly embraced by taking an Italian husband.

7

'To hie *home* and dye like a Hare upon the old *Farm*, near the Place I was *kindled* at'

In 1789, as Paris was sparking into revolution, London, in contrast, was set ablaze with royalist merrymaking as the King suddenly recovered from insanity and the threat of a regency was avoided. In the eighteenth century, the mob would often force the wealthy to support their cause by giving them the choice either to illuminate their windows by displaying burning candles – or have them broken. On the night of 10 March, it was the elite who organised a celebration in which everyone lit up their houses to show solidarity. They had commissioned artists to paint patriotic scenes on glass which were distributed to affluent householders, who then illuminated them from behind by rows of candles or oil lamps. The Piozzis were staying in their rented house in Hanover Square and Hester wrote in her diary: 'Yesterday's Illumination in Consequence of the Sovereign's being happily restored to his Throne was the most brilliant Thing ever seen in England.' She congratulated herself: 'The Transparency, & manner of Lighting up *our* house was particularly admired' (*Thraliana*, 2: 732).

Never completely accepted by the *bon ton,* Hester had to recreate her coterie which now included Florence friends such as Ippolito Pindemonte and the Greatheeds, loyal friends of former days such as Arthur Murphy, and newer acquaintances. These included rising literary talents such as the young poet Samuel Rogers and the novelist sisters from Bath, Harriet and Sophia Lee. Hester had written an epilogue for Bertie Greatheed's tragedy, *The Regent,* which was well received but had to be shelved during the King's mental illness in 1788 when the notion of a regency acquired an unintended political subtext. Sarah Siddons was their protégé having been a servant in the Greatheed household in her teens. She had been born in the Shoulder of Mutton Inn in Brecon, and came from the Kemble family of touring actors based on the border between England and Wales. Sarah became one of Hester Piozzi's closest friends. They had much in common. Both had endured unhappy marriages and lost most of their children in infancy. Sarah took the lead in making acting a respectable profession for women and, though in 1788 she had played Hamlet to her brother's Laertes, she became most famous for her heroic female victims of male tyranny. Hester Piozzi's friendship with Sarah and her success in improvising prologues and epilogues for theatrical friends, gave her the idea to write drama. At this period in her life she produced two unpublished plays: 'The Adventurer: a Comedy in Two Acts' (c.1790), which contained some brilliant dialogue but was burdened with a clumsy and vapid plot; and 'The Two Fountains, in the Manner of Milton's *Comus*' (1789), an untheatrical dramatic poem, a revision of Johnson's fairy tale 'The Fountains'. This was a blind alley. So, as France erupted into revolution, Hester turned away from play-writing and began to compose patriotic political verses for the newspapers instead, writing in her diary in the New Year of 1790:

> How thankful ought England to be for its deliverance from Sedition, Conspiracy & Rebellion, of all which we were in Danger this Time last Year; and how thankful ought I to be who begin this *1790* so happily, compar'd to the Situation I was in at the commencement of *1780*. (*Thraliana*, 2: 754)

Streatham Park was looking down-at-heel after having been let to various tenants since Henry Thrale's death. Henry had left it to his daughters, but Hester was allowed to live in it rent-free during her lifetime. Her second husband was a meticulous and thrifty manager of their finances and yet proved himself willing to spend handsomely on their building projects. They began in 1790 by not only restoring the 1730 country house to its former glory but having it redecorated in Italianate splendour. Hester commented: 'Our Nursery Garden, Shrubbery &c. is in the finest Order I ever yet saw them; & the House has an Appearance of Gayety never attempted in Mr Thrale's time' (*Thraliana*, 2: 797).

For the next five years it was their main residence. In the New Year of 1791 their festive house party included Hester's close friend, the celebrated poet, Helen Maria Williams, who was of Welsh and Scottish descent. Helen was an enthusiast in terms of her Dissenting religion and also used her verse to move the hearts of her readers on behalf of liberal causes. When Hester had to stay in bed with flu, Helen sent down a poem:

> To Cure this Cough condemn'd am I
> Within this Bed till Noon to lie;
> From the dear library am banish'd
> The Joys of Attic Breakfast vanish'd,
> And here in lonely Meditation
> Must lose my Piozzi's Conversation.
>
> (*Thraliana*, 2: 794)

Piozzi noted that 'her 'pensive Look and loveliness of Manner engages every one's Affection while her talents render her extremely respectable' (*Thraliana*, 2: 794). This latter pronouncement was true at the time, in spite of the fact that Williams had published an eye-witness account of the events unfolding on the streets of Paris which was brimming over with enthusiasm for revolutionary ideals: *Letters on the French Revolution, Written in France in the Summer of 1790* (1790). Hester conceded: 'Helen Williams's little Democratical Book is a mighty pretty Thing' (*Thraliana*, 2: 790). Yet Mrs Piozzi was much more impressed by Edmund Burke's *Reflections on the Revolution in France* (1790), which painted a melodramatic portrait of the threat the mob posed to the French royal family: ''Tis the work of a wonderful Genius' (*Thraliana*, 2: 792). The radical Helen would make republican France her home for the rest of her life, despite its descent into violence. On 4 September 1792 she wrote to Hester that she was picturing the Edenic 'dear, elegant retirement of Streatham Park amidst these scenes of tumult and death'.[1] Hester's diary shows a mixture of concern and exasperation that her friend chose to remain in France and bravely continue publishing her political opinions throughout the Terror. In 1793 Hester would write to her daughter: 'I am amazed She is still alive'.[2] She became equally shocked at Helen's close relationship with the married John Hurford Stone. Eventually, their differences in politics would end the friendship between the two.

Ironically, Mrs Piozzi was in 1789 a greater target of satire than Helen Williams, despite her own political conservatism. She already had a strong public profile, on account of her second marriage and rivalry with Boswell. Now, because of *The Florence Miscellany*, Hester Piozzi became associated in the public mind with Robert Merry, whose erotic mannered verses to 'Anna Matilda' (the playwright Hannah Cowley), and 'Laura Maria' (the beautiful actress, poet and novelist Mary Robinson), and their responses had in 1788 dazzled readers of *The World*, a fashionable newspaper published by the Prince of Wales's printer, John Bell. By April Fools' Day 1789, Hester had become disillusioned with Merry ('dissolute, wicked, and I fancy wholly worthless', *Thraliana*, 2:741) and broke with him. The antics of the 'Della Cruscans' in the newspapers were at first ignored by satirists. But that changed when the French Revolution was lauded by Merry in 'The Laurel of Liberty' (1790), challenging the British to:

> turn to France and see
> FOUR MILLION MEN IN ARMS, FOR LIBERTY!
> (ll. 419–20)[3]

Even worse, Mary Robinson replied in verse endorsing his revolutionary views in an elegant and expensive quarto volume entitled *Ainsi va le monde* (1790):

> 'Tis god-like Freedom bids each passion live,
> That truth may boast, or patriot virtue give.[4]

It was these political sentiments expressed by the most fashionable bards of the day that so alarmed the government that the Tory classicist William Gifford was prompted to respond with a Juvenalian satire, *The Baviad* (1791). His unsubtle poem brutally lambasted all the writers associated with *The World*. Because Merry was a 'Della Cruscan', Gifford included, for good measure, a quotation from *The Florence Miscellany* and lashed out at all its British contributors. In a footnote to the 1797 edition of *The Baviad*, Gifford acknowledged, in response to protests from Parsons, that he had never actually read the *Florence Miscellany*, opening it only to quote Greatheed's introductory poem. But the result was that he had therefore selected Hester Piozzi as a prime target for abuse, even though her politics were loyalist support for Church and King. Gifford did not care, as he always made a point of singling out female writers for venomous contempt:

> See Cowley frisk it to one ding-dong chime,
> And weekly cuckold her poor spouse in rhyme;
> See Thrale's grey widow with a satchel roam,
> And bring in pomp laborious nothings home;
> See Robinson forget her state, and move
> On crutches tow'rds the grave, to "Light o'Love".[5]

The beautiful Mary Robinson had been crippled, most probably by arthritis, whilst still in her twenties and Gifford's footnote that "Light o'Love" was a song that 'goes without a burden' hints salaciously that her 'state' of lameness had been caused by the after-effects of a miscarriage. The scene is set in Mrs Piozzi's salon:

> Her house the generous Piozzi lends,
> And thither summons her blue-stocking'd friends;
> The summons her blue-stocking'd friends obey
> Lur'd by the love of Poetry—and Tea.
>
> (*The Baviad*, p. 13)

Mrs Piozzi was contemptuous rather than angry, wishing that Parsons had had 'more wit than to quarrel with Mr Gifford ... for abusing Greatheed in a Poem nobody ever read'. She noted drily in her diary: 'That *I* am abused in it too, gives him no Offence they say: Tant mieux, tant mieux' (*Thraliana*, 2: 931).

By 1794 Hester Piozzi had published her next work: *British Synonymy, or, An Attempt at Regulating the Choice of Words in Familiar Conversation*. In his 1797 edition of *The Baviad and Mæviad*, Gifford, gratuitously added an attack on it, asserting that her 'jargon [had] long since become proverbial for its vulgarity'.[6] Someone told Mrs Piozzi that Gifford rhetorically asked: 'Does Mrs Piozzi ever read what she writes?' and she quickly responded 'Does any body read what Mr Gyfford [sic] writes *except* himself?' (*Thraliana*, 2: 931). Gifford followed up his attack on Della Cruscan poetasters with the lamer *Mæviad* (1795) on popular drama. His efforts brought him material rewards in the shape of the editorship of the *Anti-Jacobin or, Weekly Examiner*, which was sponsored by the Pitt government to counteract literary sentimentalism, which, it was feared, might popularize the movement for democratic reforms in Britain.

Despite the irony of these political squibs, the Piozzis settled down to a pleasant form of existence, alternating the London season with country life in Streatham, sociable sojourns in Bath and seaside holidays, where Hester loved bathing every day. But she always liked to have a literary project on hand on which to work and research. Having always shunned the novel as a genre which submerged women, as authors, readers or characters, in a sentimental dream, Hester Piozzi had come to realise that her real strength lay in non-fictional prose; her aspirations were to history and philology. On 14 December 1791 she noted in her diary that there was a need for an English book of synonyms, 'like what the Abbé Girard has done for the French'. Annoyingly for feminists, Piozzi lacked the confidence to carry out the plan properly and instead aimed only to produce some feminine light reading: 'such a Business well manag'd would be useful, but I have not depth of Literature to do it as one ought.—a good parlour-Window Book is however quite within my Compass' (*Thraliana*, 2: 837). As William McCarthy points out, she misguidedly avoided systematically basing her listing of synonyms on Johnson's Dictionary, as Girard in 1718 had based his on the French Academy's Dictionary.[7] This was presumably because she still wanted to come out from beneath Johnson's shadow, yet she did not succeed in this either – as she frequently cited him in illustrative anecdotes. Girard's book was the first of its kind in French and had already spawned one English imitator who was content with taking most of his material straight from the French.[8] Mrs Piozzi was perfectly capable of producing the first systematic study of English synonyms but chose not to do so. She made up for her lack of rigour by providing a greater number of synonyms than previous and many subsequent studies, and by illustrating the differences between them at greater length, through many entertaining examples and anecdotes. In the preface to *British Synonymy*, she once more adopted a feminine authorial persona, that of the bluestocking orchestrator of conversation in the salon and educator of her family in the parlour: 'Men teach to *write* with propriety, a woman may at worst be qualified—through long practice—to direct the choice of phrases in familiar *talk*.'

Mrs Piozzi specifically acknowledged her book was 'unworthy of a place upon a library shelf' (*Synonymy*, 1: iv). Her declaration that 'synonymy has more to do with elegance than truth' (*Synonymy*, 1: v) suggests that she was more interested in contemporary usage of the language, especially as it relates to gentility, than in producing a textbook drawing upon etymology. She imagined her reader to be a foreigner like Gabriel and pictured herself as the eloquent Welsh author who, like Glendower, can ornament the English tongue through her compositions – and indeed each entry functions as a mini-essay:

> If I can in the course of this little work dispel a doubt, or clear up a difficulty to foreigners, who can alone be supposed to know less of the matter than myself,—I shall have an honour to boast, and like my countryman Glendower in Shakespeare's Henry the Fourth, *have given our tongue an helpful ornament*. (*Synonymy*, 1: v)

Perhaps this accounts for 'British' in the title, rather than 'English', which would be more accurate, as the *Monthly Review* pointed out.[9] In the course of the book she stresses that it is Welsh that is the original tongue of the British Isles, perhaps implying that this gives her particular objectivity and authority in commenting on English:

> Mean time scholars who have had leisure and erudition to examine the language now spoken in North Wales, and prove it the true Celtic, namely, one of the primary vocal modes after the dispersion of Babel, tell us, after mentioning the affinity between that and the Hebrew tongue, that the NOMINAL DISTINCTION of *titans* came from a Gaulish or Celtic compound, *tud* earth, pronounced *tit*, and *tan* spreading, an overspreading people; while Rowlands, the ingenious author of An Archaeological Discourse on the Antiquities of Anglesey, called *Mona Antiqua Restaurata* pretends to show that these Titans were the Aborigines of our island, not descending as is commonly supposed, from the ruins of any disgraced or beaten people. (*Synonymy*, 2: 46–7)

This sort of mythologising of Welsh history on the basis of spurious etymology is reminiscent of the Welsh antiquarian and poet Edward Williams (bardic name: Iolo Morganwg) who popularised the notion that the medieval Welsh Prince Madoc and his men had predated Columbus in discovering America, and their descendants lived on as native Americans. This would justify missionary adventures of a pseudo-colonialist character by those wanting to raise the profile of the Welsh nation. In 1792 Hester had written to Lysons: 'Did you ever interest yourself about Williams the Welch poet? And how he is to go as Missionary to our newly discovered Countrymen become Savage Inhabitants of America?'[10]

British Synonymy had another agenda besides philology. It was produced whilst Britain went to war with the French republic, whilst the Jacobin Terror was at its height. On 21 October 1793, Mrs Piozzi wrote to a friend that she had invited to dinner George Robinson, 'the King of Booksellers' 'who is to buy my Synonymes'. In the same letter she declared: 'I am quite in a gasping State of Expectation; from my firm Perswasion that the Sans-Culottes will attempt a Descent upon our Island *somewhere*'.[11] The author's anxiousness to regulate the use of English on class lines was driven by Burkean fear of democracy: 'A nation like ours, where the reception depends less on established rank, than that gained by talents and manner, has a natural tendency to keep the language of high people apart from that of low' (*Synonymy*, 1:14). Piozzi puts forward the paradox that in the meritocracy of Britain, speech is strongly indicative of regional and class difference, but in Italy (and perhaps in Wales?), where class distinctions are much more rigid, the Venetian senator speaks in exactly the same dialect as his gondolier. It is only by participating in conversation that the foreigner, the child or the parvenu learns what not to say in Britain, in order to be accepted as genteel and to avoid at all costs 'base dialects, such as that of St. Giles [underworld cant]' (*Synonymy*, 1: 35). She declares that 'Nothing is so certain a brand of beggary in our country as coarse and vulgar language' (*Synonymy*, 2: 37). Mischievously, she counsels foreigners in polite society never to refer to money as '*READY RINO* [or] *CORIANDERS*' (*Synonymy*, 2: 37).

Her strings of synonyms are often politically charged, beginning with 'authority and power' where she comments bitterly: 'that these till lately venerated substantives are no longer received as synonymous, the state of Europe demonstrates at this dreadful moment' (*Synonymy*, 1: 29). Other obvious examples are: 'FREEDOM, LIBERTY, INDEPENDANCE, UNRESTRAINT' (*Synonymy*, 1: 252), 'KING, SOVEREIGN, MONARCH, PRINCE, DUKE' (*Synonymy*, 1: 330), 'MOB, POPULACE, THE LOW PEOPLE, THE VULGAR' (*Synonymy*, 2: 33), 'NATION, COUNTRY, KINGDOM' (*Synonymy*, 2: 54) and 'PARTY, DIVISION IN THE STATE, FACTION' (*Synonymy*, 2: 108). Even in illustrating the meaning of 'blameless', she intricately distinguishes between those pagan Romans who murdered Christians and 'the people now in power at Paris, who 'dismissed *all* religion: abominations had they (the Romans) in plenty,—but they worshipped something' (*Synonymy*, 1: 47). Even in the last days of the Roman empire, 'nor were men's hearts so petrified as to produce a prince of public execution EXEMPT FROM CRIME towards any earthly being' (*Synonymy*, 1: 47). Yet she concedes that the French king, though 'GUILTLESS in his own person' had erred in giving away power (presumably by accepting the constitution of the Republic in 1791). He was therefore not blameless, 'excellent, self-subdued, saint like mortal as he was' (*Synonymy*, 1: 48). The French king had been guillotined on 21 January 1793 while Piozzi was finishing her book, and it is not long before the subject recurs, in a mini-essay on the words 'DEGRADATION, DEPRIVATION OF DIGNITY, DIVESTURE' (*Synonymy*, 1: 146). The suffering Louis XVI's 'descent from the throne was more glorious than almost any King's accession' (*Synonymy*, 1: 147). Likewise 'DISMAL, GLOOMY, MELANCHOLY, SORROWFUL, DARK' evoke prisons and dungeons and the situation of the royal family in France (*Synonymy*, 1: 157).

One might assume that the political slant of *British Synonymy* was accidental: that Mrs Piozzi was merely being impressionable in allowing these gothic associations to creep into a linguistic textbook. Yet, writing to her friend and confidante Penelope Pennington, Hester Piozzi implied that her real purpose was ideological. Assuring her correspondent that the book was 'in good forwardness', she went on: 'I am only afraid the Title may prove a Millstone round its Neck: no one will think of looking for Politics in a Volume entitled *British Synonymy*'.[12] Burkean metaphors certainly abound, for example that of the oak tree, which had been co-opted into royalist mythology, and which could also be used of the national church as it evoked the ancient Britons and the sacred groves of the Druids. Under 'branches', Piozzi noted that the word could refer to genealogy. She asserted that the attachment of collateral relations to the family tree is 'still frequent in Wales and Scotland where, if these new-fangled notions of liberty and independence pervade not, good examples may yet be given perhaps of firm adherence to our old national constitution, church and king' (*Synonymy*, 1; 65–6). Another is the Burkean image of the British constitution as a dilapidated building which may either be restored or destroyed to be rebuilt: 'an old castle crumbles by time, and totters to its fall' (*Synonymy*, 1: 119). Piozzi quotes Burke on the connection between church and state, and declaims: 'Long indeed has our old Anglican episcopalian church stood like a rock among the rapids of Niagara' (*Synonymy*, 2: 93). In her definition of 'toleration' she asserts that this does not indicate equality of religious practices but is graciously granted by the Church of England: 'The last earthquakes alone will procure the complete overthrow of our large majestic venerable oak' (*Synonymy*, 2: 317).

Piozzi pays eloquent tribute to those campaigning to deliver the blacks from slavery in her piece on the synonyms 'EMANCIPATE, TO SET FREE, TO MANUMIT or DELIVER FROM SLAVERY, only to assert that even *more* commendable are those 'that never abused authority or power',

> or helped to bring forward this extraordinary yet apparently half necessary disposition in the world to close up every breach of distinction and tear away the boundaries 'twixt man and man, those once sacred limits, long prescribed by society; and permitted if not actually appointed by Heaven, as guardians of civilised life! (*Synonymy*, 1: 193–4)

Yet her fear and uncertainty at the prospect of weakening of divisions between races, ranks and species is clear. She praises the English pastime of hunting, asserting it is man's Magna Carta 'to hold dominion over inferior natures, and subjugate by reason the brute creation' (*Synonymy*, 1: 293). In 'FORTUNE, FASHION, FAMILY, RANK, BIRTH, NOBILITY', she, like Burke, regrets the passing away of belief in hereditary class distinctions as ordained by God: 'But if in this investigating age, nobility is found out to be a mere bubble, blown by the breath of kings, 'tis yet acknowledged to be an elegant, a brilliant meteor . . . a link to connect earth with heaven' (*Synonymy*, 1: 248).

She had aimed for popularity and in this she succeeded and was rewarded with a handsome £300 for her efforts. But anticipating fierce reviews of her anti-Jacobin slant, she declared: 'I may run to Brinbella [sic] myself, for if *Sans Culottism* prevails here, my Neck will be one of the first to exercise the new Guillotine upon'.[13] 'Mrs Montagu is an Enemy to My Synonymes after all—a declared one', grumbled the author, having been informed of this by a mutual friend. However, Sarah Siddons wrote acidly: 'The whole World's liking your Book will I hope content your thirst of Approbation'.[14] Mrs Piozzi admitted that the *Monthly Review* had been 'undeservedly civil' – surprised that 'these Democratic Reviewers are ten Thousand Times kinder to me than is the British Critic on whose Civilities I thought the High Church Principles of the Book had a sort of claim'.[15] This was indeed the case, as Dr. Burney in the liberal *Monthly Review* dealt with the publication seriously and at length, despite his condescending surprise that such an important 'enterprise should have been usurped in England by a female'.[16] The *Critical Review*, however, as well as noting the 'uncouth mixture of hard and inelegant words' and 'total want of plan', complained of its unwarranted ideological slant: 'she has made her book a vehicle of the most unqualified abuse against Dissenters, Frenchmen, and Democrats, on whom she takes every occasion to pour out the intemperance of her overflowing zeal'.[17] The reviewer went on: 'this lady's celebrated friend seems to have bequeathed her his narrow bigotry without the seriousness which gave it consistency, and his dogmatising spirit, without the knowledge which almost rendered it venerable'.[18] The progressive *Analytical Review* unsurprisingly also condemned 'a strange propensity to superstition, a bigoted antipathy to liberal enquiry, and a vehemence of political zeal, which can scarcely deserve a better name than frenzy'.[19]

Brynbella

During the course of this tumultuous decade in which fears of invasion came to dominate the news, the Piozzis turned for comfort to the Principality with its reassuringly traditional way of life and low cost of living. Mrs Piozzi explained: 'I should like to hie *home* and dye like a Hare upon the old *Farm*, near the Place I was *kindled* at'.[20] In 1793, when Britain went to war with revolutionary France, Gabriel became a naturalised British citizen. They had already begun to cast their dreams of building a 'cottage' in Wales into rather grander reality, for the house begun in 1792 would not be completed until 1797. Hester continued nevertheless to call the two-storey five bayed house with an extra wing 'small'. They had decided to build in the picturesque hillside village of Tremeirchion in Flintshire, not far away from Bachegraig, the sixteenth-century Flemish-style brick-built house of the Salusburys which Hester had inherited, now in decline, and whose main range would be demolished in 1817. The Piozzis' new neoclassical stuccoed house, described as 'delectable' by the modern architectural historian Edward Hubbard, had elegant interiors, bold plasterwork, mahogany doors and fine marble fireplaces. There was great attention to detail with cornices and doorcases, different in each room, and a stone staircase with a delicate iron balustrade leading upstairs where a music room housed Gabriel's chamber organ and musical instruments ornamented the chimney piece.[21] The Piozzis used the same architect and builder, Clement Mead of Charlotte Street, Fitzrovia, whom they had employed to renovate Streatham Park and decided to give the new house the macaronic name 'Brynbella' or 'beautiful hill'.

The Piozzis often stayed in the area to organise the project and, unable to rent a suitable house in 1792, they made the Crown Inn in Denbigh their headquarters. Hester wrote from there, boasting to Penelope Pennington:

> We have Coals at 10d per C – and they say how *dear* it all is! And Chickens 1s a couple—and *such* a Prospect! Well! I do think my own poor Country a very pretty one—that I do; and cheap—for tho' we are called the Squire and His Lady who live upon the *best* and Pay *for the best*: they cannot for shame ask more than seven Guineas o'Week for our Lodging and Boarding and Linnen and China and all included—four People and three Servants, and we have one very long [*storing*] room and clean Beds.[22]

They had to negotiate with the famous naturalist and friend of her father, Thomas Pennant, for some of the land that they needed, and Hester wished she had thought of asking him to lay the first stone. When she visited him, he showed her a strange fossilised beast, but she was more interested in hearing the latest news from France.

In Spring 1793, Mrs Piozzi wrote to Penelope Pennington that 'the Water surrounds the House in a full Stream ten feet deep, and the Maids may catch their Trout in the frying Pan Mead says'. Indeed, Mead had written:

> The Water is late into the Pool in order to accommodate the bricklayer, below this Canal will be extended all round the lawn to the Farm Yard at the Further end of the Field that was Mr Pennants and a Boat will be on the Same. Salmon can be kept on the Canal and Trout which is in great abundance in the brook thar runs down the bottom that to a Certainty they will live in the same water when in the Canal.[23]

Gabriel took a trip to see how everything was going along, and the lawyer, Thomas Lloyd, wrote to Hester that he did not think there could be anything he could object to except the expense. He argued in mitigation that 'there will not be a more Magnificent House in the Principality, not a House Stronger nor better executed'.[24] He was correct on both counts, as Mead's plans were exhibited in the Royal Academy exhibition of 1794, but the latter had to sue the Piozzis before they paid the full amount owed.[25] By October 1798 Mead would become bankrupt.[26]

When they both journeyed to Wales together in 1794 the Piozzis went through Shrewsbury instead of Chester and Hester was delighted at her first sight of the 'extraordinary' valley of Llangollen.[27] This time they managed to rent a house at Denbigh for a guinea and a half a week, where they stayed whilst superintending the completion of the building work. Hester's pet pug Phillis fell through the space between the joists of the unfinished mansion and hurt herself quite badly. Hester wrote proudly that the villa stood out 'white and lovely' and visible from her lodgings. From Brynbella, one could see the picturesque ruins of Denbigh Castle with the sea in the distance. She declared to a friend: 'When the Cascade roars You will like it'.[28] By August they were awaiting the arrival of Gabriel's fortepiano, and Hester was reproaching herself for forgetting to bring *The Mysteries of Udolpho* from Streatham:

it would have had such an Effect read by Owl-light among the Old Arcades of our ruined Castle here—Truth is Mrs. Radcliffe might find Scenes to describe in this part of the World without rambling thro the Pyrenees; many detached Parts of the Valley of Llangollen are exceedingly fine indeed, very like Savoy; and from the Rock above Brinbella heavy with the gathering Winters of a hundred Years is seen Snowdon; frowning in sullen Majesty like the *gros St. Bernard*.[29]

A letter from 'my dearest my loveliest Friend' Sarah Siddons finds her a little indisposed with dizzy spells, but she successfully finds a most apposite situation to present her own Brynbella tragicomedy:

> a *whorson tingling* as Sir John Falstaff says; yet if like him I go to *read the Cause of it in Galen* as he tells my Lord Chief Justice; Mr. Piozzi snatches away the Book, swearing he will burn it, because I look very well forsooth, and he is sure 'tis mere lowness of Spirits.

Sir Lucas Pepys, physician to George III, has not replied to Hester's note – from Brighton to Denbigh would represent quite a house-call – but she urges Sarah to give both the good doctor and the excellent actress her own sea-swimming prescription: 'if you see him tell what I say. Ramsgate is a good Place for the Girls, and a good Place for you as far as *Sea*-bathing goes.' What she longs for is the presence of her sublime and charismatic friend, to tempt Sarah away from her compulsive work schedule to the Romantic sublimity of north Wales:

> my recollection of the Hours spent in your Company, recur to me daily, with more and more painful delight.—*How* I do senselessly wish *you* here every day with your Baby! My Heart feels how you would like this Air, these Mountains, and the old Castle so solemn and sublime: with a self-sown Ash Tree or two growing or rather sticking between Clefts of the Rock, and measuring their Height against that of the tall Ruin.[30]

Her entertaining letter turns to the terrible theatricality of contemporary politics which has activated her own anti-Jacobin creativity:

instead of being inspired here to Performances of *Imagination*, my honest Wrath against the *Realities* of our present day, put it in my Head to make this Parody or Imitation or whatever you please to call it, of good Master Newbery's Chapter of Kings; written at first to teach Infants the History of England, but lately set and sung at Catch clubs, Bow Meetings &c. — give it Mr. Siddons for Sadler's Wells, if he thinks it good enough — turn over.

On 21 October 1794 William Siddons confirmed his receipt of the nine stanzas of Hester's 'Chapter of King-killers': 'I took it to Sadler's Wells where it has been sung with great applause for many nights together, and chiefly with loud encore'.[31]

> When France mad for Freedom her King control'd
> At first She was aw'd by Fayette the Bold;
> Then came the Assembleè Nationale,
> And then She was govern'd — by nothing at all.
> But spite of all Pother
> With this that and t'other,
>   They all lose their Heads in their Turn. (ll. 1–7)
>   [. . .]
> For Hebert who hunted his King to death,
> Resign'd at the Scaffold his guilty Breath,
> And the Wretches who join'd to accuse the Queen,
> Have all bow'd their Necks to the Guillotine.
> Whilst after all Pother
> With this that and t'other
>   They each lose their Heads in their Turn. (ll. 29–35)
>   [. . .]
> Thus let Atheists' and Anarchists' Blood be shed!
>   And never a King-killer die in his Bed!
> Till Tallien and Cambon, and curst Barrere
> Be sent for Companions to *Robespierre*.
>   And spite of all Pother
>   Each Regicide Brother
>   Like these lose their Heads in their Turn. (ll. 63–70)[32]

From Denbigh we are transported to the blood-soaked Place de la Révolution, the jeers of the *poissonières*, and then back to the encores of a patriotic metropolis.[33] With her inveterate facility of placing herself at the centre of things, Hester was arguably contributing more to the war effort than any member of the newly formed Denbighshire Huzzars. This song perfectly illustrates a remarkable breadth of reception. It might have been calculated to appeal to the rough humour of the working classes but, as we have seen, it found an enthusiastic Sadler's Wells audience. Furthermore Hester informs us, 'The Duke of Clarence is particularly fond of it,' and he 'made Mr Woodman sing it after a Bow-meeting dinner, following an archery contest, at which she and Mr. Piozzi were invited guests' (*Thraliana*, 2: 887 and n. 4). '[N]ow I write Political Ballads, and feel much pleased that you like my "King-killers"', she wrote to the scrupulous Queeney.[34]

That September she commented to Queeney that the Holy Trinity parish church in Tremeirchion, where there were monuments to her Salusbury ancestors, was in a deplorable condition: she and Gabriel would help fund its restoration. Nursing Piozzi through increasingly severe attacks of gout, and being the butt of the high-spirited Cecilia's practical jokes and often-voiced dislike of Welsh country life, failed to diminish a zest for life apparent in her frequent entertaining and visiting of local celebrities such as the Ladies of Llangollen, Eleanor Butler and Sarah Ponsonby. These ladies had scandalised their aristocratic families by leaving their native Ireland to live together in pastoral simplicity near Denbigh, devoting themselves to nature and the arts. They christened Gabriel Orpheus, so Hester named herself Eurydice. That summer, she and Gabriel enjoyed the company of the 'particularly amiable' Lewis Bagot, bishop of St Asaph, his wife Mary and sister Harriet. Mrs Piozzi wrote affectionately to her daughter Hester Maria: 'One shall seldom hear such good Preaching for example as here at Denbigh, or see so little Drinking or disorderly Manners, and we are *all* sound Aristocrates. They each invite us and Fête us. We have dined out five Times in these last eight Days'.[35]

Gabriel had furnished the dining parlour with eight Canalettos, and elegant pleasure grounds were laid out around the house.[36] A typical winter day in Denbighshire consisted of a ride in the countryside before dinner, followed by an evening's game of cards with friends, usually gambling games of casino, pool or commerce, followed by a supper of sandwiches, though they sometimes went out to dinner if there was a bright moon and Gabriel's acute attacks of gout allowed.

The Piozzis sought a retreat in Wales during the most turbulent period when many Britons feared invasion by the French, supported by home-grown radicals. Poverty was driving the lower classes to demand redress. Mrs Piozzi heard that there was unrest in Streatham, where posters appeared complaining that the rich were uncaring. That November she wrote to Hester Maria concerning her fears of invasion: 'Well! The Denbighshire Militia marched out of Town today [. . .] and marched in monstrous high Spirits too, notwithstanding that 'tis the serious Opinion of many People that they will have to defend us upon your Sussex coast'.[37] Mrs Piozzi became preoccupied with studying the sky for unusual planetary conjunctions and she sent for the visionary Richard Brothers's *Revealed Knowledge of the Prophecies and Times* (1794) among many other books of millenarian prophecies and predictions which were inspired both by the impending end of the century and the horrors of the French Revolution.[38] 'Oh Heavens! What a hash it is of Folly, Blasphemy, and Treason!' she declared.[39] She also began think of herself writing another book which would take a long view of the whole history of the world from the vantage point of the new century: 'Yet I could make a pretty Book too to bring out on the last days of 1799 or the first half of 1800 could I get materials cleverly round me, and Time for Study: as *Anecdotes* of the late Century – not a History'.[40]

When not searching the skies or the Book of Revelation for eschatological and apocalyptical signs, Hester pursued her 'career' as political propagandist with gusto, composing partisan songs to the same tunes as radical ballads, so that these could be drowned out by loyalists at rallies and marches. For example in 1793, one was sent to the Crown and Anchor Tavern in the Strand, well known as a centre for political meetings and for the distribution of partisan tracts.[41] She sent to her close friend, the classical scholar Leonard Chappelow, another 'loyal ballad' to be sung to the tune of a republican song, 'Plant, Plant the Tree'.[42] This was to galvanize the British to repulse any invasions, and began:

> See, See the mad Marauders come
>   Let loose to rob and plunder;
> They hope to find our Senate dumb,
>   Our statesmen lost in Wonder –
> But let them shun this hostile Shore
>   Or Back again we'll bang 'em;
> And of their Tree of Liberty
>   A Gallows make to hang 'em.

So eye-catching and accessible were Piozzi's anti-Jacobin ballads that a modern study of Welsh ballads of the French Revolution opens with a quotation from one of them.[43] That October Mrs Piozzi recorded in her diary:

> the parts of Tom Payne's [sic] book most easy to comprehend, have been all translated into Welch and are supposed to do no small Mischief among the low People hereabouts, I shall get Hannah More's Antidotes [i.e. her anti-Paineite story *Village Politics*] and make [the curate] Mr Mostyn translate them. (*Thraliana*, 2: 898)

Mrs Piozzi claimed in 1801 to have achieved this aim and in 1803 stated that the translator was the Revd John Roberts: 'I printed Hannah More's "Village Politics" here, and paid near twelve guineas out of my own pocket-money for its translation and dispersion' (*Autobiography*, 2: 254).[44]

On the last day of the year Hester Piozzi composed verses looking back at the tumultuous year that had passed:

> Had our brave Ancestors of Yore
> Dream'd of Deeds done in Ninety four
> Their Sons destroyd, and drain'd their Store,
> How had they curs'd this Ninety four!
> For not Afflicted France has bore
> Alone the Ills of Ninety four.
>
> (*Thraliana*, 2: 906)

On her birthday in January 1795, Hester Piozzi celebrated with the local gentry of Denbigh: the lawyer, John 'philosopher' Lloyd, who was helping them over the land negotiations with Pennant; a Denbigh physician, Dr William Makepeace Thackeray, a respected conservationist and uncle of the author of *Vanity Fair*, who had successfully treated Gabriel for excruciating seizures of gout; the Revd John Mostyn, whose sermons Hester commended; and Sarah Heaton, the dowager of Plas Heaton. All were entertained with harp music after dinner, and the Piozzis also threw a ball at the Crown Inn for the fashionable young people of the town.

The 'lower orders', as she termed them, had little recourse to festivities. The severe winter of 1794–5, exacerbating the effects of a very poor wheat harvest and the continuing war with France, led to a doubling of the price of bread. Mrs Piozzi noted uneasily: 'The poor are famishing' – even while reassuring herself that: 'The low People here in North Wales are eminently gentle, grateful & kind' and 'not to be feared' (*Thraliana*: 2: 910). Mrs Piozzi added with satisfaction in February that all the local gentlefolk contributed to have free broth distributed. However, her dream that Wales was a loyalist Arcadia was abruptly shattered on 1 April, when a riot broke out at Denbigh on account of grain shortages, and Hester's philosophical friend John Lloyd was the magistrate disturbed

> by the Sudden Entrance of 300 Men armed with Bludgeons into the Town;—a Mob collected from many Miles distance; and headed by a Fellow who in their [*sic*] own Language echoed the Sentiments of Payne [Thomas Paine] and his Jacobin Crew [. . .] The Ringleader is marked, and I hear is well known as a Correspondent of *Thelwall's* [. . .] they had Women amongst them with long Knives.[45]

According to the *Chester Courant* of 21 April, 'the acting magistrates, and a large company of gentlemen and tradesmen, together with the most reputable farmers, attended by two companies of the Somerset Horse Fencibles [. . .] set off from the town of Denbigh, at midnight [. . .] for Cerrig y Druidion (Druids' Stone).' There several rioters were apprehended, tried and imprisoned in Denbigh. It turned out that north-east Wales was actually the most unsettled region in the principality, and the *Chester Chronicle,* edited by radical William Cowdroy, published much verse on the horrors of war and social protest.[46] Mrs Piozzi suspected it of republican leanings, reporting indignantly: 'Our Chester Paper even now reproaches the rich with their Donatives of Bread and Meat, which are already styled *Insults* on the *Poor's Independence*'.[47]

The Piozzis soon left for Streatham Park where they spent the summer having most of their possessions shipped to Brynbella and commissioning new pieces of furniture for the new house. On 9 June 1795, Cecilia wrote jubilantly to her mother from Gretna Green that she had married John Meredith Mostyn of Segroid, grandson of a close friend of Mrs Piozzi's father, John Salusbury. Neither had come of age, and Cecilia anticipated Papa's blessing being mixed with mild reproofs: '*May godda bless, never I see such a people*'.[48] The young couple were staying at Llewesog Lodge, the seat of John's mother, Anna Maria and her husband Edward Watkin Wynn. Mrs Piozzi had previously withheld consent to the marriage as Cecilia was a ward in Chancery and, had Cecilia died before coming of age, this would have meant her sisters were disinherited of her portion of the Thrale inheritance. Relationships between Hester Piozzi and her eldest daughters were fragile, but they now had to accept the inevitable, doubtless blaming their mother for setting a bad example with her own love match.

In July 1795 Clement Mead was at Brynbella to conclude the negotiations with Pennant over allowing the laying of water pipes over his land and to organise the rerouting of the public road. There was some annoyance on Pennant's part over this, and by 1796 the Piozzis were also refusing to pay Clement Mead's bill. Eventually, he sued Gabriel for £6,000 and won the case on 29 January 1797.[49]

The three of them must have patched up their quarrel as Mrs Piozzi continued to employ him in renovations of Streatham Park. They had paid the enormous sum of £20,000 for Brynbella.

When the Piozzis returned to Brynbella in September 1795, the eldest daughters paid a long visit where everyone behaved in a civilised fashion despite underlying tensions. Mrs Piozzi wrote in her diary:

> All goes as it should do except Public Affairs—here are strong Dispositions towards rioting, & they have threatened to stick poor Pennant's Head upon a Pike—What Rascals! His Literature, his Virtue, his Piety;—His Charity & perpetual Almsgiving will not perhaps secure his Safety and his Peace What horrible Times are these! (*Thraliana*, 2: 943)

Pennant had been targeted because he was the chair of the Flintshire Loyalist Association. A month later, in London, the King's coach was attacked by the mob as he was going to open Parliament. The following year it was Gabriel's turn to be depressed when the French invaded Italy: 'The Ruin of his own charming Country affects him, no wonder! Such Distresses would grieve even those who had nothing to do in't' (*Thraliana*, 2: 961). The Piozzi family, who hailed from Brescia, lost most of their property when Milanese territory was overrun by Napoleon's army.

On the top of the hill, the mistress of Brynbella surveyed the preparations for war. In January of 1796 she excitedly wrote to Queeney: 'We set up our new Telescope and saw a large Fleet of forty one Sail pass by: the Glass showed every single Ship better, but the whole made a finer Appearance *to the Naked Eye*'.[50] On 22–4 February 1797 Wales itself came under threat, when French forces landed in Fishguard in support of the rising of the Society of United Irishmen. There was a quick and decisive response, and two enemy vessels were captured. Only a few months later, however, on 15 April 1797, Mrs Piozzi was outraged at the news that 10,000 seamen had refused to weigh anchor at Spithead, because their petitions to have their pay and conditions improved had been ignored. She swung into action with a ballad whose refrain turned on the sign of the tavern it was designed for:

> Ye British Seamen list to me
> And scorn the Democratic Tree
> They'll hang you on't, not make you free
> If thus for Fools you hanker . . .
> To part the Crown and Anchor.[51]

In fact, the Admiralty was forced to climb down, the mutineers were pardoned and naval reforms were instituted through an Act of Parliament.[52]

Meanwhile on the family home front, the temporary truce between Hester and her daughters was not to last long. When Hester tactlessly intervened in the Mostyns' marital affairs she was barred from attending Cecilia in her first lying-in, and comforting her daughter after a stillbirth. The bad feeling between mother and daughters triggered endless wrangling over money and legal matters. To make matters worse, while Gabriel was increasingly incapacitated by gout, Hester was weighed down by nursing him and fears that Britain would be next after Napoleon's successful invasion of Italy:

> There has the Gout gnawed and bitten for 12 entire weeks—during which Time has the truly wretched Patient suffered Torments inexpressible, and I believe rarely endured.—His letters from Italy irritating even *that* Anguish by Narrations of what Brothers, Sisters, Friends, &c endure from the Rapacity of these vile French [. . .] We are in a Leaky Ship, We must pump or drown.[53]

In another letter she mused: 'Pump or Drown would be a good title for a Political Pamphlet just now'.[54] At this juncture, while invasion fears were at their height and Pitt's government invited wealthy people to make voluntary donations to the war effort, Mrs Piozzi published an anonymous pamphlet: *Three Warnings to John Bull before he Dies. By an Old Acquaintance of the Public.*[55] It may have been technically anonymous, but the title alluded to her well-known poem 'The Three Warnings' which had been widely anthologised. The original poem had told the wry tale of a farmer who pleads with Death not to take him on his wedding day, and extorts a promise that he will go with him willingly after he has received three warnings. But even in his eighties, Farmer Dobson fails to recognise that his lameness, blindness and deafness constitute the warnings and is reluctant to agree. Now in an anti-Paine broadside in the style of Hannah More's *Cheap Repository Tracts*, Mrs Piozzi likens John Bull to Farmer Dobson, having paid no heed to calls a generation ago for patriotic spirit, support for the church and reform of manners to forestall and prevent rebellion.

Hester and Gabriel now decided not to put any more money into Streatham Park, which was expensive to maintain and would revert to her daughters on Hester's death. The Piozzis had to let it out to concentrate their resources on the new Welsh property that was their own. Hester had hoped to give birth to a son when she first married Gabriel but she had miscarried. Now as they grew old, it seemed that they were not destined to form a close bond with Hester's grandchildren. So they decided to adopt the son of Gabriel's favourite brother, Giambattista, and bring him up as their heir. They had agreed to send for him when he was old enough to emigrate to Britain and live with his uncle and aunt. In January 1798, Hester wrote in her diary:

> Italy is *ruin'd*, & England *threatened*: I have sent for one little Boy from among my husband's Nephews, he was christened *John Salusbury*: he shall be Naturalized, & we will see if He will be more grateful, & rational, & comfortable than Miss Thrales have been to the Mother they have at length *driven to Desperation*. (*Thraliana*, 2: 984)

Many years later, she gave this account of the boy to his schoolteacher, the Revd. Reynold Davies:

> My Salusbury is The Second Son I *think*—of Mr. Giambattista Piozzi, who was one of 14 Children, younger than my Husband and bred a Merchant at Brescia in Lombardy—but I fancy had more taste of Gayety than Knowledge of Commerce. He married Theresa Fracessi of a great Mercantile House at Venice and a near Relation (I believe Niece) to the noble Lord Count Lewis Fenerole—but the French Revolution destroyed all hope of Success to Trade, and its subsequent Tyranny having ruined both their Families—My Husband sent for the Boy who was bred up

by yourself and who had been previously baptized by Name of My Father John Salusbury—under the Notion probably that I might patronize his little Nephew on A Future day.[56]

8

'Each bold Cambrio Briton's a Stranger to Fear'

> The Brawn and the Books and the Turkey and the Boy are all Subjects of a thousand Thanks to Dear Mr. Chappelow;—all are safe. The Brawn nearly devoured, the books invitingly useful and desireable, The Turkey outweighing every Body's Turkey, and the Boy active and well proportioned, intelligent and merry-hearted—almost beyond anybody's Boy. I think we shall do very nicely.[1]

So wrote Mrs Piozzi to the Revd Leonard Chappelow in the New Year of 1799 of the Christmas presents he had sent along with a special passenger: John Salusbury Piozzi. She was sardonic about her daughters' resentment of the child, especially as they had never prized their Welsh inheritance: 'Little is the *all I have to bestow* compared to theirs and their Father's noble Fortunes: nor had I reason to think they esteemed that little as of any Value. To no Mortal did I ever say that I would *give him all*.' The echoes of King Lear were prophetic as she would eventually render herself homeless through making her bequests before, rather than after, her death. The last act of Mrs Piozzi's life would be shadowed by the resentment of her three daughters at her decision to pass on the Salusbury name and Welsh patrimony – while she still lived – to her young Italian nephew. This was despite the fact that her youngest daughter, Cecilia Mostyn, had also named her firstborn John Salusbury and also identified strongly with the Welsh gentry she both descended from and had married into.

Hester was careful to explain that she was merely doing her Christian duty by her nephew:

He comes here for Refuge, for Instruction, for Education—I will give him the best of each which my Country affords—In his Country I met with generous Treatment, and the Kindness experienced from his Uncle I will endeavour to repay to *him*. With proper leading, driving &c. he will want nothing from the beautiful and deserving Ladies I'm perswaded: You never saw a little Creature sharp and busy and tidy and helpful so at 5 years old. He can put on and off his own clothes, tye them all up in his little Bag and see that nothing is lost: and when he is a *General Officer* he tells me he will go back to Brescia and scold them well if they have not taken care of the *white Hens he left them in Charge*. Poor Rogue! he has seen early Service; and gave me yesterday a very clear Account of the battle he saw somewhere—in the Square he says—between French and Germans; how their Legs were broken—and the Surgeons tyed them up with Bandages &c. I asked him if they loved the French at Brescia—my Mama hates them says he because they dirtied Count Fenarolis fine House—(*Citizen* Fenaroli I mean—)—and threw his best Pictures out at Window.

The Piozzis were in regular touch with Gabriel's family and friends, who told horrific tales of the French invasion of northern Italy and the humbling of the local aristocracy. Even so, the innocent comments of her little nephew chilled his aunt, as she wrote to her close friend Lady Margaret Williams of Bodelwyddan:

[M]y poor little Boy from Lombardy said as I walked with him across our Market—These are Sheep's Heads are they not Aunt? I saw a Basket of Men's heads at Brescia. His perfect recollection of such Horrors will be however quickly lost at School, where a new Set of Play fellows speaking a Tongue wholly new to him—besides the little necessary Application to Business—will I hope and trust in a few Months wholly obliterate these Sad Ideas and substitute others less unpleasing in their Room.[2]

As the reference to 'business' suggests, Hester Piozzi had an unsentimental view of childhood and an unswerving adherence to education based on discipline and application. John (born 9 September 1793) had been put under the care of the Revd Reynold Davies, the curate at St Leonard's, who ran a preparatory school at Streatham. When her daughter Susanna visited the boy

Mrs Piozzi wondered how she would react to seeing a child 'with my name and my husband's face'. But, when she herself next saw him, would he even remember his aunt, whom he called 'merry lady'? Hester would not change her way of life or see much of the child, but she intended to provide him with the most privileged education that money could buy:

> Could I but live to see this John Salusbury a fine Fellow, and accounted one of the first Scholars at Eton; I really should think it a prodigious Happiness—and Yet a Lad is not fairly *launched* into the World till he quits the University—leaving Christ Church with *Eclat* for the Bustle of active Life.[3]

In the Autumn Piozzi wrote to the master, complaining of the high cost at the school and lack of care. She was eager that John keep up with or even pass the other pupils' attainments. Reynold Davies wrote back indignantly to defend his 'university' for infants:

> He is hard at his books for above eight hours every day with one of us teachers at his elbow. All say, and Bishop Embry, who is more than all says, it is too much; but Mrs. Piozzi's words are 'Duc invitas ipsa per ora rotas' ['Drive on, I say, over his very face, though the wheels be reluctant', Ovid *Fasti* 6.608]. Labour is the characteristic of the university at the expence of one hundred pound per annum. Idleness and extravagance are the characteristics of Eton at the expence of three hundred pounds per annum.[4]

Peace was restored and the Piozzis accepted Davies's suggestion that John should not return to them for the Christmas holidays in case he reverted to speaking Italian. Mrs Piozzi reported sadly to Davies: 'His Parents always write *so* anxiously and make such minute Enquiries for their Darling one pities them from one's heart.' John could certainly be spirited: Reynold Davies reported on 24 January that the boy 'knocked his Preceptress off the chair the other day flat on the ground'.[5] His alarmed aunt advised Davies not to overdo the cramming: 'Little Phials must be filled with a Tunning-dish however; Else much learning is spilt by the way, and the fragile Bottle is in danger of bursting,' and she gave permission that he be taught dancing, perhaps to use up spare energy. In the New Year of 1801 he visited his aunt and uncle at Bath and was thrilled to attend the theatre: 'His joy to see Mrs. Siddons on the Stage, who had called on him two Days before, was beyond all telling: She looks says he like a Peacock with that long Green Tail—and so She did'.[6]

The Piozzis now lived entirely at Brynbella, spending only the winter months in Bath, when Gabriel was most badly afflicted with gout. As well as the magnificent scenery and their elegant new house, the low cost of living was a great attraction. But the reason for that was that rural Wales was trapped in a colonial dependence on the English economy. There were few traders, middle-class people or professionals in the Principality, which had no large cities either. Poor people spent all their daylight hours at the loom and spinning wheel to earn a pittance, while their emaciated herds of cattle were regularly taken away by drovers to England for fattening and sale. As Denbighshire and Flintshire were transformed by an Industrial Revolution built on Liverpudlian capital, the Welsh peasants became starving workers at the mercy of slumps and booms. The wartime blockade hit trade and 1799 was a particularly poor harvest so Mrs Piozzi reported:

> my honest Neighbours have but just barely Bread in the strictest Sense; mere Bread, and that made of Barley too for their Families during such Winters as this cruel Summer will infallibly produce: Mr. Piozzi and I shall scarce be suffered to get thro' the Village they will so cling, and cry round us; and beg we will stay another Month, another Week, &c.[7]

The kindly Gabriel became Overseer of the Poor of the locality and did his outmost to help. By the end of the year, she reported that a famine was predicted and that: 'our Poor would starve round us but for my Masters Charitable Care, and what is more surprising than all—Oatmeal here is high prized as Wheat, and Water Gruel is grown a Dainty with us'.[8] In 1800 things only got worse and Hester wrote to friends in England:

> We have good Weather for Sowing, but the poor People cannot afford to purchase Corn here, so the Fields must lye uncultivated and Scarcity be prolonged to another Year. The Horses are not able to plough for Weakness, and the Cows give no Milk. People can't afford feeding Poultry, so Eggs are not expected.— And a Labourer's Wages does not suffice to buy Bread for his Family. Welsh Folks might eat Oats and Barley you'll say; so they might: but there is neither Oats nor Barley to be had.[9]

The Piozzis continued improving the Brynbella estate by adding to it the Bryn plantation. They funded the restoration of the dilapidated medieval Corpus Christi Church at Tremeirchion, and in 1803 would have a vault built for themselves there under the altar 'for *his* and *my* last cold residence, & narrow Apartment'. Hester composed verses to an air of Gabriel's for the opening of the newly repaired church. They also had to decide whether to demolish or repair the seventeenth-century Salusbury mansion of Bachegraig, and chose the latter.

> Bachygraig is putting into Tenantable Repair, and I do hope Edward Jones the late Tenant, will be coerced into making good at least some of the Contracts he subscribed to on entering the Premises. Mr. Piozzi was excessively kind to my Caprices in not pulling all down as He was advised, and building a Snug Farm House with the Material—His Reward is coming already; the Tithes let particularly well: he will keep the *near* Fields or Town Ships in his own Hands and yet have an equal Sum to what the whole produced him last Year.[10]

In the summer of 1800, the Piozzis decided to celebrate their wedding anniversary by laying on a feast with a difference:

> instead of feeding the Rich, We fed the poor; and every one of our 35 Haymakers had a good Noggin of Soup and a Lump of Beef in it and a Suet Dumpling and they were like the People in the Deserter who Sing—Joy Joy to the Duchess wherever She goes. And my Master's Health was *sincerely* drank tho not very *copiously* for Bread and Beer are yet considered as *Luxuries* in our poor Skin and Bone Country.[11]

The price of corn was so much lower in Wales than in the English cities that it was always sent there. Mrs Piozzi bewailed: '*Why* are the Poor so little attended to I wonder, and their wants so ill supplied. Here is a lovely Harvest, and one hears of Grain brought in to every Port every day. I thought that was only Newspaper Nonsense, till Accounts from Liverpool assured us there was plenty in *their* Town'.[12]

Retrospection

Hester worked hard to finish her ambitious new book begun back in 1796, the publication of which she intended to herald the first year of the new century: 'I should like that it should come out as early in 1801 as possible. We will not quarrel when The Century begins; but *One* will alw[ays] be the first Number; and I want Retrospection to make the *first Figure* in it, if we can'.[13]

She was working against time and described her typical author's day thus:

> 'Tis five o'clock in the Morning. I was up at *four;* shall call the Men and Maids at six, send away this Scrawl at seven, jump into the [probably cold] Bath at 8. Breakfast at 9. Work at the Book till 1. Walk till 3. Have dined by 4—fret over Gillon's Dispatches [information on her daughters' legal disputes over property] and Piozzi's misery all the rest of the Day—a pretty Biographical Sketch of the Life <of your> poor H: L: P.

Hester presented herself in *Retrospection* as a female prophet. Denying both the Whig progressivism of David Hume and the scepticism of Edward Gibbon, she read world history providentially, as leading up to the great cataclysm of the French Revolution and the conquests of Napoleon. Her diary entries and letters in the 1790s show that Hester feared that the upheaval now enveloping Europe would climax with the Apocalypse.

> What think you of Buonaparte? We shall see him Shine thro' another Campaign, and merit still more completely perhaps, his Name of Apollione.—It is at least worth remarking that no conqueror before him ever did wear the Name, tho' many have deserved the Title of *Destroyer*. The Roman Eagle now scarce able either to fight or fly seems resolved

to dye *discrowned* after all, and I respect the Resolution.—There will be fierce Deeds done ere Set of Sun this Year yet, and I expect a Grand Finale of the 18th eventful Century.[14]

In *Retrospection*, she writes: 'What is the history of mankind? A haceldama sure, a field of blood'.[15] Haceldama was the Aramaic name given to the field Judas Iscariot bought with his thirty pieces of silver. 'What would philosophers and critics have? They must return back to their Bibles after all' (*Retrospection*, 1: 60). At odds with this millenarianism is the way Hester writes in her letters of *Retrospection* as a commercial proposition rather than a personal vision. She planned that the expensive two-volume 540-page quarto designed for wealthy readers would be followed up by a cheaper four-volume octavo version, intended as a textbook for schools:

> About the Book, I am willing to be much more explicit; and hope to wind it up pretty tolerably, and to get what it is worth for it; and 1000£ will not be too much: They will make their Money twice over, because of breaking it into four Octavo Volumes for use of Schools, after the Quarto Edition is worked off. The Title page I gave in to Robinson was *this*.
>
> Retrospection —or a Glance backward upon the most Striking and Important Events, Characters, Situations and their Consequences, which the last 1800 Years have presented to the Observation of Mankind by
>
> Hester Lynch Piozzi.
>
> The Motto is an apt one, and the Quantity about equal to Watson's Philip the 2d or perhaps 50 Pages over — not more; tho' his was a full and elaborate Account of about five and forty Years particularly interesting to Europe—my Work a close-clapt Abridgment of what has past in the World since the Christian Æra—a Review of 18 Centuries, and will I really hope, be welcome to it.[16]

Hester portrayed herself as synthesising and condensing existing historical materials for a popular readership of 'young beginners' (*Retrospection*, 1: vii), so she concentrated on anecdotes and pen portraits for which she had a talent. She dispensed with the scholarly apparatus of footnotes and acknowledgements, sometimes airily declaring 'I quote from memory alone.' She did not bother to provide an index. Publishers were chary of the hybrid venture. Robinson refused the £1,000 the author asked for, and eventually she had to accept Stockdale's offer to give her a share of any profits rather than an advance.

In her preface, Mrs Piozzi declared she wanted to 'lure away' readers from fiction to 'known truths, no less extraordinary' (*Retrospection*, 1: x). 'Our flashy *Retrospect*, a mere *jet d'eau*, may serve to soothe the heats of an autumnal day with its light-dripping fall, and form a rainbow sound' (*Retrospection*, viii). Her modest metaphor of a light shower of iridescent sound somehow manages to hint at spiritual awakening at the end of days.

Like other late eighteenth-century world histories, *Retrospection* is inevitably Eurocentric, and portrays Christianity having a civilising effect both on imperial government and defeated indigenous peoples. But Mrs Piozzi paid little attention to lands far from Europe, and writing from Wales made the natives 'us' not 'them' when she was dealing with Britain in the first volume. When the Gallo-Roman Agricola became Consul or governor of 'savage' Britannia in AD 77, he conquered Wales and the north 'after making way for the sacred truths of Christianity, by driving from Druidic Mona its frantic superstitions and softening the rugged Cambrians' sullen virtue by his urbanity' (*Restrospection*, 1: 24). In Roman Britain, monasticism took hold, including the hermit Siriolis who lived on Puffin Island or Priestholme, opposite Penmaenmawr (*Restrospection*, 1: 128). But with the overthrow of Rome by the pagan Goths, Christianity was beaten yet strengthened in the forge of adversity:

> The dragon then indeed disgorged a flood out of his mouth to destroy the woman, well representing our Christian church, but the earth helped the woman, as St John saw in his Apocalypse; and that religion meant to be swept away escaped the violence; strengthening in spite of oft-repeated blows, prospering in spite of oft repeated plunder. (*Retrospection*, 1: 80)

Even in the very outposts of the old Roman empire, Celtic Christianity produced theologians, such as the proponent of free will,

Pelagius (*Retrospection*, 1: 122). When the pagan Saxons invaded Britain, 'the old inhabitants, the Welch', who, says Mrs Piozzi, 'still in 1796 declare "Dim Sasneg" [*sic*], we speak no Saxon tongue', kept their faith and independence:

> Those choosing freedom on their barren soil rather than servitude on the green banks of the Thames, flew to their yet half inaccessible mountains, where building upon every rock a castle, and almost upon every hill a fort, they made at last their utmost stand and found their final refuge in old Mona [. . .] In Anglesey, these refuged few retained the Christian faith, as they still boast, pure from all innovation many years. (*Retrospection*, 1: 181)

Whereas those Britons fixed in Wales 'had long been converted', it was the beautiful Angles whose state of ignorance and slavery so affected the Pope that he sent missionaries. Even when the English eventually adopted Christianity, Celtic Christians asserted their independence from Rome, according to Mrs Piozzi, by 'refusal of the tonsure' and 'abhorrence of the new doctrine of unmarried priesthood' (*Retrospection*, 1: 182), which she saw as Romish accretions defacing primitive Christianity. Yet when she comes to the ascendancy of the Tudors and the Reformation, Mrs Piozzi is measured in her view of Catholicism, even though Protestantism is implicitly seen as the first stage of the Enlightenment.

The apocalyptic note sounds again with the martyrdom of anointed monarchs, such as the execution of Charles I, when she imagines that the soldiers spitting in the King's face 'called up in his memory the devout recollection how his saviour had been so treated by the Jews' (*Retrospection*, 2: 244). Indeed, during her account of the French Revolution, our royalist author notes that 'the death of human martyrs now began to vie with those of our first volume [. . .] The natural alliance between the church and state had been completely proved by the proceedings of the French assembly, which overturned both at one stroke' (*Retrospection*, 2: 503). As she deals with recent days, Mrs Piozzi loses her objective stance and the prophetic vein comes to the fore. In the satanic 1790s, 'the foe of mankind found his attempt steadily opposed, his vigilance counteracted by our preachers' (*Retrospection*, 2: 512). However, he now manifested himself in the shape of a mesmerising warrior-hero who had: 'burst on Italy, amazing all mankind, not by destruction of his sword alone, but by all his powers of fascination too' (*Retrospection*, 2: 524).

Compared with traditional monarchies, Mrs Piozzi dismisses 'young governments' with elected kings such as Poland and Holland along with republican North America as mere 'unripe fruits'. She is dismissive of those 'new republics in the North of Italy which appear like funguses in fairy rings, produced by tears of the preceding night' (*Retrospection*, 2: 522). Britain was the last monarchical government to resist the democratic infection in the form of the 'seeds of mutiny' in her navy, when the French

> followed their menaces of an invasion up by a descent on Wales. These the bold Cambrians, nothing intimidated by *this* extraordinary stroke of policy, applied the remedy of ready valour, and recollecting perhaps, how a small vessel bound from Caernarvon had a few months before beaten off a French privateer only with *mop-sticks* which they chanced to have on board; the Pembrokeshire peasantry, actuated by equal spirit, came forward with their scythes and pitchforks, headed by a gentleman residing in the country, before whom these far-renowned marauders laid down their arms, whilst Sir Harry Burrard Neale caught up the frigates that conveyed them. These events happened in February 1797 [. . .] After this blissful, this decisive day, was the word mutiny erased from our seamen's brief vocabulary. (*Retrospection*, 2: 527)

At first the book sold briskly on the strength of Mrs Piozzi's reputation despite its high price of two guineas. However, after the reviews came out, the sales slowed, then halted. The *European Magazine and London Review* devoted the lead article of its March number and part of its April number to a sustained attack on *Retrospection* – pronouncing that 'female vanity never set itself forth more conspicuously not more absurdly, than in the assumption of *universal knowledge* which runs through the whole compilation'.[17] The *Antijacobin Review and Magazine* also denounced the book as 'history cooked up in a novel form reduced to light reading for boarding school misses and loungers at a watering place'.[18] The *Critical Review* pretended to be fair to this ambitious history, 'however unadapted such a labour might appear to a female pen', but found nothing but 'a series of dreams by an old lady'.[19] The *British Critic* mocked the author's pretensions by breaking down some oratorical prose passages into blank verse for the amusement of its readers.[20] Out of the 750 sets printed, only 516 were sold. The second edition in octavo was not called for and the book has never been reprinted subsequently. The author was not out of pocket, but she had made less than £100.

Why was this book a critical and commercial failure? Mrs Piozzi had laid herself open to mockery by allowing *Retrospection* to be published before she had corrected the numerous errors of the press. She had rushed because of a delay caused by a printers' strike, and she was determined it must be printed in 1801. Nevertheless, the book would probably have been panned regardless, for even the loyalist Anglican bluestockings Hester Piozzi and Hannah More were subjected to the reactionary backlash against all women writers at the turn of the century. Gone was the affectation that male reviewers treated females with chivalry in the press. In particular, for a woman to write history was to trespass on masculine territory – so Piozzi needed to be as scholarly as the pioneering Catharine Macaulay had been to be taken seriously. She knew that it was seen as acceptable for females to write for children, however, and several historical textbooks by women had been published in the 1780s. However, Mrs Piozzi's oratorical style and scholarly allusions belied her claims to be writing for the young, and she included no maps or illustrations. The critics treated Mrs Piozzi so harshly because they recognised that she was the first female to attempt the prestigious genre of universal history.[21] The fact that the reviews were so prominent and lengthy indicates the extent of her male rivals' concern to close ranks. Mrs Piozzi's refusal to use the scholarly apparatus of footnotes to acknowledge her sources and her poor proof-reading gave them ammunition to make her a figure of fun. She responded by defending herself in the *Gentleman's Magazine*. Belatedly, she also corrected and annotated by hand all the copies she could lay hands on which had been bought by acquaintances. Indeed, in her later years Hester would occupy many hours providing her friends and family with presents of Bibles and books glossed with her own marginalia. Like Blake, she took revenge on the book trade through personalizing texts. That way, manuscript took authority over print rather than acting as its hidden and disposable handmaid.

Mrs Piozzi made sure she kept up with all the latest publications in her rural retreat in Wales, particularly science, travels and history – especially accounts of the upheavals in Europe, such as Mariana Starke's 'very interesting' *Letters From Italy* (1799). Though she generally disliked romances, she had made an exception of Charlotte Smith's popular *Emmeline, or The Orphan of the Castle* (1788), set in Wales, whilst less impressed by the Lee sisters' *Canterbury Tales* (1797–1805). She was particularly excited by the anonymous *Plays on the Passions* (1798), which sought to introduce a new psychological focus on a tortured protagonist, and she correctly detected their Scottish and female authorship – the dramatist was eventually revealed to be Joanna Baillie. Though William Godwin's radical views made him anathema, Mrs Piozzi had to admit that, as a story, his historical novel, *St. Leon, A Tale of the Sixteenth Century* (1799), was 'incomparable'.

Like her Evangelical friends, Mrs Piozzi felt writing should have a purpose or respond to a specific social occasion and she was suspicious of imaginative fiction:

> When Romances first were Written They went by Name of—Incredibilities—but People soon found out that Fiction looks best, the more She endeavours to resemble Truth. It grows however a mighty Tedious Thing after a certain Age to keep filling one's Head with flitting Dreams so—turning one's Mind into a magic Lanthorn for Shadows and Ombres Chinoises to pass over.[22]

She was admiring yet fearful of the power of Madame de Staël's shocking depiction of female suicide in *Delphine*: 'I never saw any Book so voraciously devoured—but it has every Stimulant to awake the Literary Appetite, and every Power to corrode the Constitution of those who swallow it'.[23]

In 1802, on a visit to London, Mrs Piozzi made the acquaintance of the young Irish lyricist, Thomas Moore who entertained the fashionable by singing his own patriotic Irish melodies: 'There was a Mr. Moore, a new Favourite with the Public—who makes his own Music and Poetry, and pleases People very much—a Sort of English Improvisatore'.[24]

Mrs Piozzi had warmly welcomed her friend Hannah More's *Strictures on the Modern System of Female Education* (1799) and Jane West's novel *A Tale of the Times* (1799), written to repudiate the ideas of Mary Wollstonecraft, both 'of an excellent tendency'. She now contributed to the debate herself with a broadside, *Old England to her Daughters. Address to the Females of Great Britain* (1803). Interestingly, this acknowledged the good sense of Wollstonecraft's attack on conventional femininity. This was despite the fact that Hester had been sharply attacked by name in *A Vindication of the Rights of Woman* (1792) for adopting 'masculine sentiments' in conceding, in her published letter advising a young man about to marry, that that a woman's self-esteem is based entirely on her physical attractiveness. Adopting the persona of 'Old England', Piozzi now called for women of all classes to contribute rationally to the war effort should an invasion be successful.

> Women no longer have a Right to complain of a sterile Education, or to throw off their faults upon their Fathers. Nobody now hinders them from being wise, learned or courageous; nor does any one I can see pretend to like them better for being weak, ignorant, or pusillanimous. You are therefore here solemnly call'd upon, to act rationally and steadily. (*Old England to her Daughters. Address to the Females of Great Britain*)

She staunchly continued to write and circulate loyalist ballads, for the war effort, such as this one of 1803 which begins:

> Our Ancestors ever were famous in Story
> To Valour well train'd and a terror to France
> Yet Frenchmen forgetfull of all our past Glory
> To plunder and plague us are making advance
>> But let them come near
>> We'll make it appear
> Each bold Cambrio Briton's a Stranger to Fear.[25]

In 1803 Hester wrote to Mrs Pennington of the Piozzis' wedding anniversary which the devoted couple had always hitherto celebrated with a party:

> I will enclose you some Impromptu Verses which I threw across the Table to Mr. Piozzi last Monday. We had no Company — his Health tho' mended could not admit of any, only one Friend from Denbigh, and the Parson of the Parish who translates Miss Moore's [sic] admirable Stories into Welsh for Benefit of his poor and Ignorant Parishioners—but here are the Lines to Gabriel Piozzi 25 July 1803.
>
>> Accept my Love this Honest Lay
>> Upon your Twentieth Wedding Day.
>> I little hop'd that Life would stay
>> To hail the twentieth Wedding Day.
>> If you're grown Gouty, I grown Gray
>> Upon our Twentieth Wedding Day [. . .]
>
>> Marauding French have made their Prey.
>> If then of Gratitude one Ray
>> Illuminates our Wedding Day,
>> Think, midst the Wars and Wild Affray
>> That rage around this Wedding Day;
>> What Mercy 'tis, we are spar'd to say
>> We have seen our Twentieth Wedding Day.[26]

That summer, Gabriel had suffered such a severe onset of gout attacking his throat and chest that he became delirious and his wife feared for his life. The attacks became increasingly frequent, and the acute pain, which caused him to scream in agony, could only be dulled with opiates and wine. Gout is a common form of arthritis, often laughed off as a country gentleman's complaint. However, with limited understanding of its causes and lack of effective treatments in the nineteenth century, it was a life-changing and indeed life-threatening affliction. Gabriel Piozzi's fingers and feet became so deformed that he could no longer play his beloved pianoforte or walk far.

Although Gabriel feared the sea, Hester's passion for bathing amongst the auks and gannets of 'wild & savage & solitary' Prestatyn continued unabated. It was: 'Not unaccompanied by Danger—just enough for the *Sublime* I think, is the Act of dipping in these rough Billows at the Equinox—for scarce a Machine can resist the Fury of such North Westers, as we saw & felt driving Old Ocean before them.' In journeying home they unwisely attempted to cross the Rhydlan Ford, where the Clwyd and the Elwy debouch into the Irish Sea. The high-flowing tide came in so fast that: 'our new Carriage filled apace with Salt water; & but for strong Cattle & courageous Drivers, We had been surely *lost*'. Piozzi insisted that they had been very close to drowning, but Hester simply commented: 'It may be so, but I was Not afraid' (*Thraliana*, 2: 1058). By the next post she was sending comical verses to her daughters, including 'Invitation to the Ladies':

>If then you languish with Ennui,
>   And hope begins to flatten;
>Come, bathe in our bold Irish Sea
>   That roars around Prestatyn. (ll.17–20)

and 'Verse written 22^d Sept^{tr} 1804. Prestateigne—Flintshire':

>To rude Prestatyn's Sea-beat Shore
>   And salutary Gale,
>The Muse—if Health her Powers restore
>   Or Gratitude prevail:

> Should lend at least one artless Rhyme
> To celebrate the Place
> Where savage Nature's wild Sublime
> Presents an awful Face.
>
> (ll. 1–8; *Thraliana*, 2: 1059)

Three years earlier, on 17 September 1801, Queeney's thirty-seventh birthday, the sea had presented a more benign face to the thoughtful Hester: 'I was at *Prestateign* a little Bathing Place about fifteen Miles from hence, under Dysart Rock—She was at Lowestoff in Suffolk, the whole Island between us! yet in ye Sea I thought of her, & fancied she was in at the same Moment' (*Thraliana*, 2: 1028). Hester's poignant marine epiphany, with 'Gannets & Guillemots coming under one's Feet almost while Bathing', makes her think of writing a novel: "Tis a wild Place!! a Tale in modern Taste written among those Rocks would gain me more than *Retrospection* did':

> A Shipwreck in a Wintry Night—a Ladies dying Shrieks heard by the Peasants piercing the thick Air, and ending on the Blast:—a child found by a poor Woman & bred as hers—whose gentle manners shewed in due Time superior Birth—hated of Course by all his Playfellows, and driven to pensiveness for want of Sports which seemed sufficient for his young Companions: might be the Basis of a tender Story which in this Age where every body seeks to be agitated & shuns to be informed; would please a while;—then dully take its Turn & be forgotten. (*Thraliana*, 2: 1028–9)[27]

Her self-deflating coda announces that she would never approach William Lane, proprietor of the Minerva Press; she was not a writer to 'dully take her turn & be forgotten'.

If Gabriel was well enough, the couple made annual short visits to London to see her daughters and their closest friends. But gradually the life of the gregarious Hester became contracted to the sickroom, relieved only by omnivorous reading. A reading society had been established at Denbigh, a circulating library at Holyhead and a *North Wales Gazette* at Bangor (*Thraliana*, 2: 1090), and Queeney was always ready to send new publications. Hester particularly relished William Forbes's *The Life of James Beattie* (1806) and was quick to take the credit for her generic innovation: 'the present mode of publishing Biographical Anecdotes – *begun by myself* – is exquisitely pleasing'.[28] She also began studying Hebrew with the curate, John Roberts. Her ambition was to read the Bible in the original – 'better than to learn Greek, & read about Paris & Helen'. From 1805 onwards, Gabriel was almost always confined to a couch or wheeled bath chair, and travelling was torture. In what would be his final trip to Bath early in 1807, Gabriel was so ill that Hester asked him if he wanted a priest. But instead he received communion from an Anglican rector: 'My Piozzi is now a member of our own Communion' (*Thraliana*, 2: 1081).

During these sad years, momentous changes were occurring in Hester's family, for in the spring of 1807 Cecilia Mostyn became widowed and resigned herself to bringing up her lively three sons alone, but rarely visited her mother. That August the thirty-six-year-old Sophy married banker Henry Merrick Hoare and, though not invited to the wedding, the Piozzis sent the couple a beautiful wedding present: 'a Gainsborough, scarce five Feet by four—The Subject Cattle driven down to drink, and the first Cow expresses something of Surprize as if an Otter lurked under the Bank'.[29] Sophy had sold the picture by 1815. Her older sister Susanna, meanwhile, shocked everyone by openly going to live with the widowed artist, William Wells, at his house, Ashgrove Cottage in Kent. In complete contrast, only months later the forty-three-year-old Queeney announced her engagement to the wealthy and distinguished sixty-two-year-old Admiral Lord Keith and Mrs Piozzi wrote excitedly:

> I am delighted beyond all power of Expression that my dearest Girl will be so richly rewarded for all her numerous and various Virtues. I am delighted too that a British Admiral is to be made happy by accepting her pretty little White Hand; and as for Mr. Piozzi, your Letter has put quite new Life in him: and he is at this Moment rummaging over Music which till today he has looked on—only with Disgust.[30]

Gabriel was searching through his own compositions to make up a wedding present of the best of them for the couple, and he intended to compose a nautically themed march for the ceremony as well as to give his stepdaughter his beloved travelling pianoforte. By 1808 Gabriel could not leave Brynbella at all and the couple paid no visits away from home. The following year his pain from ulcerated wounds and gangrene was dulled only by drugs and delirium until on 26 March 1809 he finally passed away. The last entry in *Thraliana* read: 'Every thing most dreaded *has* ensued,— all is over; & my second Husbands Death is the last Thing recorded in my first husband's present! Cruel Death!' (*Thraliana* 2: 1099).

Gabriel was sincerely mourned by his wife, all the poor villagers and his nephew, John Salusbury Piozzi, now a handsome teenager. Mrs Piozzi had reflected two years previously on her nephew that: 'His heart is wholly an Italian one: his Resemblance in Body & Mind strong to Mr Piozzi, for whom he has I think a much more sincere Affection & Partiality than *English* Lads ever feel toward an old Parent' (*Thraliana*, 2: 1084). The devastated Hester channelled her remaining energies into arrangements for the naturalisation and education of her heir. His tutor was now the Revd T. Shephard, who resided near Newbury in Berkshire. As she did with her favourite daughter, Queeney, Mrs Piozzi conducted her relationship with him chiefly through sending him frequent, long, chatty and intimate letters. Meanwhile, Cecilia angled for due consideration of her own John Salusbury Mostyn: 'She was so warmly solicitous that I should give her Son the odd old curious Christening Bason that was bought for Catherine de Berayne's Baptism, and had remained 309 Years in the Family—Thin as a sixpence'.[31] In addition, Queeney became pregnant, and gave birth to a pretty baby girl, Georgiana, thus arousing Hester's maternal instincts but not diverting them from John Salusbury Piozzi. He now became her especial confidant, especially of all the local north Wales gossip. The desire to provide for him became her life's purpose. 'I really believe that my Attachment to you does me good; keeps me on the *Alert* and hinders Lethargic Drowsiness from taking Place,' she wrote to him.[32] All the improvements on the Brynbella estate were calculated to provide him with future income. She also began going through her many journals, selecting what she wanted to leave for posterity. On 11 October 1810 she began copying out 'Poems on Several Occasions with Anecdotes', a task which would take four years and five manuscript volumes to complete.[33] In 1811, she had his portrait painted by the talented local artist, Moses Griffith (1747-1819). The illegitimate son of local farm labourers, Griffith had been employed by Thomas Pennant to illustrate his topographical accounts, such as the renowned *Tour in Wales* (1778). No academic, Salusbury, as Hester called him, would leave Oxford without taking a degree and was destined to follow his uncle and take up the role of country gentleman, though, unlike Gabriel, he was indolent and had adopted no profession at all. Hester enjoyed the lively company of Salusbury and his old school friend Edward Pemberton in Bath in 1812. She went to the theatre and kept up with literary chat on all the latest poetry publications. For her, Bowles's edition of Pope was a treat to put Walter Scott's *Marmion* in the shade, and as for Robert Southey's *Curse of Kehama*, it was nothing but a 'Dish of Moon shine'. She was intrigued at the popularity of Byron, the grandson of her old friend, 'What an odd Performance is Lord Byron's Giaour! very fine tho', the beginning and the End'.[34]

John Salusbury Piozzi was spending freely on his social life, exceeding his generous allowance of £125 a quarter which financed him in racing and hunting. Ironically, his aunt was ineffectually attempting to curtail her own expenses in order to balance the books. Hester worried that the upkeep of Streatham Park would leave him with debts to pay after her death, so for the next two years had the estate put in order so that a suitable tenant could be found and the rent would pay for further maintenance. 'If the Place brought Money when *No* Care was taken, it will bring *more* Money when it is likely to be looked over'.[35] Mrs Piozzi's suggestion that the Thrale sisters purchase her life interest in the property had fallen upon deaf ears even though they questioned her right to sell any of the contents. Then they complained that Clement Mead, who had been commissioned to oversee maintenance of the house, had cut down too many of the trees in the park. They resented John Salusbury Piozzi extremely. They even consulted lawyers to see if they could challenge their mother's ownership of Bachegraig, and Mrs Piozzi went to London in 1813 to make sure that idea was quickly quashed. She wrote to Salusbury detailing her last wishes as to the family pictures and heirlooms in Streatham Park:

> If I come to any harm before we meet again—Shew your Executors this Letter, by which I request You to give Lady Keith the small whole Length Portrait of My Mother by Zoffanÿ,—and that of her Father, my Grandfather, painted in The Tower when he was a Child—Prisoner for his Papa's high Treason in opposing the Incroachments on Religion by James the 2d:—old Sir Robert begged the Boy might be with him. Likewise give her Mr. Thrale's Portrait by Sir Joshua Reynolds; and old Halsey's their Relation, with a Dog—and give Mrs. Mostyn the fine Baskerville Folio Bible with her Brothers and Sisters Births and Deaths written out in the first Blank Page, and an old Chair worked by My *Great* Grandmother, with her Maiden Name Vere Herbert written on the Back—If any of the Lasses wish for *my* earliest Writing Desk given me by that Lady's Daughter Philadelphia Lynch, my own Dear Grandmamma;—let them have it. Mrs. Mostyn likes any old odd Stuff of that sort, and I think you don't care about it. You should present her with the Chest at Brynbella too; 'tis marked for her, but I would not incumber my Will with Legacies.— Thraliana should be hers—or burned—but you may read it first, if t'will amuse You—only let it *never* be printed! oh never, never *never*.[36]

In November 1813 Mrs Piozzi announced that she had made her Will in her nephew's favour.[37] Salusbury had by now fallen in love with Harriet, the sister of his friend Pemberton. When he came of age and married Harriet on 7 November 1814, Mrs Piozzi generously made over Brynbella and all her Welsh property to her nephew as a wedding gift. To Hester's delight, he was made High Sheriff of Flintshire and was knighted in 1817 as Sir John Salusbury Piozzi Salusbury. She would dearly have liked this title to be hereditary to enhance the standing of her own Welsh family. Salusbury milked her of funds to procure this, but the attempt came to nothing.

With her affairs settled and peace in Europe on the horizon, Hester Piozzi retired to Bath in 1814. She could no longer afford to stay in Pulteney Street and had to count every penny until she finally settled the bills for Streatham in 1816 by selling off possessions and paintings. Then she found a pleasant residence in 8 Gay Street: 'So I am now grown one of the curiosities of Bath, it seems, & *one of the Antiquities*.' Many friends had died; yet she could sometimes relive her friendships as their correspondence was published: 'Mrs. Montagu's Letters however are delightful, and every body says so— I devour them: the Names of all one's Contemporaries do so interest one, There is no Possibility of laying down the Book'.[38] But Mrs Piozzi's charm and zest for life ensured that she would have no trouble making new and younger friends, and many sought an invitation at her house to enjoy her conversation. She took a motherly interest in the writer Edward Mangin and Sir James Fellowes, a retired naval doctor, both thirty years her junior, who became deeply attached to her. The latter became one of her executors. Perhaps unwisely, they encouraged her unsuccessful attempts to find a publisher for 'Lyford Redivivus, or, A Grandame's Garrulity', an abstruse collection of proper names with conjectural etymologies but, as in *British Synonymy*, her philological scholarship was seriously flawed.

The devoted attentions of a young, unsuccessful actor, William Augustus Conway, compensated her for the coolness of her alienated daughters and the mercenary Salusbury. Once more an impulsive search for affection was to create scandal; her effusive letters to her 'Chevalier' Conway were the subject of deliberate and salacious misinterpretation after her death. Hester's seventy-ninth birthday (she counted it her eightieth) was lavishly celebrated in January 1820 at the assembly rooms where over 600 guests enjoyed a concert, ball and supper. All admired the undiminished vigour of her intellect and the 'astonishing elasticity' of her dancing when she and Sir John Salusbury opened the ball. Though she celebrated until the early hours, Mrs Piozzi was up the next morning and entertaining callers at breakfast. Such expense dictated a year's retirement in economical Penzance, and it was on her return from this self-imposed exile that she suffered a serious fall. '[A]lways a blue', she quipped, 'now a black and blue' (*Autobiography*, 2. 462), but complications set in. Her daughters hurried to her bedside, but she was too weak to speak and could only touch their hands. Her humour still did not desert her and, when her friend and physician Sir George Gibbes entered the room, she traced the outline of a coffin in the air (*Autobiography*, 1: 363). She died, a 'stranger to fear', at 10 Sion Row, Clifton, on 2 May 1821. Two weeks later, on 16 May, she was laid to rest, according to her expressed desire, beside her beloved second husband in the vault of Tremeirchion church in the beautiful Vale of Clwyd.

Notes

I

1. *The Literary Life of the late Thomas Pennant Esq., by himself* (London: White, 1793), p. 1.
2. *Thraliana: The Diary of Mrs. Hester Lynch Thrale (later Mrs. Piozzi) 1776–1809*, ed. Katharine C. Balderston, 2 vols (Oxford: Clarendon Press, 1951), 1: 6; henceforth '*Thraliana*' in the text.
3. *Autobiography, Letters and Literary Remains of Mrs. Piozzi (Thrale)*, ed. Abraham Hayward, 2 vols (London: Longman, 1861), 2: 10; henceforth '*Autobiography*' in the text.
4. *Expeditions of Honour: The Journal of John Salusbury in Halifax, Nova Scotia, 1749–53*, ed. Ronald Rompkey (Newark, NJ: University of Delaware Press, 1982), p. 139.
5. Letter to the Proprietors of the *Monthly Mirror*, 17 June 1798, *The Piozzi Letters: Correspondence of Hester Lynch Piozzi 1784-1821*, ed. Edward Alan Bloom and Lillian D. Bloom, 6 vols (Newark: University of Delaware Press, 1991), 2: 500. Henceforth cited as '*PLetters*'.
6. Isaac Netto (Nieto), *A Sermon Preached in the Jews Synagogue, on Friday, February 6, 1756* (London: printed for the author by Richard Reily, 1756), pp. 9–10.
7. See *Autobiography*, 2: 18, and the letter from Anna Maria Salusbury to Hester of 22 July 1756, cited from John Rylands Library, Manchester, GB 133 Eng. MS 616, item 1, by James L. Clifford, *Hester Lynch Piozzi (Mrs. Thrale)*, second edn. (Oxford: Clarendon Press, 1987), p. 21; henceforth 'Clifford'.
8. Hester Lynch Piozzi, *Observations and Reflections Made in the Course of a Journey through France, Italy and Germany*, 2 vols (London: A. Strahan and T. Cadell, 1789), 2: 52–5. Henceforth '*Observations*'; *The Biographical Dictionary of Women in Science*, ed. Marilyn Ogilvie et al. (London: Routledge, 2014), p. 1056.
9. Gregorio, Mayáns Y Siscár, *Vida de Miguel de Cervantes Saavedra* (Briga-Real, 1737), p. 200.

10. See *Thraliana*, 1: 3; *The Life of Michael De Cervantes Saavedra, Written by Don Gregorio Mayáns Y Siscár, Translated by Mr. Ozell* (London: J. and R. Tonson, 1738), p. 88.
11. Cited by Clifford from the first of the five quarto notenooks known as 'Mainwarng Piozziana, 1: 19.
12. Parker's only contribution to the Royal Society's Philosophical Transactions, a translation of an extract from a letter of Mons. Grovestins concerning an earthquake experienced at the Hague on 18 February 1756, consisted of eleven and a half lines; see the *Critical Review*, 4 (August 1757), 130–49; 140.
13. 'Harvard Piozziana', Houghton Library MS Eng. 1280, 1: 26–7.
14. Letter of 26 February 1767 from Voltaire [François Marie Arouet] to James Marriott, *Voltaire in his Letters*, trans. Evelyn Beatrice Hall [pseud. S. G. Tallentyre] (New York and London: G. P. Putnam's Sons, 1919), p. 203.
15. A. M. Broadley, *Doctor Johnson and Mrs. Thrale* (London and New York: John Lane, 1910), p. 105.
16. William McCarthy, 'A Verse "Essay on Man" by H. L. Piozzi', *The Age of Johnson*, 2 (1989), 375–420; 376. See also the analysis of the poem in his *Hester Thrale Piozzi: Portrait of a Literary Woman* (Chapel Hill and London, University of North Carolina, 1985), pp. 11–15.
17. Cf. Alexander Pope, *An Essay on Man* (London: L. Gilliver, 1734), Epistle 1: 285–6.
18. Cited from Rylands, GB 133 Eng. MS 536, 23, in Clifford, p. 28.
19. James Allison, 'Mrs. Thrale's Marginalia in Joseph Warton's "Essay"', *Huntington Library Quarterly*, 19/2 (February 1956), 155–64: 156.
20. *St James's Chronicle*, 18 February 1762.
21. Any Native American information was highly valuable; that summer saw enormous public curiosity surrounding the Cherokee embassy which had come to London to cement the peace treaty ending the Anglo-Cherokee War. By a remarkable coincidence Hester's next contribution was preceded on the front page of the *Chronicle* by a supposed 'letter' from Tohanohawighton, a member of that embassy.
22. *St James's Chronicle*, 22–4 July 1762. Bute served as Lord of the Bedchamber to Frederick, Prince of Wales, and after the prince's premature death in 1751 he remained the confidant of his widow, Princess Augusta, the mother of George III.
23. For more detailed information concerning Wilkes and his attacks upon the Lord Bute ministry (1762–3), see Arthur Cash, *John Wilkes: The Scandalous Father of Civil Liberty* (New Haven: Yale University Press, 2007), ch. 4.
24. *St James Chronicle*, 29–31 July 1762.

25 *Political Controversy: or, Weekly Magazine of Ministerial and Anti-ministerial Essays*, 2 August 1762.
26 Cited from Rylands, GB 133 Eng. MS 534, in Clifford, p. 41.

2

1 *The Letters of Samuel Johnson, LL.D.*, ed. G. B. Hill, 2 vols (Oxford: Clarendon Press, 1892), 2: 98, n. 2.
2 William Levinz, Receiver-General of Customs and former MP for Nottinghamshire, had affairs with the wives of two fellow MPs, Sir George Savile, and Soame Jenyns. He was the uncle of another of Hester's suitors: 'Mr. Levinz whose partiality to me I shall ever gratefully remember, offered to settle his whole Fortune—a very large one—on his Nephew Chaworth afterwards killed by Ld. Byron [brother to Admiral Byron, the poet's grandfather] — if I would have *him*; to which no Objection but my Father's Oddity could have been made' (*Thraliana*, 1: 296).
3 Broadley, *Doctor Johnson and Mrs. Thrale*, pp. 106–8.
4 Her poem also appeared in the *Public Advertiser* and *The London Chronicle* of 13 September, *The London Magazine, or, Gentleman's Monthly Intelligencer* (September 1763), 497–8, and *Gentleman's Magazine*, 33 (1763), 459. It was subsequently reprinted in several miscellanies and collections of fables; Hester herself noted: 'I have seen it in Boarding Schools given to Girls for a Copy' (*Thraliana*, 1: 322).
5 Harvard Piozziana, 5 vols., Houghton Library, MS Eng. 1280, 1. 50, cited in Clifford, p. 50.
6 Johnson described this poem as 'very pretty, & much in Lord Lyttelton's Style', but typically he cannot resist a patronising sting: 'a good one says he—for a *Lady*' (*Thraliana*, 1: 55).
7 Firestone Library, Princeton: MS 3891.8.313, f. 24.
8 It was in the light of her second, rather than her first, marriage that Hester at 53 wrote: '[I]f FELICITY could ever be found on earth, it might most justly be expected from a marriage of two persons eminently qualified to make each other's HAPPINESS, in a union first formed by love, continued by friendship, and so cemented by virtue as may give the partners a well-founded hope of everlasting BLISS in the world to come' (Hester Piozzi, *British Synonymy*, 2 vols (London: G. G. and J. Robinson, 1794), 1: 51–2).
9 Hester Lynch Piozzi, letter of 17 June 1798 to the proprietors of *The Monthly Mirror*, *Letters*, 2: 500–3.

10   This topical joke, inspired by the archaeologist Robert Wood's popular study, *The Ruins of Palmyra* (1753), is sadly drained of its humour by the activities of twenty-first-century terrorists, unexampled in the history of the world.

3

1   This observation is supplied by the daughter of his biographer, Sir John Hawkins: Laetitia-Matilda Hawkins, *Memoirs, Anecdotes, Facts and Opinions* 2 vols (London: Longman et al., 1824), 1: 149. Lord Chesterfield's description was written fourteen years earlier in 1751: 'There is a man, whose moral character, deep learning, and superior parts, I acknowledge, admire, and respect; but whom it is so impossible for me to love, that I am almost in a fever whenever I am in his company. His figure, without being deformed, seems made to disgrace or ridicule the common structure of the human body. His legs and arms are never in the position, which, according to the situation of his body, they ought to be in, but constantly employed in committing acts of hostility upon the graces. He throws any where, but down his throat, whatever he means to drink, and only mangles what he means to carve. Inattentive to all the regards of social life, he mistimes or misplaces every thing. He disputes with heat, and indiscriminately; mindless of the rank, character, and situation of those with whom he disputes Absolutely ignorant of the several gradations of familiarity or respect, he is exactly the same to his superiors, his equals, and his inferiors; and therefore, by a necessary consequence, absurd to two of the three. Is it possible to love such a man? No; the utmost I can do for him is, to consider him as a respectable Hottentot' (*Letters Written by the Late Earl of Chesterfield to His Son*, 4 vols (London: J. Dodsley, 1774), 3: 129).
2   James Boswell, *Life of Samuel Johnson LL.D.* 2 vols (London: C. Dilly, 1791), 1: 307: henceforth 'Boswell'.
3   Madame D'Arblay, *Memoirs of Dr. Burney*, 3 vols (London: Moxon, 1832), 2: 104–5.
4   Hester Lynch Piozzi, *Letters to and from the late Samuel Johnson, LL.D,* 2 vols (London, A. Strahan and T. Cadell, 1788), 2: 421; henceforth 'SJLetters'.
5   Mary Hyde, *The Thrales of Streatham Park* (Cambridge MA.: Harvard University Press, 1977), p. 22; henceforth 'Hyde'.
6   Biographical Anecdotes, Princeton University Library, Rare Books: Manuscripts Collection: C0199 no. 840q, f. 25.

7 Anna Williams, *Miscellanies in Prose and Verse* (London: T. Davies, 1766), pp. 74–80.
8 It is quite possible that Farmer Dobson's name was chosen by Hester as a sly reference to Thrale's mother's maiden name and obscure origins.
9 Williams, *Miscellanies in Prose and Verse*, pp. 81–9; 82–3.
10 Harvard Piozziana, Houghton Library MS Eng. 1280, 1: 61.
11 Plynlimon (Anglicised from Pumlumon (five peaks) is the source of both the Severn and the Wye, as Hester would have pointed out. Interestingly she later referred to 'The Tale of Floretta or the three Fountains in Miss Williams's Miscellanies' (*Thraliana*, 1: 205), reminding us that Pumlumon is also the source of the Rheidol.
12 Her name which may well have been suggested by Hester, is reminiscent of both 'linnet' and the Welsh name for the goldfinch; Dafydd ap Gwilym in his poem 'Y Llw' (The Oath) addresses his mistress as 'Llawn yw o serch, llinos aur (She is full of love, a goldfinch): http://www.dafyddapgwilym.net/eng/3win.htm
13 Floretta's mother, like Hester's, is ever ready with advice: 'The desire after wealth was raised yet higher by her mother, who was always telling her how much neglect she suffered from want of fortune' ('The fountains: a fairy tale', in Williams, *Miscellanies in Prose and Verse*, pp. 111–41; 129).
14 'To the Rev. Dr. Carter', ll. 17–20 (Montagu Pennington, *Memoirs of the Life of Mrs. Elizabeth Carter* (London: Rivington, 1807), pp. 421–2).
15 'Boswell', 1: 269.
16 Hester Lynch Piozzi, *Anecdotes of the late Samuel Johnson, LL.D.* (London: T. Cadell, 1786), pp. 137–8; subsequently '*Anecdotes*'.
17 Hyde, p. 21.
18 *SJLetters*, 1: 12.
19 Most readers would have supplied the name of 'Mansfield' here: William Murray, first Earl of Mansfield, was Lord Chief Justice and presided over the court of the King's Bench.
20 The following year Hester published 'A Political Alphabet' reflecting the continuing disturbance, and culminating in 'W, was a Widow would make Wilkes a Wife / X, was Xantippe, his living Dear Life' (*Public Advertiser*, 4 August 1769). She later confirmed that the widow was the republican Catharine Macaulay, at whose house Wilkes and his daughter Polly frequently dined. Hester later recalled that the 'Queen of the Bluestockings' Elizabeth Montagu had remarked that General Charles Lee, who defected to the American cause, 'should be condemned to be hanged, and that Catharine Macaulay should save his Life by marrying him under the Gallows' (*Thraliana*, 1: 121).
21 *The False Alarm* (London: T. Cadell, 1770), p. 35.

22 Boswell to Hester Thrale, 5 September 1769; *The Letters of James Boswell*, ed. C. B. Tinker, 2 vols (Oxford: Clarendon Press, 1924), 1: 173.
23 That is, his fifty-ninth.
24 *Prayers and Meditations Composed by Samuel Johnson*, ed. George Strahan (London: T. Cadell, 1785), pp. 81–2.
25 *The Letters of Samuel Johnson*, vol. 2: *1773–1776*, ed. Bruce Redford (Princeton, N.J.: Princeton University Press, 1992), pp. 38–9; cf. his letter of 29 May; 'I wish you could fetch me on Wednesday. I long to be in my own room. Have you got your key? (p. 38).
26 Katharine C. Balderston, 'Johnson's vile melancholy', in *The Age of Johnson: Essays Presented to C. B. Tinker* (New Haven: Yale University Press, 1949), pp. 3–14; 8
27 *Letters of Anna Seward: Written between the Years 1784 and 1807*, 6 vols (Edinburgh: Constable et al., 1811), 2: 103–4.
28 Cited by Clifford, p. 82.
29 *The Letters of Samuel Johnson*, vol. 1: *1731–1772*, ed. Redford, p. 378.
30 *The Westminster Magazine; Or, The Pantheon of Taste*, 1 (March 1773), 178–9.
31 A subsequent 'Memoir' reveals that the 'amorous Brewer will ever be prying into the rarities of his customers'. Mr Th—le is portrayed as having debauched 'Susan D—n', fresh from boarding-school, 'the daughter of an hostess who keeps a celebrated porter-house near St Clements Church in the Strand', whom he wooed not 'in the machine of his occupation, a dray, but in a chariot'. 'No expence was spared [. . .] the Creation was her's', but such was Thrale's 'youth and fire' that he soon returned to the more inventive sexuality of 'the celebrated Mrs. R[eddish]' (Polly Hart) (*The Westminster Magazine; Or, The Pantheon of Taste*, 1 (June 1773), 374–5).

4

1 Peter Mathias, *The Brewing Industry in England, 1700–1830* (Cambridge: Cambridge University Press, 1959), p. 226.
2 A laboratory had been built at Streatham in 1771 for Johnson's experiments into distillation which coincided with Henry Thrale's brewing interests but, realising that Johnson's attempts to distil 'Ætherial liquor' represented a danger to fascinated children, servants and to the near-sighted chemist manqué himself, Thrale insisted that further studies should be exclusively theoretical. See *Anecdotes*, pp. 237–8; *Thraliana*, 2: 982; Frederick Kurzer, 'Chemistry in the Life of Dr Samuel Johnson', *Bulletin of the History of Chemistry*, 29/2 (2004), 65–88.

³ See Henry Thrale's letters to Baverstock in J. A Baverstock, *Treatises on Brewing by the Late James Baverstock* (London: G. and W. B. Whittaker, 1824); and my '"Thrale's Entire": Hester Lynch Thrale and the Anchor Brewery', in *Bluestockings Now! The Evolution of a Social Role*, ed. Deborah Heller (London: Routledge, 2016), pp. 121–38.
⁴ Johnson to Hester, 24 October 1772, *SJLetters*, 1: 59.
⁵ Johnson to Hester, 9 November 1772; *SJLetters*, 1: 65.
⁶ 'You will not let me burst in ignorance of your transaction with Alexander' (Johnson to Hester, 9 March 1773; *The Letters of Samuel Johnson*, ed. Redford, 2: 17).
⁷ Hester to Johnson, 10 March 1773, cited in Hyde, p. 60.
⁸ Johnson to Hester, 20 March 1773; *SJLetters*, 1: 78–9.
⁹ Rylands MS 616.
¹⁰ Lawrence Stone, *The Family, Sex, and Marriage in England 1500–1800* (New York: Harper and Row, 1977), p. 463.
¹¹ *Dr Johnson and Mrs Thrale's Tour in North Wales*, ed. Adrian Bristow (Wrexham: Bridge Books, 1995), p. 90; henceforth 'Bristow'.
¹² James Boswell, *The Life of Samuel Johnson, including A Journal of a Tour to the Hebrides*, 2 vols (Boston: Carter, Hendee and Co., 1832), 1: 485.
¹³ *British Synonymy, or an Attempt at Regulating the Choice of Words in Familiar Conversation*, 2 vols (London: G. G. and J. Robinson, 1794), 1: 82. Henceforth '*Synonymy*' cited in parentheses in the text.
¹⁴ *A Diary of a Journey into North Wales, in the year 1774*, ed. R. Duppa (London: Robert Jennings, 1816), p. 93. Duppa also cites a letter of Johnson to Mrs Thrale of 15 September 1777: 'Boswell wants to see Wales; but except the woods of *Bach y Graig*, what is there in Wales, that can fill the hunger of ignorance, or quench the thirst of curiosity' (p. 53).
¹⁵ I should like to underscore the anonymous reader's comment: 'Few eighteenth-century Welsh writers long resident in England continued to identify as strongly with their homeland.'
¹⁶ *Cambrian Register*, 3 (1818), 500–2; also published in the Bangor weekly English-language newspaper, the *North Welsh Gazette*, 24 May 1818, p. 4. A certain mystery surrounds the authorship of this poem, suggesting that 'Lines on Bodfel Hall' was written by Edmund Hyde Hall (d. 16 October 1824) who was born in the parish of Trelawney, Jamaica, and whose links with Wales encouraged him to complete *A Description of Caernarvonshire (1809–1811)*, ed. Emyr Gwynne Jones (Caernarvon: Gwenlyn Evans, 1952). In a letter to her eldest daughter (now Viscountess Keith), of 31 July 1810 Hester inquires: 'Did you see a Journey thro' Caernarfonshire advertised? The Traveller has done poor little Bodvel my Birthplace, the Honour to write Verses on it; and as he

sent me several Copies I will enclose one if it will not overweight the Frank. The Author is unknown to me, — Doctor Thackeray says his Name is *Hall*. But it is high Time to sign my own Name to all this Nonsense. Could it indeed have been written by anyone except Dear Lady Keith's Affectionate Mother' (*PLetters*, 4: 301–4). The conscientious editors, the Blooms, accept Hall's authorship, apparently ignoring Hester's typically playful rhetorical question. Alexander Lindsay, however, places 'Lines on Bodfel Hall' amongst HLTP's verse in his *Index of English Literary Manuscripts* (London and Washington: Mansell, 1997), vol. 3, part 4, p. 168. The jury must remain out on this matter.

17. *The Patriot. Addressed to the Electors of Great Britain* (London: T. Cadell, 1774), pp. 15–16.
18. A letter of Hester to Johnson, dated 19 April 1773, reads: 'Mrs. Plumbe & her Daughter & young Mr. Rice the Girls Lover are now here, begging my Master's Influence over Old Sammy or his consent for the Clandestine Marriage' (cited in *Thraliana*, 2: 711).
19. Letter of 1 June 1773 from Hester to Frances Rice, cited in Percy Melville Thornton, *Some Things We Have Remembered* (London: Longmans, 1912), p. 72.
20. *The Works of Dr. Jonathan Swift* (London: C. Bathurst and J. Hinton, 1765), 4: 54–68; 61.
21. Mary Wollstonecraft, *A Vindication of the Rights of Woman* (London: J. Johnson, 1792), pp. 228–9.
22. *The Letters of Samuel Johnson with Mrs. Thrale's Genuine Letters to Him*, ed. R. W. Chapman, 3 vols (Oxford: Clarendon Press, 1952), 2: 59: henceforth 'Chapman'.

5

1. *The French Journals of Mrs Thrale and Doctor Johnson*, ed. Moses Tyson and Henry Guppy (Manchester: Manchester University Press, 1932), p. 69; henceforth *'French Journals'*.
2. *European Magazine and London Review*, 13 (May 1788), 313–14.
3. *The Letters of Samuel Johnson*, ed. Redford, 2: 311.
4. *The Letters of Samuel Johnson*, ed. Redford, 2: 313.
5. Clifford, p.144.
6. *Mrs Montagu 'Queen of the Blues': Her letters from 1762 to 1800*, ed. Reginald Blunt, 2 vols, (London: Constable, 1923), 2: 154.
7. Clifford, p.164.

8   *Diary and Letters of Madame D'Arblay*, ed. Charlotte Barrett, 7 vols (London: Colburn, 1842–6), 1: 61.
9   Clifford, p. 157.
10 Reginald Blunt (ed.), *Mrs Montagu 'Queen of the Blues': Her letters from 1762 to 1800*, two vols (London: Constable, 1923), 2: 43, 60.
11 'A Tale for the Times. To Sir Philip Jennings Clarke', the last line of which described the opponents of the American war as 'No longer Hounds—but *Newfoundlanders*', *Public Advertiser*, 28 November 1778.
12 Clifford, p. 175; Hyde, p. 220.
13 *Three Dialogues by Hester Lynch Thrale from the Hitherto Unpublished Original Manuscript Now in the Possession of the John Rylands Library*, ed. Morris Zamick, *Bulletin of the John Rylands Library*, 16/1 (January 1932), 97–114; 101.
14 *Diary and Letters of Madame D'Arblay*, 2: 46. Hester thought Elizabeth 'a monkey though to quarrel with Johnson so about Lyttelton's Life; if he was a great character, nothing said of him in that book can hurt him' (*Thraliana*, 1: 495).
15 *Diary and Letters of Madame D'Arblay*, 1: 312.
16 *Diary and Letters of Madame D'Arblay*, 1: 325.
17 Clifford, p. 187.
18 See James Van Horn, *The Rise of the Public in Enlightenment Europe* (Cambridge: Cambridge University Press, 2001), p. 25.
19 *Diary and Letters of Madame D'Arblay*, 2: 8.
20 *The Queeney Letters, being letters addressed to Hester Maria Thrale by Doctor Johnson, Fanny Burney and Mrs. Thrale-Piozzi*, ed. Henry William Edmund, Marquis of Lansdowne (New York: Farrar & Rinehart, 1934), p. 60. See *Thraliana*, 1: 550.

6

1   *The Additional Journals and Letters of Frances Burney*, ed. Stewart Cooke and Elaine Bander (Oxford: Oxford University Press, 2015), p. 139.
2   *PLetters*, 1: 81–2.
3   Hester might well have been reading Richard Jago, *Poems, Moral and Descriptive* (London: J. Dodsley, 1784), p. xxiv, who 'thought a preface as essential to the figure of a book, as a portico is to that of a building'.
4   Clifford, p. 262.
5   *Monthly Review*, 76 (May 1786), 373–83; 379–80.
6   See Piozzi's Postscript, dated Naples, 10 February 1786, *Anecdotes*, concluding page.

7   *London Chronicle*, 18–20 April 1786.
8   Quoted by McCarthy, *Hester Thrale Piozzi*, p.109.
9   This strange tract introduces Piozzi as 'the priestess of our Pig; [Johnson] a lady who had acquired the Greek language without losing her own, and whose manners and latinity were both equally pure'. But even this Johnson-loather reveals a certain sympathy for his abandoned boar/bore: 'How great therefore must have been his grief, when he afterwards saw his fair provider melt away into the arms of a soft, but doubtless sinewy Signor, and bathe herself, as it is yet her fortune to do, in the voluptuous warmths of Italy', *Anecdotes of the Learned Pig* (London: T. Hookham, 1786), p. 20.
10 *The Florence Miscellany* (Florence: Printed for G. Cam, 1785), p. 6.
11 Steve Clark, '"Amphibious Grown": Hester Thrale, Della Crusca and the Italian origins of British Romanticism', in *British Romanticism in European Perspective: Into the Eurozone*, ed. Steve Clark and Tristanne Connolly (Basingstoke: Palgrave Macmillan, 2015), pp. 89–112; 103.
12 Reginald Blunt (ed.), *Mrs Montagu 'Queen of the Blues': Her Letters and Friendships from 1762 to 1800*, 2 vols (London: Constable, 1923), 2: 278.
13 William Roberts (ed.), *Memoirs of the Life and Correspondence of Mrs Hannah More*, 2 vols (New York: Harper, 1834), 1: 282.
14 *Diary and Letters of Madame D'Arblay*, 2: 444.
15 McCarthy, *Hester Thrale Piozzi*, p. 141.
16 *Gentleman's Magazine*, 58/1 (1788), 233.
17 See Bruce Redford, *The Converse of the Pen: Acts of Intimacy in the Eighteenth-Century Familiar Letter* (Chicago and London: University of Chicago Press, 1986), pp. 206–44; 227, 213.
18 Giuseppe Baretti, *The Sentimental Mother, A Comedy in Five Acts; The Legacy of an old Friend, and His Last Moral Lesson to Mrs. Hester Lynch Thrale, now Mrs Hester Lynch Piozzi* (London: Ridgway, 1789).
19 *Diary and Letters of Madame D'Arblay*, 5: 30.

7

1 Quoted by Deborah Kennedy, *Helen Maria Williams and the Age of Revolution* (Lewisburg: Bucknell University Press, 2001), p. 90.
2 To Hester Maria Thrale, 13 November 1793 (*PLetters*, 2: 150).
3 *The Laurel of Liberty, by Robert Merry, A.M. Member of the Royal Academy of Florence* (London: John Bell, 1790), p. 26.
4 Laura Maria, *Ainsi Va Le Monde* (London: John Bell, 1790), p. 8.
5 *The Baviad* (London: R. Faulder, 1791), p. 8
6 William Gifford, *The Baviad and Mæviad* (London: J. Wright, 1797), p. viii.

7 McCarthy, *Hester Thrale Piozzi*, p. 186.
8 John Trusler, *The Difference, between Words, esteemed Synonymous, in the English Language; And the Proper Choice of them determined: Together with, So much of Abbé Girard's Treatise, on this subject, as would agree, with our Mode of Expression. Useful to all, who would, either write or speak, with Propriety, and, Elegance* (London: Parsons, 1766).
9 *Monthly Review* 15 (November, 1794), 241–51, 371–80; 241.
10 To Samuel Lysons. 5 March [1792] (*PLetters*, 2: 50).
11 To the Revd Leonard Chappelow, 21 October 1793 (*PLetters*, 2: 144).
12 To Penelope Sophia Pennington, 2 December 1793 (*PLetters*, 2: 152).
13 To Penelope Sophia Pennington, 11 February 1794 (*PLetters*, 2: 167).
14 To Penelope Sophia Pennington, 26 April 1794 (*PLetters*, 2: 172–4, and see note 6).
15 To the Revd Leonard Chappelow, 22 December 1794 (*PLetters*, 2: 221, and see note 3).
16 *Monthly Review*, 15 (November, 1794), 241–51, 371–80; 243.
17 *Critical Review*, 12 (October, 1794), 121–8; 122.
18 *Critical Review*, 12 (October, 1794), 121–8; 124.
19 *Analytical Review*, 19: 3 (July, 1794), 146–52; 151.
20 To Penelope Sophia Pennington, 22 May [1793] (*PLetters*, 2: 120).
21 Edward Hubbard, *The Buildings of Wales: Clwyd and Denbighshire* (New Haven and London: Yale University Press, 1986), pp. 450–1.
22 To Penelope Sophia Pennington. 15 September 1792 (*PLetters*, 2: 68).
23 To Penelope Sophia Pennington, 22 May 1793 (*PLetters*, 2: 119, and note 8).
24 *PLetters*, 2: 130, note 11. Lloyd had already received £1,280 15s. 0d, paid £1,384 16s. 0d and would have to 'pay large sums more'.
25 *The Exhibition of the Royal Academy*, 26 (London: Joseph Cooper, 1794), p. 21.
26 *Universal Magazine*, 103 (1798), 375.
27 To Penelope Sophia Pennington, 25 July 1794 (*PLetters*, 2: 185).
28 To the Revd Leonard Chappelow, 2 August 1794 (*PLetters*, 2: 187).
29 To Penelope Sophia Pennington, 4 August 1794 (*PLetters*, 2: 189).
30 To Sarah Siddons [née Kemble], Wednesday, 27 August [1794] (*PLetters* 2: 197–200).
31 Rylands MS.574.19, cited in *PLetters*, 2: 197–200, n. 4.
32 To Sarah Siddons, 17 August [1794] (*PLetters*, 2, 197). The poem was also published in *The Oracle and Public Advertiser* of 24 June 1796; see *PLetters*, 2: 359, note 11.
33 Hester refers to the 'swift-speeding guillotine' as banishing the horrors of the rack, in her *British Synonymy*, 2: 397. She had also read of the 'Halifax Maiden', a machine long predating that of Dr Joseph-Ignace

Guillotin, in her friend Thomas Pennant's A *Tour of Scotland*, 2 vols (London: Benjamin White), 1776), 2: 363–5.

34   To Hester Maria Thrale, 17 September 1794 (*PLetters*, 2: 208).
35   To Hester Maria Thrale, 17 September 1794 (*PLetters*, 2: 208).
36   To Samuel Lysons, 5 September 1794 (*PLetters*, 2: 201).
37   To Hester Maria Thrale, 19 November 1794 (*PLetters*, 2: 214).
38   She pointed out to Mrs Pennington the articles in *British Synonymy* on 'SYMBOL, TYPE, EMBLEM, FIGURE, SIGN, IMPRESE, DEVICE &c' and 'NAME, NOUN, PROPER, NOMINAL DISTINCTION, APPELATIVE' which revealed her belief in biblical prophecy in the Book of Revelation; to Penelope Sophia Pennington, 11 February 1794 (*PLetters*, 2: 168, note 5).
39   To Samuel Lysons, 14 March 1795 (*PLetters*, 2: 247).
40   To Hester Maria Thrale, 28 January 1795 (*PLetters*, 2: 233).
41   To Penelope Sophia Pennington, 7 February 1793 (*PLetters*, 2: 106 and see note 15).
42   To the Revd Leonard Chappelow, 27 January 1795 (*PLetters*, 2: 230).
43   Ffion Mair Jones, *Welsh Ballads of the French Revolution 1793–1815* (Cardiff: University of Wales Press, 2012), p. 1.
44   To the Rt. Revd Dr Robert Gray, bishop of Bristol, Wednesday 13 May 1801 (*PLetters,* 3: 281). The Blooms ascribe the translation to the Methodist Edward Barnes, as does Marion Loeffler, *Political Pamphlets and Sermons from Wales 1790–1806* (Cardiff: University of Wales Press, 2014), p. 52. In 1803, however, Hester cites Denbighshire-born John Roberts (1775–1829), curate of Tremeirchion, as the translator; to Penelope Sophia Pennington, 31 July 1803 (*PLetters*, 3: 423, and note 4).
45   To Hester Maria Thrale. 3 April [1795] (*PLetters*, 2: 256–7). Note 4 gives details from the *Chester Courant*, 21 April 1795.
46   See Elizabeth Edwards, 'The voices of war: poetry from Wales 1794–1804', in *'Footsteps of Liberty and Revolt': Essays on Wales and the French Revolution*, ed. Mary-Ann Constantine and Dafydd Johnston (Cardiff: University of Wales Press, 2013), pp. 271–90; 277.
47   To the Revd Daniel Lysons, [24 March 1796] (*PLetters*, 2: 325).
48   Cecilia Margaretta Mostyn to Hester Lynch Piozzi, 9 June 1795 (*PLetters*, 2: 264).
49   To Penelope Sophia Pennington, [21 December] 1796 (*PLetters*, 2: 409, note 1).
50   To Hester Maria Thrale, [8] January 1796 (*PLetters*, 2: 294).
51   To Hester Maria Thrale, 21 December [1796] (*PLetters*, 2, 411; see note 16).

52   See Ellen Gill, *Naval Families, War and Duty in Britain, 1740–1820* (Woodbridge: Boydell and Brewer, 2016), p. 217.
53   To Penelope Sophia Pennington. 10 January 1798 (*PLetters*, 2: 467).
54   To Robert Ray, 20 January 1798 (*PLetters*, 2: 470; see note 9).
55   *Three Warnings to John Bull before he Dies. By an Old Acquaintance of the Public* (London: R. Faulder, 1798), p. 4. See also letter to Penelope Sophia Pennington, [29] April 1798 (*PLetters*, 2: 491 and note 6).
56   To the Revd Reynold Davies, 7 November 1813 (*Letters*, 5: 214)

8

1   To the Revd Leonard Chappelow, *c*.6–7 January 1799 (*PLetters*, 3: 49).
2   To Lady Margaret Williams, 10 February 1799 (*PLetters*, 3: 55).
3   To the Revd Leonard Chappelow, 22 May 1799 (*PLetters*, 3: 99).
4   To the Revd Reynold Davies, 9 November 1799 (*PLetters*, 3: 143).
5   To the Revd Reynold Davies, 22 January 1800 (*PLetters*, 3: 162, note 6).
6   To Lady Margaret Williams, 1 February 1801 (*PLetters*, 3: 262).
7   To Penelope Sophia Pennington, 21 August 1799 (*PLetters*, 3: 120).
8   To the Revd Leonard Chappelow, 2 December 1799 (*PLetters*, 3: 152).
9   To the Revd Leonard Chappelow, 21 April 1800 (*PLetters*, 3: 179).
10   To the Revd Leonard Chappelow, 7 July 1800 (*PLetters*, 3: 214).
11   To Penelope Sophia Pennington [née Weston], *c*.26 July 1800 (*PLetters*, 3: 216, and n. 11).
12   To the Revd Leonard Chappelow, 19 September 1800 (*PLetters*, 3: 225).
13   To the Revd Reynold Davies, 29 March 1800 (*PLetters*, 3: 176).
14   To Hester Maria Thrale, 23 September 1800 (*PLetters*, 3: 228).
15   Hester Lynch Piozzi, *Retrospection: or A Review of the Most Striking and Important Events, Characters, Situations, and Their Consequences which the Last Eighteen Hundred Years Have Presented to the View of Mankind*, 2 vols (London: Stockdale, 1801), 1: 243. Henceforth '*Retrospection*' in the text.
16   To the Revd Leonard Chappelow, 30 June 1800 (*PLetters*, 3: 211).
17   *European Magazine and London Review*, 39 (March 1801), 188–93; (April 1801), 271–6.
18   *Antijacobin Review and Magazine*, 8 (March 1801), 241–6.
19   *Critical Review*, 32 (May 1801), 28–36.
20   *British Critic*, 19 (April 1802), 355–8.
21   See McCarthy, *Hester Thrale Piozzi*, p. 211. Marnie Hughes-Warrington, 'Writing on the Margins of the World: Hester Lynch Piozzi's "Retrospection" (1801) as Middlebrow Art?', *Journal of World History*, 23: 4 (December 2012), 883–906; 884, claims Piozzi was preceded by Lucy

Peacock, *A Chronological Abridgement of Universal History: To Which is Added, an Abridged Chronology of the Most Remarkable Discoveries and Inventions Relative to the Arts and Sciences* (1800). However, this was a translation from the French of M. La Croze.

22. To Penelope Sophia Pennington, 17 July 1799 (*PLetters*, 3: 113).
23. To the Revd Leonard Chappelow, 2 March 1803 (*PLetters*, 1: 397).
24. To Penelope Sophia Pennington, 2 June 1802 (*PLetters*, 1: 356).
25. To Hester Maria Thrale, 20 September 1803 (*PLetters*, 3: 430, note 1).
26. To Penelope Sophia Pennington, 31 July 1803 (*PLetters*, 3: 423).
27. Cf. 'Now the lone Traveller his Pathway lost / Creeps by old Oceans Edge, and shuns the Vale; / Sees strew'd with Wreck our Billow-beaten Coast / And hears the hoarse Gull screaming to the Gale', 'A Winter in Wales to Mrs Hoare', ll. 5–8, *Thraliana* 2: 1085. One of Hester's most powerful poems, which she sent to her daughter Sophia, receives a masterly analysis from William McCarthy, *Hester Thrale Piozzi*, pp. 88–90.
28. To Hester Maria Thrale, 11 August 1807 (*PLetters*, 4: 147).
29. To Hester Maria Thrale, 17 October 1807 (*PLetters*, 4: 153).
30. To Hester Maria Thrale, 22 November 1807 (*PLetters*, 4: 159).
31. To John Salusbury Piozzi, 9 September 1809 (*PLetters*, 4: 246).
32. To John Salusbury Piozzi, 16 July 1810 (*PLetters*, 4: 296).
33. John, however, never attempted to have them published after her death, and indeed would not allow access to her papers. He had urged her to burn *Thraliana* as he dreaded more scandal and notoriety.
34. To Hester Maria Elphinstone, Viscountess Keith [née Thrale], 17 January 1814 (*PLetters*, 5: 235).
35. To Alexander Leak, 6 February 1813 (*PLetters*, 5: 171).
36. To John Salusbury Piozzi, 19 April 1813 (*PLetters*, 5: 179). In 1816 she had to sell the contents of Streatham Park, including most of the Reynolds portraits in order to settle the costs the house had incurred. She then installed a tenant who agreed to pay all further maintenance in return for a low rent.
37. To the Revd Reynold Davies, 7 November 1813 (*PLetters*, 5: 214).
38. To Hester Maria Elphinstone, Viscountess Keith, 17 January 1814 (*PLetters*, 5: 234).

Bibliography

Manuscript Sources

Bath Central Library, letters to Sophy Pugh.
British Library (BL), correspondence with her daughter and others, RP 812, 5318.
BL, letters to Charles Burney and his family, M/440.
BL, correspondence with Frances Burney, Egerton MS 3695, RP 5318.
BL, letters to Alexander Leak, M/572, RP 766 (copies).
BL, letters to Clement Mead, RP 293 (copies).
Harvard University, Houghton Library, letters, mainly to Mr and Mrs Edward Mangin.
Harvard University, Houghton Library, 'Harvard Piozziana', MS Eng. 1280.
Hertfordshire Archives, letters to the Rice family of Tooting, Misc. Vol. X, D/X44, D.X98,
National Library of Wales (NLW), Bachegraig estate papers, incl. diaries and correspondence.
NLW, correspondence with Hugh Griffith.
NLW, letters to John Lloyd.
Princeton, Firestone Library: MS 3891.8.313.
Princeton University Library, Biographical Anecdotes, Rare Books: Manuscripts Collection: C0199 no. 840q, f. 25.
John Rylands Library (JRL), letters to Williams family of Bodelwyddan.
JRL, GB 133 Eng. MS 534.
JRL, GB 133 Eng. MS 536, 23.
JRL, GB MS.574.19.

Newspapers and Periodicals

Analytical Review.
Antijacobin Review and Magazine.
Cambrian Register.
Chester Courant.
Critical Review.
European Magazine and London Review.
Gentleman's Magazine.
North Welsh Gazette.
Political Controversy: or, Weekly Magazine of Ministerial and Antiministerial Essays.
Public Advertiser.
St James's Chronicle.
The London Chronicle.
The London Magazine, or, Gentleman's Monthly Intelligencer.
The Monthly Mirror.
The Monthly Review.
The Oracle and Public Advertiser.
The Westminster Magazine; Or, The Pantheon of Taste.
Universal Magazine.

Hester Lynch Thrale Piozzi: Principal Published Writings

Piozzi, Hester Lynch Thrale, 'The Three Warnings. A Tale'; this first appeared in Anna Williams, *Miscellanies in Prose and Verse* (London: T. Davies, 1766), pp. 174–80.
— *The Florence Miscellany* (Florence: Printed for G. Cam, 1785).
— *Anecdotes of the late Samuel Johnson, LL.D.* (London: T. Cadell, 1786).
— *Letters to and from the late Samuel Johnson, LL.D*, 2 vols (London: A. Strahan and T. Cadell, 1788).
— *Observations and Reflections Made in the Course of a Journey through France, Italy and Germany*, 2 vols (London: A. Strahan and T. Cadell, 1789).
— *British Synonymy*, 2 vols (London: G. G. and J. Robinson, 1794).
— *Three Warnings to John Bull before he Dies. By an Old Acquaintance of the Public* (London: R. Faulder, 1798).
— *Retrospection: or A Review of the Most Striking and Important Events, Characters, Situations, and Their Consequences which the Last Eighteen Hundred Years Have Presented to the View of Mankind*, 2 vols (London: Stockdale, 1801).

— *Autobiography, Letters and Literary Remains of Mrs. Piozzi (Thrale)*, ed. Abraham Hayward, 2 vols (London: Longman, 1861).
— *Three Dialogues by Hester Lynch Thrale from the Hitherto Unpublished Original Manuscript Now in the Possession of the John Rylands Library*, ed. Morris Zamick, *Bulletin of the John Rylands Library*, 16/1 (January 1932), 97–114.
— *The French Journals of Mrs. Thrale and Doctor Johnson*, ed. Moses Tyson and Henry Guppy (Manchester: Manchester University Press, 1932).
— *The Queeney Letters, being letters addressed to Hester Maria Thrale by Doctor Johnson, Fanny Burney and Mrs. Thrale-Piozzi*, ed. Henry William Edmund, Marquis of Lansdowne (New York: Farrar & Rinehart, 1934).
— *Thraliana: The Diary of Mrs. Hester Lynch Thrale (later Mrs. Piozzi) 1776–1809*, ed. Katharine C. Balderston, 2 vols (Oxford: Clarendon Press, 1951).
— *The Piozzi Letters: Correspondence of Hester Lynch Piozzi 1784–1821*, ed. Edward Bloom and Lillian D. Bloom, 6 vols (Newark: University of Delaware Press, 1991).

Primary Sources

Allison, James, 'Mrs. Thrale's Marginalia in Joseph Warton's "Essay"', *Huntington Library Quarterly*, 19/2 (February 1956), 155–64.
Anon., *Anecdotes of the Learned Pig* (London: T. Hookham, 1786).
Baretti, Giuseppe, *The Sentimental Mother, A Comedy in Five Acts; The Legacy of an old Friend, and His Last Moral Lesson to Mrs. Hester Lynch Thrale, now Mrs Hester Lynch Piozzi* (London: Ridgway, 1789).
Boswell, James, *The Letters of James Boswell*, ed. C. B. Tinker, 2 vols (Oxford: Clarendon Press, 1924).
Bristow, Adrian, *Dr Johnson and Mrs Thrale's Tour in North Wales* (Wrexham: Bridge Books, 1995).
Broadley, A. M., *Doctor Johnson and Mrs. Thrale* (London and New York: John Lane, 1910).
Chesterfield, Philip Dormer Stanhope, fourth Earl of, *Letters Written by the Late Earl of Chesterfield to His Son*, 4 vols (London: J. Dodsley, 1774).
D'Arblay, Madame, née Frances Burney, *Diary and Letters of Madame D'Arblay*, ed. Charlotte Barrett, 7 vols (London: Colburn, 1842–6).
— *The Additional Journals and Letters of Frances Burney*, ed. Stewart Cooke and Elaine Bander (Oxford: Oxford University Press, 2015).
Duppa, R., *A Diary of a Journey into North Wales, in the year 1774* (London: Robert Jennings, 1816).

Gifford, William, *The Baviad* (London: R. Faulder, 1791).
— *The Baviad and Mæviad* (London: J. Wright, 1797).
Gill, Ellen, *Naval Families, War and Duty in Britain, 1740–1820* (Woodbridge: Boydell and Brewer, 2016).
Hall, Edmund Hyde, *A Description of Caernarvonshire (1809–1811)*, ed. Emyr Gwynne Jones (Caernarvon: Gwenlyn Evans, 1952).
Hawkins, Laetitia-Matilda, *Memoirs, Anecdotes, Facts and Opinions*, 2 vols (London: Longman et al., 1824).
Johnson, Samuel, *The False Alarm* (London: T. Cadell, 1770).
— *The Patriot. Addressed to the Electors of Great Britain* (London: T. Cadell, 1774).
— *Prayers and Meditations Composed by Samuel Johnson*, ed. George Strahan (London: T. Cadell, 1785).
— *The Letters of Samuel Johnson, LL.D.*, ed. G. B. Hill, 2 vols (Oxford: Clarendon Press, 1892).
— *The Letters of Samuel Johnson with Mrs. Thrale's Genuine Letters to Him*, ed. R. W. Chapman, 3 vols (Oxford: Clarendon Press, 1952).
— *The Letters of Samuel Johnson*, ed. Bruce Redford, 5 vols (Princeton: Princeton University Press, 1993).
'Laura Maria' [Mary Robinson], *Ainsi va le monde* (London: John Bell, 1790).
Merry, Robert, *The Laurel of Liberty, by Robert Merry, A.M. Member of the Royal Academy of Florence* (London: John Bell, 1790).
Netto (Nieto), Isaac, *A Sermon Preached in the Jews Synagogue, on Friday, February 6, 1756* (London: printed for the author by Richard Reily, 1756).
Pennant, Thomas, *The Literary Life of the late Thomas Pennant Esq., by himself* (London: White, 1793).
Pindar, Peter [John Wolcot], *Bozzy and Piozzi, or The British Biographers, A Town Eclogue* (London: G. Kearsley, 1786).
Pope, Alexander, *An Essay on Man* (London: L. Gilliver, 1734).
Rompkey, Ronald (ed), *Expeditions of Honour: The Journal of John Salusbury in Halifax, Nova Scotia, 1749–53* (Newark: University of Delaware Press, 1982).
Seward, Anna, *Letters of Anna Seward: Written between the Years 1784 and 1807*, 6 vols (Edinburgh: Constable et al., 1811).
Swift, Jonathan, *The Works of Dr. Jonathan Swift* (London: C. Bathurst and J. Hinton, 1765).
Trusler, John, *The Difference, between Words, esteemed Synonymous, in the English Language; And the Proper Choice of them determined: Together*

with, So much of Abbé Girard's Treatise, on this subject, as would agree, with our Mode of Expression. Useful to all, who would, either write or speak, with Propriety, and, Elegance (London: Parsons, 1766).
Williams, Anna, *Miscellanies in Prose and Verse* (London: T. Davies, 1766).

Secondary Sources

Anon., *The [Twenty-Sixth] Exhibition of the Royal Academy, 1794* (London: Joseph Cooper, 1794).

Balderston, Katharine C., 'Johnson's vile melancholy', in *The Age of Johnson: Essays Presented to C. B. Tinker* (New Haven: Yale University Press, 1949).

Baverstock, J. A., *Treatises on Brewing by the Late James Baverstock* (London: G. and W. B. Whittaker, 1824).

Blunt, Reginald (ed.), *Mrs Montagu 'Queen of the Blues': Her letters from 1762 to 1800*, 2 vols, (London: Constable, 1923).

Boswell, James, *Life of Samuel Johnson LL.D*. 2 vols. (London: C. Dilly, 1791).

Cash, Arthur, *John Wilkes: The Scandalous Father of Civil Liberty* (New Haven: Yale University Press, 2007).

Clark, Steve, '"Amphibious Grown": Hester Thrale, Della Crusca and the Italian origins of British Romanticism', in *British Romanticism in European Perspective: Into the Eurozone*, ed. Steve Clark and Tristanne Connolly (Basingstoke: Palgrave Macmillan, 2015).

Clifford, James L, *Hester Lynch Piozzi (Mrs. Thrale)*, second edn. (Oxford: Clarendon Press, 1987).

D'Arblay, Madame, *Memoirs of Dr. Burney*, 3 vols (London: Moxon, 1832).

Edwards, Elizabeth, 'The voices of war: poetry from Wales 1794–1804', in *'Footsteps of Liberty and Revolt': Essays on Wales and the French Revolution*, ed. Mary-Ann Constantine and Dafydd Johnston (Cardiff: University of Wales Press, 2013).

Franklin, Michael J., '"Thrale's Entire": Hester Lynch Thrale and the Anchor Brewery', in *Bluestockings Now! The Evolution of a Social Role*, ed. Deborah Heller (London: Routledge, 2016), pp. 121–38.

Hubbard, Edward, *The Buildings of Wales: Clwyd and Denbighshire* (New Haven and London: Yale University Press, 1986).

Hughes-Warrington, Marnie, 'Writing on the Margins of the World: Hester Lynch Piozzi's "Retrospection" (1801) as Middlebrow Art?', *Journal of World History*, 23/4 (December 2012), 883–906.

Hyde, Mary, *The Thrales of Streatham Park* (Cambridge MA.: Harvard University Press, 1977).

Jones, Ffion Mair, *Welsh Ballads of the French Revolution 1793–1815* (Cardiff: University of Wales Press, 2012).

Kennedy, Deborah, *Helen Maria Williams and the Age of Revolution* (Lewisburg: Bucknell University Press, 2001).

Kurzer, Frederick, 'Chemistry in the Life of Dr Samuel Johnson', *Bulletin of the History of Chemistry*, 29/2 (2004), 65–88.

Lindsay, Alexander, *Index of English Literary Manuscripts* (London and Washington: Mansell, 1997).

Mathias, Peter, *The Brewing Industry in England, 1700–1830* (Cambridge: Cambridge University Press, 1959).

Mayáns Y Siscár, Gregorio, *Vida de Miguel de Cervantes Saavedra* (Briga-Real, 1737).

Mayáns Y Siscár, Gregorio, *The Life of Michael De Cervantes Saavedra, Written by Don Gregorio Mayáns Y Siscár, Translated by Mr. Ozell* (London: J. and R. Tonson, 1738).

McCarthy, William, *Hester Thrale Piozzi: Portrait of a Literary Woman* (Chapel Hill and London, University of North Carolina, 1985).

— 'A Verse "Essay on Man" by H. L. Piozzi', *The Age of Johnson*, 2 (1989), 375–420.

McIntyre, Ian, *Hester: The Remarkable Life of Dr. Johnson's 'Dear Mistress'* (London: Constable, 2008).

Peacock, Lucy, *A Chronological Abridgement of Universal History: To Which is Added, an Abridged Chronology of the Most Remarkable Discoveries and Inventions Relative to the Arts and Sciences* (1800).

Pennington, Montagu, *Memoirs of the Life of Mrs. Elizabeth Carter* (London: Rivington, 1807).

Redford, Bruce, *The Converse of the Pen: Acts of Intimacy in the Eighteenth-Century Familiar Letter* (Chicago and London: University of Chicago Press, 1986).

Roberts, William (ed.), *Memoirs of the Life and Correspondence of Mrs Hannah More*, 2 vols (New York: Harper, 1834).

Stone, Lawrence, *The Family, Sex, and Marriage in England 1500–1800* (New York: Harper and Row, 1977).

Thornton, Percy Melville, *Some Things We Have Remembered* (London: Longmans, 1912).

Van Horn, James, *The Rise of the Public in Enlightenment Europe* (Cambridge: Cambridge University Press, 2001).

Voltaire [François Marie Arouet], *Voltaire in his Letters*, trans. Evelyn Beatrice Hall [pseud. S. G. Tallentyre] (New York and London: G. P. Putnam's Sons, 1919).

Wollstonecraft, Mary, *A Vindication of the Rights of Woman* (London: J. Johnson, 1792).

Index

Accademia della Crusca 106
Accademia Fiorentina 106
Addison, Joseph 31
Alexander, Thomas 57, 58
Alfieri, Count Vittorio 105
Alighieri, Dante 106
American Revolutionary War 66, 83, 87, 153
Amiens Cathedral 72
Analytical Review 117, 130
Anchor Brewery 20, 44, 52, 53–9, 83–4, 87, 90
Anglicanism 87, 94, 128, 130, 154, 160
Anglo-Cherokee War (1759–60) 17
Anti-Jacobin or, Weekly Examiner 123–4
anti-Jacobinism 102, 103, 123–4, 133, 137, 138–9, 141–2, 163
Antijacobin Review and Magazine 153
Arianrhod 25
Ariosto, Ludovico 14
Arouet, François-Marie (known as Voltaire) 14
Ashbourne 51, 60, 61, 67
Astell, Mary, *A Serious Proposal to the Ladies* 73

Bach, Johann Christian 28
Bachegraig 1, 16, 59, 61, 77, 91, 131, 148
Bagot, Lewis, bishop of St Asaph 135
Baillie, Joanna, *Plays on the Passions* 155
Balderston, Katharine C. 48
Bangor 112, 159
Barbauld, Anna Laetitia 42
Barclay, David 90
Barclay, Robert 90

Barère de Vieuzac, Bertrand 134
Baretti, Giuseppe Marc'Antonio
    Baretti 70, 71, 72, 73, 74, 75, 76, 77, 82, 116
    French translation of Johnson's *Rasselas* 73
Bath 76, 77, 78, 86, 92, 94, 119, 147, 160, 162, 163
Bathurst, Richard 49
Baverstock, James 53
Beauclerk, Topham 101
Beaumaris Castle 64
Bell, John 122
Berain, Catrin of, 'Mam Cymru' 3, 161
Bible 7, 107, 150, 155, 160, 163
Blake, William 155
Blount, Martha, 'Patty' 46
Bluestockings 37, 68, 79, 80, 81, 89, 94, 96, 100, 125, 154
Boccaccio, Giovanni 106
Bodvel or Bodfel Hall 1, 2, 3, 63–4
Boileau-Despréaux, Nicolas, 'Epistle to his Gardener' 36
Boothby, Mrs Hill 111
Boscawen, Frances 80, 81
Boston Tea Party 66
Boswell, James 38, 45, 47, 48, 71, 96, 101, 111, 113, 116, 122
    Account of Corsica 45
    Journal of a Tour to the Hebrides 96, 100, 115
Bowdler, Henrietta Maria 86
Bowdler, Thomas (brother and sister collaborated on *The Family Shakespeare*) 86, 89
Bowles, Revd William Lisle 162
Brescia, Lombardy 140, 142 144

Index

brewing 27, 34, 53–8, 76, 85, 115
Bridges, Edward 5–6
Brighton 32, 33, 55, 69, 77, 80, 85, 88, 90
British Critic 130, 154
Bromfield, Robert 51, 67
Brooke, Francis 46
Brothers, Richard, *Revealed Knowledge of the Prophecies and Times* 136
Brynbella 129, 130–3, 139, 140, 147, 148, 161–2, 163
Burke, Edmund 65, 82, 113, 127, 128, 129
  Reflections on the Revolution in France 121
Burney, Charles 41, 82, 88, 101
  A General History of Music 80
Burney, Frances x, 31–2, 80, 84–5, 86, 89, 92, 93, 95, 102, 111, 113, 117
  Evelina or, A Young Lady's Entrance into the World 81
  'The Witlings' 81
Butler, Eleanor 135
Butler, Mrs 4
Byron, Admiral John ('Foulweather Jack') 83
Byron, Lord, *The Giaour* 162
Byron, Sophia 83, 86

Cadell, Thomas 100, 112
Caernarfon 64–5,
Caernarvonshire 63, 109, 112, 153
Calais 71
Calvert, Felix 54
Cambon, Pierre-Joseph 134
Canal, Giovanni Antonio (known as Canaletto) 136
Carter, Elizabeth, translator of Epictetus 38, 81, 94
Catholicism 4, 87, 93, 94, 105, 106, 107, 152
Cator, John, MP for Wallingford 85, 90
Cavendish, William, fifth duke of Devonshire 61
Cervantes Saavedra, Miguel de, *Don Quixote* 8
Chambers, Robert 43, 82
Chapone, Hester 81
Chappelow, Leonard 137, 144
Charles I 152

Chaucer, Geoffrey, translator of Boethius' *De consolatione philosophiae* 32
Chester Chronicle 139
Chester Courant 139
Chirk Castle Hill 109
Chronicle 17
Chudleigh, Elizabeth, Duchess of Kingston 72
Clarence and St Andrews, William, Duke of (the future William IV) 135
Clark, Steve 105
Clerke, Sir Philip Jennings-, MP for Totnes 83, 86, 87
Clifton 165
Clinton, Lord John 89
Collier, Dr Arthur 9–10, 11, 12, 13, 19, 32, 42
Columbus, Christopher 126
Combermere Abbey 61
Conway, William Augustus 164
Conway Castle 110
Cook, James 89
Cornelys, Teresa, the 'Circe of Soho Square' 28
Cotton, Philadelphia Lynch 5, 163
Cotton, Sir Lynch Salusbury, MP for Denbighshire 4, 5, 19, 61
Cotton, Sir Robert Salusbury 2, 61, 163
Cowdroy, William
Cowley, Hannah 102, 122, 123
Cowper, Lady 106
Crane, Dr Edward, prebendary of Westminster 4, 19, 20
Critical Review 101, 108, 114, 130, 154
Crutchley, Jeremiah 90

Darwin, Erasmus 60
Davies, Revd Reynold 142, 145, 146–7
D'Elci, Conte Angelo 103
Denbigh 135, 136, 138, 139
Denbigh Assembly Rooms 1
Denbigh Castle 132
Denbighshire 147
Descartes, René 11
Devaynes, William 86
Dilly, Charles 96
Dolbadarn Castle 65

188

Dovedale 61
Drury Lane 30
Dunk, George Montagu, 2nd Earl of Halifax 4, 6, 15, 20

East Hyde, Berkshire 5
Edgecumbe, Lady 69
Edward I 65
Eisteddfod 111
Eliott, General George Augustus, 1st Baron Heathfield of Gibraltar 107, 108
Elliot, Ann, 'Miss Hooper' 30
Elphinstone, George Keith, Viscount Keith 160
Elphinstone, Georgiana 161
English Review 101
European Magazine 103, 153
Eyles, Mr 57

Fellowes, Sir James 164
Fenarole, Conte Luigi 142, 145
Fielding, Sarah 9
Fiquet de Bocages, Anne-Marie, née La Page
  Les Amazones 75
Fishguard 140, 153
Flintshire 5, 16, 108, 109, 131, 140, 147, 158, 163
Florence 109, 119
Fontaine, Jean de La, 'Death and the Dying Man' 36
Foote, Samuel
  A Trip to Calais 72
Forbes, William, *The Life of James Beattie* 160
Fordyce, Alexander 55
French Revolution 102, 119, 120, 121–3, 130, 135, 136, 137, 142, 149, 152
French Tour 71–5

Gainsborough, Thomas 160
Garrick, David 4, 81, 82
Genoa 108
Gentleman's Magazine 103, 114, 154
George III 18, 75, 100, 133
Gibbes, Sir George 165
Gibbon, Edward 149

Gibraltar 105
Gifford, William
  The Baviad 123
  Mæviad 124
Gillon, John 149
Girard, Abbé 124, 125
Globe, the 27, 30
Goch, Owain 65
Godwin, William, *St. Leon, A Tale of the Sixteenth* Century 155
Gogynfeirdd 37
Goldsmith, Oliver 31, 82
Gordon, Lord George 87, 88
Gordon Riots 86-7, 94
Gray, Miss 72
Gray, Thomas 14
  'The Bard' 37
Greatheed, Bertie 103, 105, 111, 119, 120, 122 124
  The Regent 119
Greene, Richard 60
Gregorio, Mayáns Y Siscár, *Vida de Miguel de Cervantes Saavedra* 8
Griffith, Moses 162

Hankin, William 56
Harris, James 'Hermes', *Hermes, or, A Philosophical Inquiry Concerning Universal Grammar* 12
Hart, Polly 19, 30, 52
Hastings, Warren 112
Hawkins, Sir John 96
Haynes, Mrs 4–5
Heaton, Sarah 138
Hébert, Jacques René 134
Hebrides 48, 71, 100, 115
Hoare, Henry Merrick 160
Hogarth, William 48
  The Lady's Last Stake 8
Holles, Thomas Pelham, duke of Newcastle upon Tyne and first duke of Newcastle under Lyme 18
Hopson, Peregrine Thomas, Lieutenant-governor of Acadia (later Nova Scotia) 6
Hotham, Sir Richard, MP for Southwark 86

Index

Howard, Henry, sixth duke of Norfolk 72–3
Howell, James 110
Hubbard, Edward 131
Hume, Alexander, MP for Southwark 33
Hume, David 149
Hyde, Mary 59, 70

Ilam 60–1
Italy 59, 75, 91, 92, 94, 96, 100, 105, 106, 109, 127, 140, 141, 142, 145, 153

Jackson, Humphrey 34, 53, 54, 55
Jebb, Sir Richard 75, 76, 78, 85
Johnson, Elizabeth 44
Johnson, Dr Samuel, the 'Great Cham' 28, 30, 31, 33, 34, 36, 38, 39–40, 42–4, 45–50, 55, 56–7, 58, 59, 60, 61–3, 65–6, 67, 70, 71, 72, 73, 74, 75, 76, 77, 78, 80, 81, 82, 84, 86, 90, 91, 92, 93, 94, 97, 95, 98–9, 106, 112, 113, 114, 115–16, 117
  The False Alarm 45
  The Fountains: A Fairy Tale 37–8
  The History of Rasselas, Prince of Abissinia 61, 73
  The Patriot 66; *Lives of the Poets* 83
Jones, Edward 148
Jones, William 69
Joseph II, Holy Roman Emperor and ruler of the Habsburg Empire 107

Kedleston 61
Kent, North Downs 45
King, Peter, sixth Baron King 30
King, Mrs Sarah, later Lady Salusbury 16, 28, 91
Knowles, Mary 49
Krafft-Ebing, Richard von, *Psychopathia Sexualis* 48

Lade, Lady Ann, née Thrale 76
Lade, Sir John 76
Lafayette, Marie-Joseph Paul Yves Roch Gilbert du Motier, Marquis de 134

Lane, William 159
Lawrence, Herbert 43
Lawrence, Thomas 85
Lee, Harriet 119
  Canterbury Tales 155
Lee, Sophia 102, 119
  Canterbury Tales 155
Leopold, Peter, Grand Duke of Tuscany 105, 106
Levet [Levett], Robert 63
Levinz, William, jun., MP for Nottinghamshire 22
Lichfield 40, 49, 56, 60, 76, 111, 114
Lisbon earthquake 7, 15
Liverpool 147, 149
Llangollen 132, 133
Llewellyn the Great 65
Lleweni Hall 1, 2, 3, 5, 6, 61
Llyn Peris 65
Lloyd, Dick 64
Lloyd, Thomas 132, 138
London Chronicle 101, 103
Loreto 108
Lorrain, Claude 65
Louis XVI 127–8
Lunar Society, The 60
Luttrell, Simon, first Earl of Carhampton, the 'King of Hell' 30
Lysons, Samuel 100, 111, 113,
Lyttelton, George, first Baron Lyttelton 84–5
Lyttelton, William Henry, Lord Westcote 82

Macaulay, Catharine 154
Macpherson, James, *Fingal, an Ancient Epic* 17
Maintenon, Françoise d'Aubigné, Marquise de 113
Malone, Edmond 96, 100
Mangin, Edward 30, 164
Mangin, Mrs 30
'Massacre of St George's Fields' 44
Marriot, Dr James, 'Verses from Ariosto addressed to Miss Salusbury' and *Poems written chiefly at the University of Cambridge* 14, 22
Mason, William 14

Mathias, Peter 53
Matlock Bath 61
Mawbey, Sir Joseph, MP for Southwark 43
McCarthy, William ix, 125
Mead, Clement 131, 132, 139, 162–3
Medmenham 44
Merry, Robert 103, 106
  'The Laurel of Liberty' 122
Mi'kmaq (indigenous natives of Nova Scotia) 17
millenarianism 7, 136, 149–50
Montagu, Edward, MP for Huntingdon 79
Montagu, Elizabeth, 'Queen of the Bluestockings' x, 79–80, 82, 84, 86, 90, 92, 94, 100, 113, 129, 164
  Essay on the Writings and Genius of Shakespear 79, 100
Montgolfier, Joseph-Michel 105
Monthly Review 101, 108, 116, 126, 130
Moore, Thomas 156
More, Hannah 101, 102, 113, 154
  Cheap Repository Tracts 142
  Strictures on the Modern System of Female Education 156
  Village Politics 137
Morelli, Maria Maddalena (known as Corilla) 110
Mostyn, John Meredith of Segroid 139, 141
Mostyn, John Salusbury 161
Mostyn, Revd John 138
Murphy, Arthur 49, 82, 116, 119
  The Citizen 30, 31
Murray, William, first earl of Mansfield 44, 87

Naples 108
Napoléon Bonaparte 140, 141, 149–50
Neale, Sir Harry Burrard 153
Nesbitt, Arnold 83
Newbery, Elizabeth 41–2
Newbery, Francis 134
Newcastle 79
Newgate Prison 87
Nieto, Isaac, *haham* (rabbi) of Bevis Marks Synagogue 7

North, Frederick, second earl of Guilford (known as Lord North) 66
North Wales Gazette 159
Nova Scotia 4, 5, 6

Offley Park, Hertfordshire 5, 6–7, 9, 12, 13, 15, 16, 59
Osborne, Mary, née Lady Mary Godolphin, duchess of Leeds 4
Osborne, Thomas, fourth duke of Leeds 4
Ovid, *Fasti* 146
Owen, Margaret 'Peggy' 77
Oxford 43
Oystermouth 86
Ozell, John, translator 8

Paine, Thomas 137
Paoli, Pasquale 45, 65
Parini, Abate Giuseppe 103
Paris 72, 74, 110, 119, 121, 127
Parker, Revd Dr William 11, 15
Parsons, William 103, 123
  'To Mrs. Piozzi in Reply, Written on the Anniversary of Her Wedding' 104
Pelagius 14, 151–2
Pemberton, Edward 162
Pemberton, Harriet 163
Pembrokeshire 34, 153
Penmaenmawr 112, 151
Pennant, Thomas, 131, 132, 139, 140
  The Literary Life of the late Thomas Pennant Esq., by himself 1; *Tour in Wales* 162
Pennington, Penelope Sophia, née Weston 89, 128, 131, 132, 157
Penrice, Sir Henry 5
Penzance 164
Pepys, Sir Lucas 80, 88, 100, 133
Pepys, William Weller 80, 84, 85, 89
Perkins, John 54–5, 56, 58, 59, 76, 84, 85, 87, 89
Petrarch, Francesco 106
Petty, William, second earl of Shelburne and first marquess of Lansdowne 91
Pignotti, Lorenzo 103

Index

Pindemonte, Marquis Ippolito 103, 119
  'Hymn to Calliope' 105
Piozzi, Gabriel 88, 89, 91–2, 93, 94, 95, 110, 112, 125, 130, 131, 132, 135, 136, 139, 141, 142, 146, 147, 157–8, 159, 160–6
Piozzi, Giambattista 142
Piozzi (née Salusbury; other married name Thrale), Hester Lynch
  adopting Gabriel's nephew 142–3, 144–4, 162, 163
  anchored to the brewery 27, 34, 44, 52, 53–8
  Anecdotes an instant bestseller 100–2
  anti-Jacobin songs for Sadler's Wells 133–4, 135, 137–8, 156–7
  arrival of the Bluestocking Queen 79–80
  Brynbella 130–2, 139–40
  the Burneys 31–2, 41, 80–1, 84–5, 88, 89, 91, 92, 93, 95, 101, 102, 111, 113, 117, 130; character 3, 5, 6, 10, 11, 12, 13, 15, 19, 24, 81–2
  'Chevalier' Conway 164
  collaboration and psychological aid 32, 46–50
  combative conversation 32, 39, 42, 45, 49, 79, 86, 89, 96, 97, 98, 107, 121, 125, 164
  comparative geography 109–10, 111–12
  death of her first-born Henry 75–6
  death of her mother 58–9
  editing Johnson's letters; 112–16
  education 7–8, 9–10, 11, 38, 41–3, 50
  election business 33, 43, 54, 66, 86, 88
  feminism 1–2, 8, 18–19, 34, 38, 41, 46, 47, 56, 60, 69, 73, 75, 79, 80, 107, 124, 156
  French tour 71–5
  Gabriel's decline and death 157–8, 160–1
  genealogy and birth 1–3
  'heiress' 4, 7, 14, 24, 26
  Johnson's death and literary plans 95–100
  literary celebrity and new friends 102–8
  marriage to Thrale 24–5
  efforts to capture his love 25–6
  meeting and marrying a *musician* 88, 89, 91–2, 93–4
  model for Hogarth 8
  mother, Hester's 'total failure' as 60
  new life and a Grand Tour 94–5
  patriarchal husband 26–7, 28
  perpetual pregnancies 29–30, 32, 33, 43, 50, 52, 56, 59, 67, 83
  personal appearance 8–9
  'The poor are famishing' 138–9, 147–9
  'the poor Woman is mad' 93–5
  presence of Johnson 31, 32, 33–4, 38
  rating one's friends 81, 86
  Retrospection 149–55
  romanticism 15, 21, 62, 67, 88, 105, 106, 111, 133
  sea-bathing 88, 92, 124, 133, 158–9
  societal etymology 124–9
  suitors 13, 14,16, 20
  target for satire 103, 116–17, 122–4
  Thrale's illness and death 83, 84, 85, 86, 89
  tour of north Wales 60, 61–5
Pitt, William 18, 124, 141
Plasnewydd 64
Plumbe, Alderman Samuel 67
Ponsonby, Sarah 135
Pope, Alexander 15, 46, 162
  Iliad 50
Pott, Percivall 67
Prestatyn 158–9
Priestholm or Puffin Island 151
Prince Madoc, son of Owain Gwynedd 126
Public Advertiser 44
Pughe, William Owen, *Cambrian Register* 63
Pwllheli, 1, 64

Queen Charlotte of Mecklenburg-Strelitz 118
Queen Marie Antoinette 75
Quin, James 4

Racine, Louis, first 'Épitre sur l'homme' 15
Radcliffe, Ann, *The Mysteries of Udolpho* 132, 133
Rambler, The 114
Ramsgate 133
Ranelagh 70
Redford, Bruce 114
Reynolds, Joshua 82, 163
  Streatham Portraits 97
Rhuddlan Castle 62
Rice, Frances Plumbe 67
Rice, John 67, 68
Rice, Morgan 67
Richardson, Samuel, *Sir Charles Grandison* 73
Riquet, Antoine 36
Roberts, John 160
Robespierre, Maximilien François Marie Isidore de 134
Robinson, George 126, 151
Robinson, Mary 122, 123
Rochefoucauld, François VI, Duc de La 47
Roffette, Abbé 73
Rogers Samuel 119
Rome 198
Rousseau, Jean-Jacques 99
Rowlands, Henry
  Mona Antiqua Restaurata 126
Rural poverty 136, 138, 139, 147–8
Russell, John, fourth Duke of Bedford 24

Sadler's Wells 134
St James's Chronicle 17–18, 23, 100
Salusbury, Lady Anna Maria, née Penrice, heiress of Offley 5, 6–7, 13, 43, 61
Salusbury, Hester Maria, née Cotton 1, 12, 15, 18, 19–20, 21, 27–8, 34–5, 48, 50, 58, 60, 114
Salusbury, John 1, 4, 6, 7, 9, 12, 13, 14, 15–16, 18–19, 139, 144
Salusbury, Revd Thelwall 24
Salusbury, Sir John Salusbury Piozzi (nephew of Piozzi) 142–3, 144, 145–6, 161, 162, 163, 164

Salusbury, Sir Thomas (brother of John Salusbury), knighted as an Admiralty Judge, married Anna Maria Penrice 5–6, 10, 15, 16, 18, 19, 20 28, 58, 59
Salusbury Estate 77
Salusbury y Bodiau, Sir John 3
Salzburg, Adam of (son of the Duke of Bavaria) 3
Sandys, Edwin, second Baron Sandys 82
Sayer, James 116
Scott, Sarah, *Millenium Hall* 73
Scott, Sir Walter, *Marmion* 162
Scrase, Charles 56
Sea-bathing 88, 92, 124, 133, 158–9
Sévigné, Marie de Rabutin-Chantal, marquise de 113
Seward, Anna 49, 102, 111
Shakespeare, William 27, 30, 32
Shephard, Revd T. 161
Siddons, Sarah 120, 129–30, 147
Siddons, William 134
Smith, Charlotte 102
  Emmeline, or The Orphan of the Castle 155
Smith, Henry 90
Smollett, Tobias (editor of *The Briton*) 18–19
Snowdon 65, 109, 133
Society of United Irishmen 140
Soho 24, 27, 28, 29, 50
Somerset Horse Fencibles 139
Southey, Robert, *Curse of Kehama* 162
Southwark 20, 25, 27, 29, 30, 33, 34, 40, 43, 44, 53, 65, 66, 84, 85, 86
'The Southwark Macaroni' 22
Spenser, Edmund 12
Spinoza, Baruch 15
Spithead 140
Staël, Madame Anne-Louise-Germaine de
  Corinne, or Italy 106, 110
  Delphine 155-6
Starke, Mariana, *Letters From Italy* 154
Stockdale, John 151
Stone, John Hurford 122

Index

Stone, Lawrence 60
Streatfeild, Sophie 81, 83
Streatham Park 24, 27, 38, 39, 43, 45, 48, 50, 53, 64, 65, 70, 76, 77, 80, 82, 83, 87, 90, 91, 120, 122, 132, 136, 139, 142, 162, 163, 164
Strickland, Cecilia (née Towneley) 72, 73, 77
Stuart, John, third earl of Bute 18, 66
Swift, Jonathan 45, 46, 84
 'A letter to a very young lady on her marriage' 68

Tallien, Jean-Lambert 134
Taylor, Dr John 51, 60, 98, 114
Thackeray, Dr William Makepeace (uncle of the author of *Vanity Fair*) 138
Thelwall, John 138
Thomas, Nathaniel 17
Thompson, Edward
 The Court of Cupid 52
 The Metriciad 52
Thrale, Anna Maria 43, 50–1, 115
Thrale, Cecilia Margaretta 77, 92, 111, 135, 139, 141, 144, 160, 161, 162–3
Thrale, Frances 33
Thrale, Frances Anna 67, 75
Thrale, Henrietta Sophia 82, 92
Thrale, Henry 16, 18–19, 20, 21–2, 24–5, 29, 31, 33, 38, 39, 45, 51–2, 53–8, 61, 63, 64, 70, 71, 74, 76, 77, 78, 83–4, 86, 87, 88, 89–90, 91, 112, 115–16, 159–60, 163
Thrale, Henry Salusbury 40, 50, 75, 77, 115
Thrale, Hester Maria ('Queeney') 29, 39, 40, 42, 50, 61, 63, 65, 67, 70, 71, 72, 74, 75, 76, 77–8, 80, 88, 90, 91, 92, 93, 111, 135, 136, 160–1, 163
Thrale, Lucy Elizabeth 50, 51, 59, 77, 115
Thrale, Mary 22
Thrale, Penelope 56
Thrale, Ralph (Henry's father) 22, 24
Thrale, Ralph (8 November 1773–13 July 1775) 59, 66, 67, 69, 70, 115

Thrale Sophia 78, 92, 160, 162–3
Thrale, Susanna Arabella 51, 76, 145–6, 162–3
Townsend, John 90
Tremeirchion 61, 112, 131, 135, 148, 165
Tunbridge Wells 83, 85
Turk's Head Club 38
Turner, Joseph Mallord William 65
Tuscany 105, 110, 117

Vale of Clwyd 2, 108, 158, 165
Vesey, Elizabeth 80, 93
Vesuvius 112

Wales 1, 3, 15, 17, 59, 60, 61–5, 71, 72, 77, 85, 109, 110, 111–12, 120, 126, 128, 130, 132, 133, 136, 138, 139, 140, 147, 151, 152, 153, 155, 161, 162
Warton, Joseph, *Essay on the Genius and Writings of Pope* 15
Watkin Wynn, Anna Maria 139
Watkin Wynn, Edward 139
Wells, William 160
Welsh culture 31, 37, 63, 65, 67, 79, 82, 102, 108–9, 110, 111, 118, 125, 126, 127, 137, 144, 152
Welsh Tour 59, 61–5
West, Jane, *A Tale of the Times* 156
West Malling 45
Westminster Magazine 52
Weymouth 92
Whalley, Thomas Sedgwick 86
Whitbread, Samuel 54
Wilkes, John, *Essay on Women* 44
 The North Briton 18, 43, 44, 75
Wilkes, John Caesar (Brookes), *Political Controversy* 18
William the Conqueror 3
Williams, Anna 34, 37
Williams, Edward (Iolo Morganwg) 126
Williams, Helen Maria 102, 121, 122
 Letters on the French Revolution, Written in France in the Summer of 1790 120
Williams, Lady Margaret, of Bodelwyddan 145

Willoughby, Francis *Ornithology* (1678) 1
Wilson, Richard 65
Wolcot, John (*pseud*. Peter Pindar), *Bozzy and Piozzi, or The British Biographers, A Town Eclogue* 101
Wollstonecraft, Mary 69, *Vindication of the Rights of Woman* 156
Woodhouse, James, *Poems on Sundry Occasions* 30

Woodman, Mr 135
World, The 122, 123
Wynn, Colonel Glyn, MP for Caernarfon Boroughs 65
Wynn, John, County Commissioner for the Suppression of Piracy 1
Wynn, Mrs Bridget 65

Ynys Enlli 1, 115
Ynys Môn 64, 151–2

Zoffany, Johann 39, 163